DAD,
I'm so glad you enjoy
these types of books. May
we never have to experience
this type of war again.
   Love,
   Scott

G Company's War

TWO PERSONAL ACCOUNTS OF THE CAMPAIGNS IN EUROPE, 1944–1945

Bruce E. Egger
&
Lee MacMillan Otts

Edited and with Commentary by

Paul Roley

The University of Alabama Press
Tuscaloosa and London

First Paperback Edition 1998

2 3 4 5 6 7 8 9 • 06 05 04 03 02 01 00

Copyright © 1992 by
The University of Alabama Press
Tuscaloosa, Alabama 35487–0380
All rights reserved
Manufactured in the United States of America

The paper on which this book is printed meets the minimum
requirements of American National Standard for Information
Science-Permanence of Paper for Printed Library Materials,
ANSI Z39.48-1984.

designed by zig zeigler

Library of Congress Cataloging-in-Publication Data

G Company's war : two personal accounts of the campaign in Europe.
1944-1945 / by Bruce E. Egger and Lee MacMillan Otts ; edited and
with commentary by Paul Roley.
    p. cm.
Includes bibliographical references and index.
ISBN 0-8173-0978-0 (alk. paper)
    1. Egger, Bruce E., 1923– . 2. Otts, Lee MacMillan, 1922– .
3. World War, 1939–1945—Campaigns—Western. 4. World War,
1939–1945—Personal narratives, American. 5. Soldiers—United
States—Biography. 6. United States. Army.—Biography. 7. United
States. Army. Infantry Regiment, 328th. G Company—History.
I. Otts, Lee MacMillan, 1922– . II. Roley, Paul, 1927– .
III. Title.
D756.3.E35   1992
940.54′21—dc20   91-31408

British Library Cataloguing-in-Publication Data available

Contents

Maps

Acknowledgments

As word of this undertaking began to spread among former G Company members, a number of them stepped forward to offer important documentary materials, words of encouragement, and reminiscences. Foremost was former G Company 1st Sgt. Rocco Clemente, who provided us with some helpful company rosters, his personal journal, some pictures, and information concerning dimly remembered comrades from another era. Bill Frost, the former company clerk, sent us the definitive roster of G Company from the time it went overseas and a yellowed, beat-up pocket journal in which were recorded all changes in status of G Company personnel from September 1944 until the end of the war. Former Lt. Ernie Greup gave us original platoon rosters plus an elusive photo we had been trying to track down. These documents were essential in our efforts to account for all the men who had appeared on G Company's wartime rolls.

A number of other G Company veterans have eagerly shared bits and pieces of information concerning their roles in the events described in these pages. Mrs. Jack Hargrove kindly gave us copies of her late husband's scrapbook and wartime pictures from his collection, and Mrs. Donald Thompson also contributed some snapshots. We thank them all. Then there is former T/Sgt. Larry Treff, who not only led forty men in battle when he was barely twenty years old but set a personal example of courage and devotion to duty that would be remarkable at any age. We appreciate his interest and encouragement throughout this project.

My personal thanks also to Mrs. Mary Parker of the National Personnel Records Center in St. Louis for her help. Her decisiveness in overcoming a monumental bureaucratic snafu and making available G Company's microfilmed morning reports to a frustrated academic who had traveled 2,500 miles to examine them borders on the heroic. Bob Clapp, the affable secretary of the 328th Combat Team Veterans' Association, was most gracious in providing addresses of some former G Company men.

I am indebted to a number of individuals and agencies at Western Washington University for their help in this project. Tops on the list is Ms. Joy Dabney of the university's Educational Media Services, who is responsible for the beautifully executed maps in this volume. My thanks also to Dean Maury Schwarz and the Bureau of Faculty Research for underwriting the preparation of the maps.

I also much appreciate the efforts of my student assistant, Ms. Susan Flynn, in her painstaking work with the copies of the sometimes badly preserved morning reports. The index cards she prepared on each of the 625 men who appeared on G Company's wartime rolls proved to be invaluable. And of course my wife, Joan, showed her usual dedication in cheerfully helping out with a number of clerical chores during the preparation of this work.

But above all my thanks go to those two true gentlemen, and now dear friends, Bruce Egger and Lee MacMillan Otts, whose remarkable wartime journals are the reason for this book. Never was an editor whose task it was to hack up and blue line so much of their work blessed with more cooperative authors. Nor is it possible to conceive that there could be more supportive wives than Leora Egger, Mary Frances Otts, and Joan Roley. All three are terrific ladies and a reflection on our good judgment in marrying them in the first place. [P.R.]

Introduction

The smallest detail taken from an actual incident in war is more instructive . . . than all the [histories] in the world. They speak for the heads of state and armies, but they never show me what I wish to know—a battalion, company, or platoon in action. The man is the first weapon of battle. Let us study the soldier, for it is he who brings reality to it.

—Charles Ardant du Picq

This is an account of an American rifle company in Patton's famed Third Army during World War II as detailed in the journals of S/Sgt. Bruce Egger and Lt. Lee M. Otts, both of G Company, 328th Infantry. What distinguishes it from other accounts of the wartime experience is that these are the voices of ordinary GIs, two of the hundreds of thousands of mud-bespattered, footsore riflemen who were at the tip of those thrusting arrows that mark the advance of armies on the historians' maps. There are numerous World War II memoirs from the pens of the mighty—the generals and statesmen who viewed events from on high—but only a handful from the frontline soldiers who did the actual fighting.

We believe this work to be unique in that it embodies parallel accounts of the same events as seen by two men in the same company who did not know each other at the time. There is a high degree of correlation in their individual recollections of G Company's war, even down to some minor details. But there are also differences that are perhaps even more important than the similarities.

The most obvious is the difference between the experiences of an enlisted man and an officer, but in a frontline rifle company these are not so pronounced as one might expect. More striking is how these two distinctly different personalities recorded the same experiences. What we get, in fact, are two views of the same war; the details are much the same but the psychology and tone of the two accounts differ markedly.

Bruce Egger was a serious-minded, sensitive young soldier for whom the war was a grim ordeal. His account is packed with detailed descriptions of the dead and wounded of both sides, of the privations he and his comrades endured and the destruction they witnessed. In all this he is a strikingly perceptive observer, but we get from him few instances of the horseplay and humorous repartee that are a normal part of male fellowship, whether in the locker room or the foxhole.

For Lee Otts the war was no less an ordeal, but his sunny disposition responded to it differently. Despite the fear and privation, the grinding fatigue and the discomfort, all of which he recorded, Otts reacted to the war as a once-in-a-lifetime experience, sometimes even fun. He says so in his letters home and in his memoirs, and it is clear that he was not simply putting the best face on things. In his account he unfailingly records the high jinks and the pranks, the sometimes ludicrous side of the life of a combat infantryman, and, in a self-mocking tone, his own pratfalls and foibles.

This work, then, presents two different perceptions of the combat experience. Each is accurate in its own right, but it is our belief that the combination of the two into a single, interwoven account provides a more comprehensive truth about war and the men caught up in it.

Pfc. Bruce Egger arrived in France as part of a replacement draft in October 1944, and went on line with G Company of the 328th Infantry Regiment—a unit of the 26th (Yankee) Division—on November 6. He served out the remainder of the war in close to continuous frontline action without missing a day of duty. There were some close calls—most notably a piece of shrapnel stopped by the New Testament in the breast pocket of his field jacket—but he came through it all without a nick. He rose from private first class to staff sergeant and became one of the old-timers in the company. Most of all he survived, which is all that really counts in war.

2nd Lt. Lee Otts was initially assigned as a replacement platoon leader to Easy Company of the 328th Infantry on November 18, 1944. Some two weeks later he was transferred to G Company. He, too, experienced some near misses but served continuously until that unlucky day of March 13, 1945, when he sustained two serious wounds in G Company's last major engagement. For Lee Otts, now a first lieutenant, the war was over except for an extended period of hospitalization in England and the United States.

I encountered Bruce Egger's journal through his daughter, who was in one of my history classes at Western Washington University. In his foreword Bruce explained that he had written the account for his family and did not believe it would merit publication. I thought otherwise, and he agreed to a collaborative effort to shape his manuscript into a book.

Egger's major concern was that some of his remarks about certain individuals in G Company might cause them or their families embarrassment. Yet the fact that he speaks forthrightly of the malingerers, the goldbricks, and the outright cowards is one of the unusual and most valuable aspects of his journal. As Bruce later wrote to me concerning a World War II memoir I had lent him, "Everything seemed to run a little too smoothly in his company to be realistic. Nothing is mentioned of shirkers and disciplinary problems—just a bunch of good old boys."

He was right. Whatever the other virtues of American fighting men in World War II, they were not all exemplary soldiers. Neither were some of Egger's G Company comrades, and I thought it necessary to retain certain incidents, even though they might reflect poorly on some individuals, to present as accurate an account of the combat experience as possible. We have therefore resorted to the use of pseudonyms (which are identified as such the first time they are used) for those members of G Company whose conduct in combat left something to be desired and who might be embarrassed to have their derelictions revealed today.

The origins of Egger's account are in a diary he kept in which he jotted down brief entries each time he came off the line. He fleshed these out into a full journal in June of 1945 while on occupation duty in Czechoslovakia. Then in the winter of 1982–1983, after his retirement from the U.S. Forest Service, Egger reworked and expanded the journal with the aid of the letters he had written to his parents during the war, adding more descriptive detail and insights gained over the years. Excerpts from his letters are included in the body of the text.

Lee Otts also kept a diary that became the basis of an account of his wartime experiences which he wrote in the summer of 1947. When I placed a note in the Yankee Division Veterans Association newsletter, *Yankee Doings*, asking to hear from old G Company members, Lee wrote, telling me of his manuscript and offering to let me read it. I found it a lively, well-written account that remarkably complemented Egger's journal. Where Bruce's work is detailed and precise, Lee's is colorful and descriptive, particularly of people and the atmosphere of battle. In this sense their writings resemble, respectively, the memoirs of Generals Grant and Sherman, as described by the eminent historian, Page Smith: "Grant's style is a proper measure of the man. Simple, austere, reserved, direct, informed by a severely suppressed passion, by the determination to do justice to everyone concerned, friend and foe alike. . . . Where Grant is spare and almost dry, Sherman is vividly anecdotal and discursive, . . . lively, even garrulous, but unfailingly interesting."[1] More importantly, because Otts was an officer and therefore privy to operational plans most enlisted men would not know about, he is able to supply details on tactics that Egger's journal lacked.

The three of us agreed that the two accounts should be combined. This required that both manuscripts be trimmed of repetitious material and generally tightened up, which in turn involved some rewriting and rephrasing and supplying of bridging sentences or short passages to connect the gaps where material has been omitted. In addition, I broke Otts' material into daily entries (it had originally been a continuous narrative) to conform to Egger's format.

Although I have done some stylistic editing of both accounts, the main body of this work remains theirs. My major contribution has been the passages labeled "Operational Background" and "After Action Summary," which are provided to assist the reader in better understanding the military situation as it pertained to G Company's operations. Also, I am the author of the introduction, the prologue, the epilogue, and the appendixes. All passages written by me are identified by my initials in brackets [P.R.].

The footnotes scattered thoughout the main text are mostly based on information culled from photocopies of G Company's morning reports—the daily record kept by each company—I secured during a visit to the National Personnel Records Center in St. Louis to verify the dates of specific events and check the names of individuals mentioned in the two accounts. Bruce Egger and I later combed through these records in mind-numbing detail. This led to his making a number of minor revisions and additions to his manuscript, usually having to do with precise dates and the inclusion of additional names, even though his original journal had proved to be remarkably accurate on both counts.

The experiences Lee Otts and Bruce Egger relate in the following pages are now more than four decades in the past, but their afterglow burns on in the two men's memories, impacting their lives in ways nobody can articulate. There is no need to try. All combat veterans of World War II, not least of all the men of G Company, can understand how the memories of that great and terrible endeavor can both warm and sear the lives of those who experienced it. They will never forget. Let us hope that this work will help others remember.

PAUL ROLEY
Bellingham, Washington

Prologue

The burden of fighting the wars that old men make is disproportionately the lot of the young, and never more so than in World War II. The authors of the two accounts contained in this book are cases in point. S/Sgt. Bruce Egger was twenty-one years old during the entire time he was leading a squad of twelve men in combat; Lt. Lee Otts was twenty-two while in charge of forty men in a rifle platoon.

It is difficult to conceive today that their government regularly put so much responsibility on such young shoulders. In the case of Egger and Otts, however, they had what we would today call "the right stuff." Both were sustained by a firm religious faith; both possessed excellent leadership qualities and had the respect of the men they led; both were directed by a strong sense of duty, so much so that neither missed a day of duty in several months of service in a frontline rifle company. Both were, in fact, uncommonly conscientious soldiers who were driven by an inner toughness that helped sustain them through the ordeal they faced.

Yet the two men had little in common other than their soldierly qualities. While they suffered equally the hardships and horrors of extended infantry combat in the European Theater of Operations, to the shy, sensitive Egger the war was a soul-scarring experience; to the ebullient Otts it was often an adventure.

The contrast in personalities was almost total. Lee Otts was a genial, fun-loving son of the South who would bend an elbow with friends and, in his words, "give out with the fancy talk" with the girls, but it was all with the innocence of Andy Hardy at a frat party. Lee was, in fact, a very moral young man with a strong sense of responsibility.

So was Bruce Egger, except that Bruce possessed a stern ascetic streak that was in part a legacy of his fundamentalist background. In an age when the smoking habit among American males was almost universal, he did not use tobacco in any form. Although to be sociable he would sometimes sample the local spirits, note in the following pages how Egger consistently spurned the alcoholic booty of war in favor of other prizes. Like Otts, he had retained a sturdy set of moral values in an environment where so many had set theirs aside for the duration.

With Egger the anomalies abound. Despite his impatience with malingerers, we often find him speaking with compassion for those who did not have the strength to keep up on forced marches. His own remarkable endurance gives the impression that he must have been an imposing physical specimen. He was not. At five-foot-ten and 155 pounds, Bruce Egger was far from robust, but that slight physique concealed an inner strength that drove him in the performance of his duty, even to the extent on one occasion of refusing to report to the aid station with a case of jaundice on the eve of an attack. It was this willed toughness that at one point made Egger consider joining the paratroops and, in the postwar years, to spend three summers as a smoke jumper, parachuting in to fight forest fires.

Here, then, was a shy, physically unimposing young soldier who willed himself the strength and endurance to meet all the rigorous demands placed upon the combat infantryman, a frontline rifleman with a tender digestive tract—Egger's stomach problems are a recurring theme in his journal—that frequently caused him as much misery as the enemy or the elements.

Otts, too, possessed impressive endurance for a young man who had been overweight and unathletic as a boy. But he had loved hunting and shooting, pastimes that no doubt contributed to the enjoyment he at times found in the war. The fatigue and deprivation were no fun, however, and Lee's character shows up in the fact that as a platoon leader he always shared the hardships of his men, riding in the back of the truck with the troops instead of in the cab on cold, rainy trips and plodding along with his platoon on exhausting marches instead of hitching a ride in one of the company jeeps. Lee Otts was also a gutsy guy who shared the dangers as well as the discomforts of his men and did not panic in tough situations. It is of such qualities that leadership consists.

The two men sprang from markedly different backgrounds. Lee MacMillan Otts was a Southerner to the core, whereas Egger was very much a product of the mountains of central Idaho. Otts was from a family that had resided in Greensboro, Alabama, for generations. His mother worked as a clerk in the local post office and his father was a rural mail carrier who was determined that his two children would have the best he could afford. Because he was a frugal man, he was able not only to send young Lee to the University of Alabama but also to support his membership in a fraternity.

In high school Otts had excelled academically, showing a particular flair for math and the sciences. When he entered college and became involved in fraternity life, Lee bloomed socially, but he was a capable enough student to graduate in three years with a major in chemistry.

Bruce Egger was the son of a working-class, fundamentalist family that had been hit hard by the depression. His father, Emil, was a hard-working, unskilled laborer of Swiss extraction with little formal education whose life was directed by a strong Christian faith. The Scottish girl he married, Alice Bruce, matched her husband in piety and in strength of character.

During the early depression years Bruce's father worked, when he could, as an agricultural laborer, and the Eggers moved several times before finally settling down in Boise. In 1941 he got a permanent job in the little town of McCall, Idaho, where Bruce attended his senior year of high school. After graduating in May 1942, young Egger worked for six months in the same sawmill where his father was employed, until he was inducted into the Army on January 12, 1943, at nineteen years of age.

In March, after completing basic training at Camp Kerns, Utah, Bruce was assigned to Fitzsimmons Hospital in Denver for training as an X-ray technician. Had he stuck with this program it is likely he would have had a secure billet in a medical facility for the remainder of the war, but in April Egger took a test for the Army Specialized Training Program (ASTP), which provided college training in a number of civilian specialties the Army thought it would need before the war was over. Having passed, he was sent to Kansas State College, Manhattan, Kansas, to study civil engineering. He arrived there in late May 1943.

On August 10, however, Bruce wrote home, "I don't feel like I should be going to school while the rest of the men fight." No doubt that view arose in part because "they keep throwing the fact at us all the time," "they" being the Army cadres at Kansas State, since scorn for the ASTP men seems to have been widespread in the service at that time. One of Egger's G Company buddies later reported that in 1943 there were frequent clashes between soldiers at a training camp near Raleigh, North Carolina, and ASTP "Whiz Kids" at a nearby university. The joke among the former was that ASTP stood for "All Safe Till Peace."[1]

Bruce need not have worried about sitting out the war in college, however. On February 10, 1944, the Army, scraping the bottom of the manpower barrel as it prepared for the invasion of France, terminated the college training of 120,000 ASTP men, 73,000 of whom were assigned to the Army Ground Forces.[2] In March 1944 the surviving trainees at Kansas State, Private Bruce Egger included, were sent to the 97th Infantry Division, which was then undergoing advanced training at Fort Leonard Wood, Missouri.

Millions of Americans who served in the armed forces during World War II will recognize the bitter irony in this turn of events. First the Army combed through its inductees, selecting out its best and brightest, and sent them to college. Since the Army Ground Forces usually came last in the distribution of manpower, these same ASTP trainees would otherwise have ended up in secure stateside or noncombat-zone billets such as Egger's initial assignment to receive training as an X-ray technician.[3] Then the Army cut the ground out from under its Whiz Kids and fed them into rifle companies, where they would never have ended up except for having been assigned to a specialized program that was phased out.

Not that Egger was unhappy with this abrupt shift in his fortunes. "I enjoyed the infantry training and the active life with the 97th," he later recalled in his journal. He had an affinity for the outdoor life that came naturally to a boy raised in communion with the mountains of western Idaho. It was a taste that would help him cope with the hardships he would later face in France and Germany.

In July the 97th Division was transferred to San Luis Obispo, California, for amphibious training preparatory to deployment in the Pacific.[4] But on August 28 the Army selected a number of men from each rifle company of the 97th Division to be shipped to Europe as replacements. The next day Pfc. Bruce Egger was among the contingent that entrained for Fort Meade, Maryland, preparatory to shipment overseas.

One of Egger's close friends in the group from the 97th Division was Pfc. Robert Dixon, whose wife and mother visited him at Fort Meade on September 9. One of the men assured the ladies they would take good care of Dixon, prompting his wife to reply, "I think Bob can take care of himself." Both promises proved to be hollow.

The next day Egger's group left by overnight train for Camp Shanks, New York, their port of embarkation. On September 17 the replacement draft was transported to the harbor, where eight thousand men filed onto the English troopship *Mauretania* as their names were called out. "The Army made sure there were no last minute deserters," Egger commented.

In the meantime, Lee Otts was heading in the same direction by a different route. At the University of Alabama he had joined an ROTC unit of the Coastal Artillery and, in May 1942, the Army Reserves. He graduated in June 1943, a month after his twenty-first birthday, and was inducted into the Army two months later and sent to Officers' Candidate School (OCS) for antiaircraft personnel at Camp Davis, North Carolina. While trying to keep fit waiting for an OCS class to open, he suffered a fractured elbow. As a result, when the class got underway two weeks later Lee was hard put to meet the physical demands of the training. Neither was he up to par in the spit and polish department, but he managed to get by on a strong academic performance and received his commission as a second lieutenant on January 13, 1944.

At OCS the candidates could specialize in one of three different types of antiaircraft weapons—quadruple .50 caliber machine guns mounted on a half-track, 40mm guns, or 90mm cannons. Otts confessed that his choice of the 90s was dictated by the consideration that they were the least likely of the three types to operate close to the front.

By that time there was a surplus of antiaircraft officers, and the Army transferred a large number, Otts among them, to that old dumping ground, the infantry. Lee was eventually sent to Fort Benning, Georgia, for an eight-week infantry course and in June was assigned to Camp Blanding, Florida, as part of the permanent cadre at the Infantry Replacement Training Center. In early October he was transferred to Fort Meade, Maryland, preparatory to being shipped overseas. One of the other officers in that replacement draft was 2nd Lt. Law Lamar, an old friend of Otts from the University of Alabama. Their paths were to cross frequently in the European Theater of Operations over the next six months.

On October 12 Otts' group was sent by train to Camp Shanks, New York, and on the 20th the contingent of some thirty infantry officers, six field artillery liaison pilots, and about twelve hundred enlisted men boarded the U.S. Army Transport *Thomas H. Barry*. They set sail for Southampton, England, the following morning, arriving there on November 2.

The privileges of rank—and possibly the differences in accommodations on British and American troop transports—were revealed in Egger's and Otts' respective accounts. Bruce remembers that his company, which drew KP for the entire voyage, slept on the mess hall floor; Otts and ten other shavetails shared a cabin approximately ten by twenty feet. The food, Lee wrote, was the best he had ever eaten in the Army, with printed menus and a variety of entrees for each meal. Egger, on the other hand, found the English food on the *Mauretania* "not very tasty—thin watery oatmeal, stewed prunes, coffee, and hard-boiled eggs for breakfast. There was no lunch and the evening meal was usually canned corned beef." He noted wryly that it "wouldn't have been difficult to meet the requirements as a cook on this ship."

Egger's replacement draft arrived in Liverpool on September 25 after an eight-day passage. The GIs disembarked the next day, loaded on a train for an hour's ride to a small village in central England, and then marched the four remaining miles to Camp Pillemore. Bruce's disgust with shirkers surfaced as he noted in his journal, "Some of the men discarded their packs. I suppose they considered themselves winners since vehicles were dispatched to pick up the gear."

Life in transit at Camp Pillemore had more than its normal share of frustrations. It rained every day, and the so-called training, which was mostly intended to keep a mob of disorganized troops occupied, consisted of close and extended order drill. On one occasion there was a call for volunteers for the paratroopers. Bruce was tempted but decided otherwise when none of his friends would join him.

On October 7 Egger noted that the inevitable "rumors were going around that we would be leaving soon." The next day the transients underwent yet another clothing inspection, which seemed to Bruce to lend credence to this latest scuttlebutt. That same evening they entrained for Southampton, where they were marched on board a ship for passage across the Channel. They disembarked on Omaha Beach via landing craft the afternoon of October 10.

Lee Otts and his group were denied—or spared, as the case may be—the opportunity to spend any time in England this trip. At Southampton they moved directly off the *Thomas H. Barry* and onto an old English ship, *Antenor*, for transport across the Channel on November 4.

Their first week in France was a miserable one for Bruce Egger and his group. It rained daily and, while their tiny two-man pup tents shed the water, they could do little about the sodden ground. Trying to keep their blankets, clothing, and gear from getting soaked and caked with mud proved futile. There were no field kitchens and their meals usually consisted of cold Spam, orange marmalade, crackers, and lukewarm coffee. "The Army didn't furnish bicarbonate of soda or anti-acid pills to relieve the heartburn I suffered after each meal," Egger noted.

After marking time in the vicinity of Omaha Beach for five days, and on one occasion working on an ammunition unloading party, the replacements departed by truck on October 15 for the front lines, their sodden cargo packs seemingly weighing 150 pounds. They passed through Caen, Orleans, and Toul, enduring the rain and mud at night in their pup tents. On the 17th, near Toul, many of the men came down with diarrhea and beat a path back and forth to the latrine throughout the night. Egger escaped with just stomach cramps, but he recorded in his journal how "one man slipped and fell in the mud and crapped in his clothes. He lay there and cried in frustration."

The next day the group was trucked on to Neufchateau, which was the winter quarters for the 17th Replacement Depot. There Egger and some of his buddies were able to find quarters in the attic of an old French barracks, thus being able to sleep out of the weather for the first time since they had arrived in France. After marking time there for a week, the replacements were trucked to the nearby city of Nancy on October 25 and assigned to the 26th Infantry Division.

Lee Otts' experience as a replacement in transit in France was much the same as Egger's. For the first four days there was a muddy bivouac area near Omaha Beach with continuous rain and the same cold rations. Then on November 8—the day Bruce Egger and his new unit got their first taste of serious combat—Otts' replacement group loaded into open trucks in the rain and traveled eastward all afternoon and a good part of the night. "I have never been so cold in my life," Lee wrote his parents. About ten o'clock they arrived at a replacement depot near Le Mans, where the officers enjoyed the luxury of being quartered in pyramidal tents.

The sun came out the next day and life became more bearable. Otts and a fellow officer got a pass into Le Mans that Sunday night, November 13. They didn't find much to do there but it was still nice to enjoy a break from camp life.

The respite was short-lived, since the next day the contingent was marched four miles with full packs to a loading area and crammed into the notorious *Quarante-et-huit* French boxcars—forty men or eight horses. Even with thirty-five men in Otts' car, it was still insufferably crowded and the ride rough and cold. They arrived at their destination about ten o'clock on the night of the 15th. The next morning the group debarked from their packed boxcars and marched a short distance to the 17th Replacement Depot just outside Neufchateau. On the afternoon of November 17 they were trucked through Nancy and, in a downpour, out into the countryside to the regimental train area of the 328th Infantry Regiment, 26th Infantry Division, to which they had been assigned. After carrying all their baggage out into a bivouac area and setting up their tents, all in the pitch dark at eleven o'clock at night, they were exhausted.

The 26th Infantry Division, to which Pfc. Bruce Egger was assigned on October 25 and 2nd Lt. Lee Otts on November 17, had been formed in 1917 out of the New England National Guard—hence the nickname "The Yankee Division" and the patch bearing the big "YD" initials— and reactivated in January 1941. Most of the men were from Massachusetts, although eventually the YD contained draftees from all over the United States. The 26th Division was composed of the 101st, 104th, and 328th Infantry Regiments. The famed World War I hero, Sgt. Alvin York, had served in G Company of the 328th, which was destined to be Egger's and Otts' outfit.

The Yankee Division had landed in France at Utah Beach on September 7–8. It had supposedly been in strategic reserve over the next month, but some three thousand men from the 26th had been formed into nineteen provisional truck companies and assigned to the famous "Red Ball Express" to haul supplies from the beaches of Normandy to the fighting front. On October 7 the 26th Division had been assigned to the Third Army in anticipation of the forthcoming offensive in Lorraine, which was expected to break the stalemate that had developed in the early fall.[5] Egger and Otts and the other new replacements assigned to the Third Army in October and November of 1944 would soon find themselves involved in that costly campaign. [P.R.]

S/Sgt. Bruce E. Egger, 1945

Lt. Lee MacMillan Otts, 1945

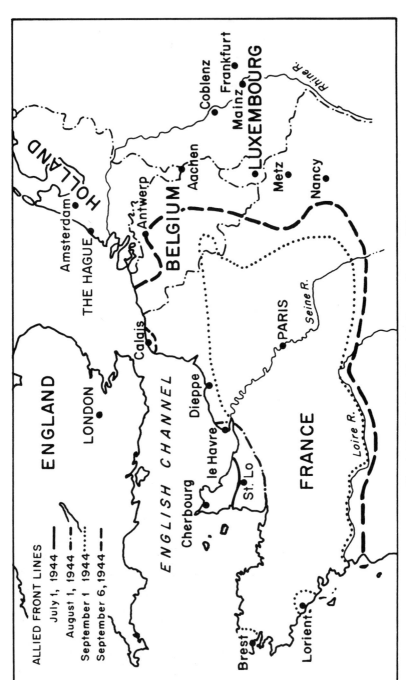

ENGLAND

LONDON

HOLLAND

Amsterdam
THE HAGUE

ENGLISH CHANNEL

Calais

Dieppe

le Havre

Cherbourg

St. Lo

Brest

Lorient

FRANCE

PARIS

Seine R.

Loire R.

BELGIUM

Antwerp

Aachen

LUXEMBOURG

Coblenz
Frankfurt
Mainz

Metz

Nancy

Rhine R.

Map 1. The Allied Breakthrough in France, Summer 1944

1 First Blood
October 25–November 17, 1944

OPERATIONAL BACKGROUND Following the invasion of France on June 6, 1944, and a protracted slugging match in the hedgerows of Normandy, the Allies had been able to effect a breakout at St. Lo in late July. Suddenly the war had been transformed from a series of bloody assaults into one of movement as the Anglo-American armies swept across northern France.

Leading the way in this spectacular advance was General George Patton's much publicized Third Army. But in late August, as a severe fuel crisis loomed, General Eisenhower had made the difficult decision to give first priority on supplies to Field Marshal Sir Bernard Montgomery's 21st Army Group in its northeastward thrust into Belgium and toward Germany's vital Ruhr industrial area. This meant that the Third Army's advance would have to halt for lack of gasoline. (See Map 1.)

Although Patton was able to resume operations within a few days, the pause had proved to be fatal to Allied momentum. The Germans had been busy feeding in reinforcements, particularly on the Third Army's right flank, which faced the main invasion corridor leading to the Saar Basin and on to Frankfurt. The days of easy pursuit were over; the Wehrmacht had made a remarkable recovery, and the American advance in Lorraine during September was bitterly contested. The Third Army quickly moved to the Moselle River, but the attempt to advance beyond that line provoked strong resistance.

By late September, also, a new logistical squeeze was developing. The operations in Holland, against Aachen in the northeast, and the attempt to advance east of the Moselle all combined to strain to the breaking point the existing port facilities and the supply and communications systems in northern France. The shortage of artillery ammunition was becoming critical, and another gasoline famine was looming. Eisenhower therefore decided that priority had to be given to Montgomery's efforts to secure the port of Antwerp, which had long been considered the only solution to the Allies' supply problems. The corollary of this decision was that the Third Army would have to go over to the defensive. Thus it was that in early October, when the 26th Division was assigned to Patton's forces, a period of quiet had settled in on the Third Army front that was to last until early November.[1]

In the meantime, the Yankee Division was being fed into the lines to give it combat experience for the coming offensive. On the morning of October 22 the 328th Infantry suffered its first serious losses when the 1st Platoon of Fox Company (2nd Battalion) ran into a buzzsaw on a combat patrol just south of the little town of Vic-sur-Seille and lost twenty-four of the original forty-three men, including several who were captured. (Of the twenty-eight replacements sent to the 2nd Battalion on October 25, F Company got twenty-five; the remaining three, including Egger, were assigned to G Company.)

Four days later the 328th moved in to relieve its sister regiment, the 104th Infantry, in the vicinity of Bezange-la-Petite on the extreme right flank of the Third Army sector (see Map 2),[2] where Egger and his fellow replacements would soon join their units. With Lee Otts still en route to England, we now pick up Bruce's account. [P.R.]

EGGER *Oct. 25, 1944.* A shipping list, which included our entire company, came out this morning assigning us to the 26th Infantry Division, Third Army. Trucks took us to division headquarters near Nancy, where we had a clothing inspection before being assigned to regiments. Two of my friends from the 97th Division went to the 101st Regiment and Bob Dixon and I were sent to the 328th.

On the way to regimental headquarters we drove through Nancy, a bustling city with large numbers of people and soldiers on the streets. The traffic was mostly military vehicles. It was after dark when we arrived at the headquarters of the 328th. I wanted to stay in a barn full of hay, but we were moved to a field where we were told to dig a foxhole. The guards told us a German patrol was supposed to be in the area, but Dixon and I thought that might be a story to impress the replacements.*

Oct. 26, 1944. We had a hot breakfast with the medics before moving by vehicle to 1st Battalion HQ. On the way we passed a jeep that had been blown up when it ran over a mine. The two occupants were lying at the edge of the road with all but their feet covered by blankets. Artil-

---

*The Germans had in fact been conducting bold, large-scale patrols in this sector at the time. No doubt the headquarters personnel at the 328th were genuinely nervous about these enemy probes.[3]

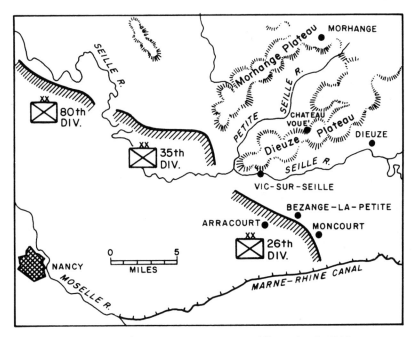

Map 2. XII Corps Front on the Morning of November 8, 1944

lery pieces were dug in on both sides of the road. Whenever one fired we involuntarily jumped.

Dixon, Erickson, Giovinazzo, and about twenty others from our replacement group were assigned to F Company. Cullison, Davidson, and I went to G Company in the 2nd Battalion.* We were to stay with the 1st Battalion until our outfit came off the line.

Oct. 27, 1944. Dixon and I improved our foxhole, which was at the foot of a slope near a creek. We also visited with the others and wrote letters. Occasionally a German artillery shell went over, but none landed near us. Not used to being on the receiving end of artillery, we wasted no time running to our holes.

Dixon was twenty-five years old and although he had been married three years, he and his wife didn't have any children, which he regret-

---

*An American infantry regiment in World War II normally had three battalions, each with four companies. The latter were lettered consecutively within the regiment, so that Companies A, B, C, and D would always be in the 1st Battalion; E, F, G, and H in the 2nd Battalion, etc.

ted. He had been an Air Force cadet at Kansas State College while I was there in ASTP. He was one of what we called "grounded butterflies." The Air Corps had decided they had an adequate supply of pilots, bombardiers, and navigators, so the program was disbanded along with ASTP. Dixon had been in my company with the 97th Division but in a different platoon, so I didn't know him until we shipped out as replacements.*

Oct. 28, 1944. It had been raining, so we pitched a tent over our foxhole. We spent most of the day visiting, sleeping, and writing letters. Dixon spent time studying a book to learn German.

Oct. 29, 1944. The 1st Battalion had church services this morning in an open field. The service was interrupted by a barrage of 88mm artillery, which the Germans used for antiaircraft, antitank, and antipersonnel. Their tanks were also equipped with 88s. The shells didn't land near us, but the shelling broke up the church service.

Oct. 30, 1944. It started to rain again after two days of sunshine. Our foxhole, which was at the base of a slope, was receiving water seepage, but we managed to plug the leaks with sod. All the foot and vehicle traffic was causing the area around the kitchen to become muddy.

A company filed past us this morning on the way to the front lines. The men didn't seem very enthusiastic about moving up.

The replacements for the 1st Battalion had been assigned to their respective companies and we 2nd Battalion replacements were moved up to join our companies on the front lines. A jeep took Cullison, Davidson, and me to G Company Headquarters in a small village near Bezange-la-Petite. On the way up we passed several burned-out American and German tanks. The G Company Command Post, or CP, was in the basement of a building whose upper stories had been almost leveled by artillery. Only portions of the walls were left standing. The sounds of machine gun fire and exploding shells were much closer. The mail clerk, jeep drivers, and several helpers stayed in the basement. We didn't tell them we had eaten our evening meal before we left, so they

---

*Although the rifle company was supposed to be the basic unit of the infantry, the outfit with which its members most closely identified, in the American army it never worked out that way. This is in contrast to the considerably more cohesive German infantry company.[4] The reader will note that throughout the following pages Egger identifies primarily with his squad and only secondarily with his platoon. He was rarely very well acquainted with the members of the other three platoons in George Company.

prepared canned eggs for us over a small gas stove. The basement had a musty smell, but it was warm and dry and more comfortable than a foxhole. Candles furnished our light.

Oct. 31, 1944. The front lines were only about three-hundred yards from town. Captain Paul Carrier, the Commanding Officer of G Company, decided to leave us at the Company CP, since it was only possible to move into position under the cover of darkness and the 2nd Battalion was due to be relieved soon. I went upstairs several times to look around, but it was not safe to venture very far from the security of the basement. The small farm village where we were located had no civilian population left. There wasn't a building in town that hadn't suffered damage from artillery.

Pfcs. Larry Treff and Carl Anderson came in from the front after dark. They both had diarrhea, a messy situation when you can't leave your foxhole. They heated water on the gas stove, bathed, and changed underwear. They were keyed up and talkative after being confined to a foxhole and so close to the Germans.

Nov. 1, 1944. The 1st Battalion relieved the 2nd Battalion after dark and we went back into reserve. I was one of the four guides assigned to take the G Company platoons back to the rear-area positions the 1st Battalion was vacating. Fog had settled in, providing good cover, and there were no problems during the exchange or the walk back to the rear. The kitchen had hot coffee for the men. I could hear some of them talking most of the night while I was on guard duty.

Nov. 2, 1944. Cullison and I had taken over the foxhole I had shared with Dixon, who had gone to F Company. It was still raining and the water table was rising. We kept throwing sod in the hole so we wouldn't be sleeping in the water. By the time the leaks were stopped the hole was almost at ground level. We were not that concerned about artillery, since none had landed in our vicinity.

A thousand pair of feet on top of the previous traffic soon turned the kitchen area into a sea of mud. The troops who had come off the line were unshaven and dirty and most were taking action to remedy the situation since being clean shaven was one of General Patton's requirements. Three hot meals were served daily. We had two hours of guard duty at night. George Company had suffered one man killed and three wounded so far. All the casualties had been from shrapnel.

Nov. 3, 1944. Cullison and I dug a hole on higher ground to avoid the seepage and pitched our tent over it. A stray cow wandered into camp this morning and some of the fellows promptly killed and butchered it. A bottle of wine was issued to every three men. By the time I went on guard at 2200, the one-third of a bottle I had drunk was causing stomach cramps. Before I got off guard I had diarrhea and spent the rest of the night and morning running to the latrine. The water was all right here. It was the wine you had to watch out for.

Harold Clark [pseudonym], Captain Carrier's runner, shot himself in the foot today while cleaning his carbine.*

General Patton talked to most of the officers in the 26th Division today and told them the Third Army would be making a big drive soon.

FROM EGGER'S LETTER OF NOVEMBER 3

I haven't seen any action yet, the closest I have been is about a half mile from the front. The men who have been there say I don't have much to look forward to.

Mud and rain are two things I'll remember about France.

If I make it through this winter I'll be satisfied as long as I have a roof over my head and three meals a day. A person never appreciates anything until conditions worsen. You would be surprised at how little the men here complain.

They gave us a bottle of wine for every three men. Don't worry, we are drinking it very sparingly and it isn't very strong. . . .

I guess there is no picnic ahead for me. I only hope and pray that I can take it like a man and do my part. . . . I know if your prayers and everyone else's mean anything that I'll come through alright.

Nov. 4, 1944. I felt weak and sick this morning so I went to the medics, who gave me some pills. The runs stopped by mid-morning and I felt good enough to ride back to Regimental HQ for a shower. I saw several dead cows, killed by artillery, lying in the pastures on their backs, legs sticking straight up. As they began to decompose the body cavities filled with gas, causing the carcasses to roll onto their backs. The people here had lost their homes, livestock, and probably most of their possessions.

The quartermasters had set up big tents with shower stalls and

---

*The G Company morning report for Nov. 3 listed this man as "seriously wounded (self-inflicted) in the right foot."

wooden slat floors. I don't know how the water was heated, but I know that we hated to leave the warmth of the shower and return to the cold and mud of the foxholes.

Nov. 5, 1944. A Red Cross clubmobile was at the battalion area in the afternoon with coffee, doughnuts, phonograph music, and two pretty American girls to remind us of home.

It had rained all day and the foxholes were full of water. It was impossible to keep ourselves or our blankets dry and free of mud. I felt discouraged today, probably because I was not feeling good.

OPERATIONAL BACKGROUND   Despite the strong resistance encountered on all fronts in September and October, the Allied high command was convinced the German army would crumble under continued pressure. The unremitting rains of October may have made the lives of the troops miserable and complicated the battlefield situation, but the generals considered that, with victory seemingly so close, operations had to continue. The decision of late September to halt the advance of the Third Army had been dictated by an untenable logistical situation, but that problem was well on the way to resolution. By mid-October, then, Eisenhower's headquarters was cranking out plans for a general offensive on all fronts.

The broad strategy would remain the same. Primary emphasis would be on Montgomery's northern thrust, assisted by Hodges' First American Army, toward the Ruhr industrial area, thence across the Rhine, and ultimately on to Berlin. At the same time Patton's Third Army would drive northeastward through Lorraine and in the direction of Frankfurt.[5]

In the Third Army sector, XX Corps would envelop Metz while General Manton Eddy's XII Corps, to which the 26th Division was attached, would advance on the right. The Yankee Division's 328th Infantry, with Pfc. Bruce Egger one of the new replacements in its 2nd Battalion, would be on the extreme right, or southern flank of the XII Corps (and the Third Army) line, which abutted on the Marne-Rhine Canal. The date of the attack was set for November 8.

General Patton was brimming with his usual confidence. "It is 132 miles to the Rhine from here," he told the new 95th Division on November 4, "and if this army will attack with venom and desperate energy, it is more than probable that the war will end before we get to the Rhine." What he failed to foresee is that a total of 7.2 inches of rain would fall on Lorraine in November, as contrasted to the normal precipitation of three inches for that month, turning the terrain into a sea of mud and exacting a heavy toll upon troops not equipped by their government for such miserable combat conditions.

The role of the 2nd Battalion of the 328th Infantry was to take the town of Moncourt. The more than two hundred men who ended up as casualties there were not informed that this was merely a diversionary action; the main attack was occurring farther to the north.[6] [P.R.]

━━━━━━━━━━━━━━━━━━━━━━━━━━━━━

EGGER *Nov. 6, 1944.* Orders came down this morning that the 2nd Battalion was to relieve the 3rd Battalion on line in the late afternoon.

I was assigned to the 1st Squad, 3rd Platoon. Cullison was sent to the 1st Platoon and Davidson went to a machine gun section of the 4th Platoon. The supply sergeant gave me a duffel bag and I turned in my extra clothes, a blanket, gas mask, razor, notebook, and some other personal gear. Gas masks were not carried in the field; the high command evidently thought there was not much risk of the Germans using poison gas.

We moved out shortly after I joined the platoon, so I didn't have a chance to become acquainted with the members of the squad. Carl Anderson, whom I had met at the Company CP, introduced me to Ed Evans, Charles Foster, Joe Treml, Frank Kuchyt, Harry Lee, Allan Parlee, Ernie Viscio, and Tom Twardziewski. Anderson, Evans, Foster, and Treml were all transfers from ASTP. S/Sgt. John Saulenas and Sgt. George Kearny [pseudonym] were the squad and assistant squad leaders, respectively. The men spoke highly of Saulenas, although of late he had been nervous and irritable. Some of the men thought Kearny was not very intelligent and mostly talk. T/Sgt. Edward Zabloski was the platoon sergeant and S/Sgt. Wallace Sullivan was platoon guide. Larry Treff was the only other man I knew in the platoon.

We moved out just before dark in single file. Traveling was difficult. At times we would sink to our knees in the mud, and I was soon wishing I had left more of my gear back in my duffel bag. We passed through a draw in which the burned-out hulks of four American tanks stood. We walked about two miles before the squad split up. Kearny took Foster, Evans, Kuchyt, Lee, and me to a small cement pillbox on a hill, while Saulenas and the rest of the squad went to a bunker about four hundred yards away, near the woods. The rest of the platoon and the 1st and 4th Platoons dug in behind us while the 2nd Platoon was in the woods to our right. Kearny immediately posted a guard. He did not pull guard, but the rest of us were on two and off eight.

The pillbox was drier than the holes we had left, but it was crowded for five men. There was no room to stretch out, so I sat on my pack and tried to sleep. By 2000 the roof had begun to leak and by midnight the floor was muddy and water was running in the open doorway.

When I went on guard at 2000, it was still raining and so dark that I could only see a few feet. The wind was so strong it would have been difficult to hear or see anyone approaching or for a patrol to find their way. German artillery kept landing close enough that I could hear the shrapnel whistle as it passed overhead.

Standing guard on the front lines was a heavy responsibility, since the safety of the other men depended on the vigilance of the sentry. Because of the inactivity, it was easy to daydream, reflect on the future, think of home, and wonder what your loved ones were doing. I fought to stay alert and was glad to be relieved at 2200.

Nov. 7, 1944. We learned this morning that a German patrol had attacked a squad of the 2nd Platoon the night before and had killed one man, wounded two, and taken two prisoners.*

It rained all day and about six inches of water was standing on the floor of the pillbox. Foster reminded me of a small boy playing in the mud as he tried to dam out the water flowing in the doorway. Kuchyt was a funny guy and kept everyone laughing except Lee, who tended to be moody.

I was on guard from 0600 to 0800 and from 1600 to 1800. Enemy artillery periodically landed on the platoons to our rear. Some of the men would get out and stretch their legs and dive for the foxholes when a round came in. One man did not make it in time and caught a piece of shrapnel in the buttocks. Kearny thought we would be here for several more days before another unit relieved us.

We sat with our feet in the water most of the day. I was the only one who didn't have overshoes and my feet, which had not been dry for four days, were starting to itch and burn and felt swollen. The pillbox was full of steam from our wet clothes, cigarette smoke, and fumes from the stove we used to heat our rations.

Nov. 8, 1944. It was still raining at 0200 when I relieved Evans on guard duty. I wore a raincoat over my overcoat and, except for my feet and lower legs, managed to stay dry.

While I was on duty the mortar platoon from M Company set up their weapons near the pillbox. I asked their sergeant if they were relieving us. "No," he said, "we will be providing you with mortar sup-

---

*Pvt. Clarence C. Spake was killed in action, S/Sgt. Stanley Twardzik and Pfc. Harry O. Anderson were wounded, and Pfcs. Charles D. Barnes, Jr., and Henry B. Bobrow were taken prisoner, all on the night of Nov. 6, 1944, near Moncourt. Anderson returned to duty with G Company on Mar. 10, 1945.

port this morning while you attack Moncourt." Moncourt was a small village to our right front beyond the wooded area. About ten minutes later T/Sgt. Zabloski and S/Sgt. Sullivan arrived and confirmed what I had been told.

We left our overcoats and packs in the pillbox and headed out about 0345 to join the rest of the squad. Kearny didn't have any trouble finding Saulenas and the other men, despite the inky darkness and heavy rain.

There was only room for six in their bunker, so half the squad had to wait outside. I got a ten-minute turn in the bunker, which smelled of wet wool clothes and was full of cigarette smoke and steam from wet bodies and clothes. I didn't have any hand grenades so Saulenas gave me one. I noticed that the dirt seemed ingrained in the skin of his hands and his fingernails were dirty. I looked at my hands and they were the same.

Six of us waited in the rain outside the bunker for close to an hour; as usual with the Army, it was hurry up and wait. Kuchyt found an unoccupied bunker with a log roof and stood in a crouched position in water up to his knees. I couldn't see that his situation was any better than ours; maybe this was the only way he could keep his cigarette lit.

Before we moved out I took off my raincoat, folded it, and put it behind my cartridge belt over my hips. I wanted to be able to move if need be and didn't want a long coat binding my legs. In five minutes the rain had penetrated my jacket, wool shirt, and wool underwear.

We met the rest of the platoon on a path at the edge of the woods and moved through in single file. Kearny was the last man in the platoon and I was just ahead of him. The path we were following was full of water, and the mud, brush, and communication wire strung on the ground made it difficult to keep up in the darkness.

I'll never forget how I felt that morning. The Army had been preparing me for this for months, and I had ignorantly been anticipating combat. I had been better off being ignorant because I had worried very little about going into battle, but now that the time had arrived I was not feeling so eager. I had the same gut-wrenching feeling in the pit of my stomach that I used to get before the beginning of a sports contest in high school, except that it was more intense because I realized that this was no game and that some of us were going to die or be wounded today. I not only feared for our safety, but for our success and my performance. But I knew I had no choice but to face whatever would happen and to pray that God provide the strength and courage to face the day and, of course, to spare my life if it was His will.

The plan was for F Company to take Moncourt; George Company was to take the high ground to the left and hold it while tanks moved through our positions.* It sounded very simple in conception, but the execution proved to be another matter.

THE ACTION AT MONCOURT WOODS
(as described in Ed Zabloski's letter of June 4, 1991, to Bruce Egger)

Nov. 8th and Moncourt woods are like a nightmare to me. . . .

We were to attack with the 1st and 3rd Platoons—2nd in reserve—and the 4th supporting. The 101st Mechanized Cavalry [an incorrect designation for elements of the 2nd Cavalry Group] was behind us and their mission was to drive through the break once that was accomplished.

We knew that the Germans had a pillbox on our right flank and a machine gun emplacement on our left flank, located in a patch of woods.

Prior to the general attack, two men were assigned to take the pillbox out, and a squad from the 2nd Platoon was to destroy the machine gun emplacement on our left flank.

. . . I saw the two men make their way up to the pillbox, throw a couple of grenades in, and destroy it. We moved forward on command and were immediately pinned down by machine gun fire from our left flank.

Two of our squad leaders were killed and other members of the 3rd Platoon, including myself, were wounded.

I sent Sgt. Sullivan back to Co. headquarters to tell them that we were still pinned down by heavy fire from our left flank. Sully was also hit and wounded. By 9:00 a.m. the 3rd Platoon was no longer able to contribute. . . .

While we were moving through the woods our artillery was passing overhead, landing in the town and the woods to our front. Our platoon stopped for a few minutes at the edge of the woods and waited while Captain Carrier briefed the platoon leaders. We spread out and crouched low, since our artillery was landing near us. H Company's heavy machine guns were located nearby and were firing into the trees to our right front. Day was breaking and we could hear shouting along with the deep report of our M-1 rifles and the sharp clatter of the enemy

---

*Two former members of G Company state that the attack was supposed to have been supported by tanks but that they didn't appear until that afternoon.

machine guns and burp guns to our right where Fox Company was attacking.

Our squad moved to the left across a road and along the edge of the woods, where Saulenas signaled us to stop and get down. From this position we could observe a squad from the 2nd Platoon firing their rifles while they ran across an open field toward a grove of trees. Enemy artillery was landing in a low area beyond the trees and at the foot of a slope that extended upward to Moncourt. The ground was soft from the constant rain and the shells sank into the ground, sending geysers of mud into the air as they exploded.

The 1st Battalion was attacking Bezange-La-Petite, which was almost two miles to our left. American artillery landing in the town had set fire to many of the buildings. Rifle and machine gun fire from both sides indicated that the Germans were putting up a stiff resistance. Soon the automatic weapons fire was being turned on us. I hugged the ground as the bullets passed over me and tore up the earth about two feet to my left. Fortunately our squad suffered no casualties.

The fire was coming from our right front. Evidently pressure from the attack in F Company's sector occupied the machine gunner's attention, since we received no fire when we jumped at a signal from Saulenas and ran for the grove of trees the 2nd Platoon had taken. The 2nd Platoon had caught the Germans by surprise. They had suffered no casualties while killing a number of the enemy and taking five prisoners. The three young, fair-haired dead Germans lying on the ground near their bunkers were the first war dead I had observed at close range. The color had drained from their faces and blood was running from the nose of one. A German pistol was lying beside one of the dead, but I didn't have time to collect war trophies. Their dugouts were deep and were covered with logs and dirt, which had provided them with excellent protection from our artillery.

The 1st Squad's objective was the high ground on the left edge of Moncourt. The squad formed a skirmish line at the edge of the woods in preparation for crossing the pasture that sloped gently upward to Moncourt. We moved out with two men running forward and hitting the ground to provide fire cover while two more moved up. We were spaced about twenty or thirty feet apart to lessen the chances of a shell getting more than one man.

We had moved about seventy yards in this manner when Evans, who was to my immediate right and in the prone position, started firing his BAR (Browning Automatic Rifle). I couldn't see his target. Suddenly Evans' helmet appeared to jump from his head. As it rolled away from him the helmet liner came out and rolled in tight little circles. He never moved. Saulenas, who was to the right of Evans, was shot in the neck when he started to crawl towards Evans. Saulenas groaned, grabbed his neck, rolled over several times and lay still.* The Germans apparently didn't see the rest of our squad as we were not fired on. It appeared that we would have been less visible if we had approached from farther to the left. The Germans must have expected an attack from that area because they continued to bombard it with artillery and mortars.

Kearny, who was now in charge, held a hurried conference with several members of the squad and decided to pull back to the main part of the woods. A first aid station had been set up there and it was overrun with the wounded. Fox Company, which was moving up the right side of the road, had been pinned down by machine gun fire and mortars and had suffered heavy casualties.

There was a field about 150 yards wide between the woods and the town. Part of our company had taken a pillbox and had almost reached the town from the left side of the road. We moved up the left edge of the road toward town, stopping to wait with a squad of the 2nd Platoon in a clump of trees and brush while Kearny tried to find out where we were needed. A German observer apparently spotted us and within a few minutes a barrage of 88s and mortars fell on us. The sound of the exploding shells was deafening. The concussions from the explosions shook the ground so violently that I felt like I was bouncing and in danger of sliding off the face of the earth. I pressed myself to the ground and covered my head with my arms for added protection. I looked up and all I could see was black smoke. The smell of the powder was overpowering. After each explosion I was amazed to find myself unscathed and gritted my teeth as each new screaming 88 or whispering mortar shell approached. I was continually showered by mud from the exploding shells and the shrapnel, which tore up the ground around me.

When the shelling let up in about fifteen minutes, I could hear the cry, "Medic!" all around me. Anderson and Foster, who were near me, had been wounded, but not seriously. Lee was sitting in a hole half filled with water. The heel of his left foot was shattered. Parlee and Treml had been hit, but they were able to walk to the aid station. Twardziewski was dead, propped in a sitting position against the trunk of a tree, blood running from his nose.† A man from the 2nd Platoon lay dead; his body had been nearly severed by a large piece of shrapnel. Another soldier had severe chest wounds. He wheezed as he breathed and was coughing

---

*Pfc. Edward J. Evans and S/Sgt. John M. Saulenas were both listed in subsequent G Company morning reports as killed in action.

†Pfc. Carl E. Anderson was listed as "slightly injured [as opposed to wounded] in action." He had suffered a contusion on the left knee and was hospitalized but re-

up blood. Kuchyt and I were the only ones left from the squad—I had lost contact with Viscio, and Kearny had gone to the aid station with a nicked nose. There were no medics in the area, so the survivors administered first aid.

My first inclination was to get out of there as fast as possible before the Germans started shelling again. An ammunition bearer for one of our forward machine guns who was returning from the rear with belts of cartridges had been caught in the barrage. When the shelling had let up he had got up and started forward, which is the best way to get out of the artillery's range. I was torn between following him and staying to help the wounded.

I decided to go back for a medic and litter bearers. I offered to help Lee, but he didn't want to move. He seemed to be in shock from the wound or the shelling or perhaps both. I had only gone a short distance when I noticed a lieutenant lying on his back underneath a tree. He had a gaping wound at the junction of his right leg and stomach. He had treated the wound as well as he could and had stopped the bleeding, but he was weak and pale from the loss of blood. I continued to the aid station and came back with a medic and five litter bearers. The medic gave the lieutenant a shot of morphine and we lifted him to the litter and started back.* The medic and other litter bearers went on to administer to the other wounded. We could not travel on the road because the Germans had mined and felled trees across it. I know the trip was rough for the lieutenant, but he never complained.

I didn't note and don't remember whether the litter bearer and I made more than one trip to the aid station with the wounded. We must have, because the events described so far would not have occupied the entire day. I know I only stayed at the aid station a short time.

The aid station was located in the area where F Company had attacked at daylight, and the ground was dotted with dead soldiers from both sides. As I started back toward Moncourt I passed a dead Amer-

---

turned to duty two weeks later. Pfc. Charles N. Foster was reported to have been "seriously wounded in action" but was able to return to duty on Nov. 12.

Pfc. Harry D. Lee was listed as "seriously wounded in action" and died of his wounds that same day. Pfc. Thomas J. Twardziewski was killed in action.

Pfc. Allan W. Parlee and Pfc. Joseph S. Treml were both listed as "slightly wounded" and were hospitalized. Parlee does not appear on G Company records again, but Treml returned to duty on January 13, 1945. He was wounded again on March 13, 1945.

---

*Egger's inquiries have led him to conclude that this was 2nd Lt. Elmer L. Stevens of H Company. He died of his wounds that same day.

ican soldier lying face down and facing toward town. His size, build, and the color of his hair reminded me of Bob Dixon, but I could not bring myself to turn him over. I learned later that he had been killed in action on November 8.

1st SQUAD, 3rd PLATOON AT MONCOURT, NOVEMBER 8, 1944

S/Sgt. John Saulenas, KIA	Pfc. Frank Kuchyt*
Sgt. George Kearny*	Pfc. Harry Lee, DOW
Pfc. Carl Anderson, Injured	Pfc. Allan Parlee, WIA
Pfc. Bruce Egger	Pfc. Joseph Treml, WIA
Pfc. Edward Evans, KIA	Pfc. Thomas Twardziewski, KIA
Pfc. Charles Foster, WIA	Pfc. Ernest Viscio

*Slightly wounded but not hospitalized

It was now about 1600. As I reached the thicket that had been the scene of the morning shelling, I met what was left of the company pulling back from Moncourt. Easy and Fox Companies had finished taking the town and we were to dig defensive positions at the edge of the woods. Some of the wounded, including Cullison, who had been shot in the leg, walked back.* The other wounded were carried. Davidson had made it, but I didn't know any of the other men.

We moved back to the edge of the woods to wait for the company to regroup. The wounded were transported by jeep to the aid station. Suddenly I felt exhausted. I had been up since 0200 and had not eaten all day. I sat at the edge of the road and ate a K ration while I listened to some of the men talk about their experiences.

Frosty [Pfc. William F. Frost], the assistant to the company clerk, and Junior Servoss, the G Company jeep driver, parked near me and asked me about the day's events. I told them as best I could what had happened to the squad. They were heading to Rechicourt and offered to take me with them, but I felt I should stay with the company. They said it would be OK since they had to come back in a half-hour. But while

---

*Pfc. Carl R. Cullison was listed as "seriously wounded in action." He was hospitalized but returned to duty with G Company on March 14.

we were at Rechicourt we learned that the 2nd Battalion was being relieved by the 2nd Cavalry and that the men would be trucked to Arracourt. Since the jeep was not going back to Moncourt, I was told to stay with the kitchen and help the cooks move the next day.

I was issued dry clothes and treated like royalty at the kitchen. The supply sergeant, the mess sergeant, and the cooks had been with the company for a long time and were anxious to learn how their friends had fared. Kearny, his "wound" covered by a Band-Aid, was with the kitchen. I heard him tell the cooks he had killed five Germans today. What a blowhard! I had been with him up until the time he went back to the aid station and never saw him fire a shot. I felt that he had run out on the squad and that he could at least have stayed and helped move the wounded.

It had been a confusing day for me and I wondered if anything had gone as planned. But I had found that I could do what had to be done without being immobilized by fear or squeamish at the sight of the dead and wounded.

Neither words nor film can fully describe war. You have to be there, smell the cordite, hear all the sounds, see a broader field than the camera can cover, feel the fear and fatigue, the personal loss of friends, and see more than a fleeting glimpse of death and suffering. There was no way the Army could have prepared me for this day.

I was dead tired but had trouble falling asleep as my legs were cramping. I was thankful to be alive and all in one piece and to have dry clothes and a dry floor to sleep on.

Nov. 9, 1944. I believe Lt. Shipman, G Company Executive Officer, suspected that I had deserted the platoon yesterday, as he questioned me about being with the kitchen. I explained what had happened and asked him to check with Frosty and Servoss. He told me, and I agreed, that I should not have left the rest of the men. I ended up being the loser because I worked while the men at Arracourt rested.

Lt. Shipman, Supply Sergeant Aras, and two other men and I took a truck to the positions the company had left yesterday morning to pick up equipment that had been left behind. It was a desolate looking place. In the foxholes, which had filled with water, were shelter halves, blankets, sleeping bags, overcoats, and field packs. I had a good view of Moncourt and Bezange-La-Petite from the high ground. The fighting had moved on and the rumble of artillery was in the distance. We knew that the graves registration unit was probably gathering the dead at yesterday's two battle sites. After we finished collecting the equipment we joined G Company at Arracourt.

Kearny, Kuchyt, Viscio, and Treff were the only men left in the 3rd

Platoon that I knew. During the action at Moncourt the company lost sixty men from all causes, twenty-two of them killed, which is an extremely high ratio of killed to wounded.* Two of the 3rd Platoon squad leaders—Saulenas and S/Sgt. Gaetano Iovanni—had been killed. T/Sgt. Zabloski, the platoon sergeant and acting platoon leader, and S/Sgt. Sullivan, the platoon guide, had both been wounded.†

I had thought it was difficult to go into combat as a replacement with men you hardly knew, but after Moncourt I could see some advantages to it. I hadn't had time to get close to anyone in the company, as I had with Dixon, Carlson, Brown, and Hummel. I believe the loss of so many friends destroyed the spirit of some of the men in the company; a number of them went back with trench foot and illness during the next few weeks.

Nov. 10, 1944. We spent most of the day cleaning our rifles and drying clothes and equipment. The Red Cross clubmobile was in town to provide coffee, doughnuts, and music and to remind us what women looked like.

Seventy-nine replacements joined the company in the evening and we were reorganized. Lt. Ernest Greup and T/Sgt. Willard Straw from the 2nd Platoon were our platoon leaders and S/Sgt. Ed Sorel was platoon guide. S/Sgt. Dan Rankin from the 1st Platoon was leader of the 1st Squad and Sgt. Paul Nickel was his assistant. Kearny and Stashin had the 3rd Squad. I was glad I was not in Kearny's squad.

We were told to be prepared to move that night. The Germans were falling back and we were to keep applying the pressure. I wondered if we were ever going to have a chance to rest. We learned that the main push of XII Corps was being made to the north by the 80th and 35th Divisions and by our 101st and 104th Regiments. Our attack on Moncourt and Bezange-La-Petite had been a diversionary action.

The replacements with their clean clothes and smooth faces were conspicuous and almost treated us old men with reverence. Two weeks ago I had looked the same as these men. It would have been interesting to know what Kearny told the replacements in his squad.

It started to rain at 2000 when we were loading onto the trucks. The vehicles used cat's-eye blackout lights, which provided light enough to

---

*G Company's losses since going on line on Oct. 6 had numbered some 82 men killed, wounded, and whatever. The table of organization for a World War II rifle company called for 6 officers and 187 enlisted men, of which about 160 were assigned combat roles.[7]

†T/Sgt. Edward J. Zabloski and S/Sgt. Wallace L. Sullivan were both listed as "seriously wounded." Sullivan returned to duty on Mar. 13.

permit the trucks to travel about ten miles an hour. The truck ahead of us ran off the road, injuring three men when it rolled over. The road was too congested with traffic for us to make any progress, so we went back to Arracourt to spend the night.

OPERATIONAL BACKGROUND While the 328th Infantry was conducting its costly diversionary attacks toward Moncourt and Bezange-la-Petite, its two sister regiments, the 101st and the 104th, had been attempting to advance through a meat grinder a bit farther north. On November 10 the 328th was dispatched to join them in that bloody effort.

The 26th Division was being funneled into what is considered the classic invasion route between France and Germany, but it was far from being an open gate. The initial problems were two elongated hill bastions running roughly east and west that guarded the gateway routes through the valleys below. The northern ridge was known as the Morhange Plateau, named for the little town located at its southeastern base. Running parallel on the south was the Dieuze Plateau, also named after a nearby town. The latter ridge is commonly referred to as the Foret de Bride et de Koecking, which overlay most of it. Between these two plateaus there is a constricted valley through which runs the Little Seille River.

The plan was for elements of the 4th Armored Division, supported by the 104th Regiment, to drive through the valley of the Little Seille while the 101st Infantry was taking the Dieuze Plateau on the right (see Map 2). Both efforts were eventually successful, but at a terrible cost. The 104th took heavy casualties, and the 101st was so badly cut up in gaining a foothold on the heavily wooded ridge that General Willard Paul, commander of the 26th Division, had to send in the 328th to help.[8] [P.R.]

EGGER *Nov. 11, 1944.* During the night the platoon sergeant of the 2nd Platoon shot himself in the foot and a sentry wounded a GI who didn't respond with the proper password. As I recall there were about seven cases of self-inflicted wounds in the company from October to May. All but one of the wounds were in the foot, and I only know of one man who returned to the company. I don't know how the Army handled these cases or what went on the soldiers' records. I doubt that any of them were awarded the Purple Heart.

We left by truck at 0400, rode for about ten miles, and detrucked in an orchard near the little town of Vic-sur-Seille. We were issued rations and water and we stacked our bedrolls and packs in squad bundles. The bedrolls were brought to us if and when the occasion permitted. I left my overcoat in the squad bundle and threw my leggings away, as they were too much bother to lace and unlace. I had obtained a pair of oversized overshoes at Arracourt.

Treff and I were assigned to be the scouts but he stayed with the Company CP because his appendix was bothering him.* We had a K ration for breakfast and moved out at 0600, a column in single file on each side of the road. We walked for two hours and stopped for a short break. We passed the burned-out frames of six German trucks that had been shot up by our fighter planes or tanks. An artillery unit dug in along the road was firing into the woods, which were about two miles to our front. The fields were full of shell holes and many of the trees had been shattered by artillery.

We turned right at a road junction; a sign on the road to the left indicated that it was thirty-five kilometers to Metz. Along the road to the forest, which took us through a small village, were four dead German soldiers. One soldier appeared to be about 16 or 17 years old. Two of our tanks had stopped at the edge of the woods and were firing their cannons and machine guns. They soon moved out of sight into the forest.

The road was congested with vehicles from the 101st Regiment and with tanks, so we left the road and crossed a field over which the infantry and some tanks had just passed. We walked past two dead American soldiers lying face down about ten feet apart. One of them had a head wound and an untied open compress bandage rested on his head. Either he or a medic had tried to treat the wound and he had died before the job was completed.

It was about noon when we entered the woods, and we stopped and waited for three hours. While we were waiting it occurred to me that this was Armistice Day and wouldn't it be nice if history repeated itself? We heard church bells that afternoon. Since it wasn't Sunday, probably the French in a liberated village were observing the end of World War I.

We were in reserve to the 101st Regiment, which was leading the attack. I ate a dinner ration and dug a foxhole, which soon filled with water. The clouds had lifted enough so that our fighter planes were diving and strafing a mile or so ahead of us.

---

*Pfc. Larry Treff was in fact recuperating from a most unusual accident that had befallen him on Nov. 8 at Moncourt. He had stepped on a German "Bouncing Betty" mine, setting off a weak charge that throws up a fragmentation device that detonates on contact. The device had hit Treff in the groin, lifting him off the ground and hurling him several feet, but fortunately it did not detonate. In a couple of days, however, the bruise in his groin area was so purple and swollen he couldn't walk. This is why he didn't lead as a scout with Egger on Nov. 11.

S/Sgt. Rankin told me that the battalion would be relieved as soon as we cleared the woods. I was to hear that statement many more times: "When the objective is taken we will be relieved and go back for a rest."

We moved out at 1500 over a road through a conifer forest. We could hear small arms fire to our front and on the high ridge to our right. Our route of travel took us across a clearing about three hundred yards wide where we saw two dead GIs and an American tank with an 88 hole through the turret. Bayoneted rifles had been stuck in the ground beside the bodies. This was a common practice to indicate the location of the dead for the grave registration unit. At the far edge of the clearing and just inside the timber were a number of dead Germans. One of them must have taken a direct hit from a tank cannon, as he was badly mangled.

We turned left and walked another fifteen minutes deeper into the woods, and then stopped while the platoon leaders made a reconnaissance of the positions we were to occupy that night. A few mortar shells landed on us, causing some casualties in the 1st and 2nd Platoons. By then I could tell by the sound whether a mortar or artillery shell was a threat to me. The replacements were as jumpy as I had been two weeks ago.

After Captain Carrier and the platoon leaders came back, we moved to our positions and dug in for the night. I was paired with one of the replacements in the last foxhole on the squad's right. A machine gun from Howe Company was on our right.

E Company repulsed a counter attack just before dark and some of the wounded Germans called for help throughout the night.

The hardwood forest offered no protection from the rain that started falling about dusk. It was dark and damp; the woods smelled of rotting leaves. One of us was supposed to be awake at all times, but neither of us slept much as we had no blankets and we were wet and cold. A machine gun to our left fired periodically during the night and a German burp gun replied.

Nov. 12, 1944. At daylight we were surprised to discover that the 3rd Platoon had moved during the night. We walked to our left until we found some men from F Company and they directed us to G Company. When we found the 1st Squad, rations were being handed out and they were making preparations to move. Rankin was a little put out with us, but I told him that I thought it was his or Nickel's responsibility to see that we got the word to move.

My overshoes had not kept my feet dry and had rubbed my heels raw with blisters so I left them along the road. My toes were swollen and my feet itched and tingled from dampness and cold.

A battalion from the 101st Regiment was to move up the left side of the road, Easy and Fox Companies were to attack up the right side and G Company was in reserve guarding the right-rear flank. The attacking companies moved ahead, encountering a few snipers and machine gun nests. G Company, in the rear, was catching all the artillery. One heavy barrage fell to our rear, killing Major [Robert J.] Servatius, the Battalion CO, and wounding the Regimental CO and several others.*

A few prisoners were brought back through us during the day. They looked as wet and miserable as we did.

In the afternoon, as we were waiting along the road for E and F Companies to move ahead, a platoon from the 101st Regiment walked past on the way to the rear. Among them I recognized Bolton, who had been with me at Kansas State, Fort Leonard Wood, and in my replacement company. He was crying. I assumed it was because he was miserable and frustrated—at least he certainly looked miserable—or perhaps he had just lost a buddy. He didn't see me and I didn't speak to him as there was no time to visit and I didn't want to embarrass him.

We stopped along the road in a grove of pine trees for the night. We were soaking wet; it had rained all day and we had been making our way through wet brush. Our bedrolls could not be brought up to us, so we prepared to spend the night as best we could by digging a hole and covering the bottom with pine boughs. We put one raincoat on the bottom of the hole and the other over the top of us.

Kuchyt and a replacement dug in alongside us underneath a pine tree. Some of the limbs were cracking from the weight of the moisture, but Kuchyt thought a German was in the tree. Despite my explanation, he fired a clip from his BAR into the tree top, but only succeeded in shooting down a few limbs. I soon fell asleep, despite the drip from the trees and the water that ran into our hole.

Nov. 13, 1944. We slept through the storm, which put down about six inches of snow during the night. We were wet, muddy, and shivering from the cold. A barrage of 88s greeted us at daylight, but most of them landed on Easy Company to our left. Kuchyt had taken a prisoner during the night, a German soldier who had come strolling down the road. Kuchyt said, "I knew there was a man in that tree."

A number of men, including Kearny, Rankin, Sorel, and a replace-

---

*Lt. Col. David O. Byars, the 2nd Battalion CO, had become sick during the night and Major Servatius, the executive officer, had taken command. Byars resumed command the next morning.[9] Colonel Ben R. Jacobs, Regimental CO, was wounded in action but returned to duty on Nov. 18.[10]

ment from our squad went back with trench foot.* Nickel was now squad leader and I was designated acting assistant squad leader. Our company was in reserve again, and we followed the same procedure as the day before. We had moved ahead about three thousand yards yesterday. The snow soon turned to slush and it was another damp, raw day.

Machine gun fire killed E Company's CO [Captain Clifford Lierman] during the first few minutes of the attack. Fox Company ran into some stiff opposition during the afternoon and we were held up for several hours. Shortly after our forward progress had stopped, 88s started landing in our area. Stacks of cordwood provided us some protection from the shrapnel.

During a lull in the shelling the company moved forward about a hundred yards and stopped again. The 1st Squad was at the rear of the 3rd Platoon and the 1st Platoon was behind us. Word had been passed back that Fox Company had called for artillery on the German position. As soon as I heard the shells approaching I knew they were going to fall short and I hollered at the men to stay down. There was no cover or protection. The mistake was corrected in a few minutes, but it seemed like an eternity. Three replacements in front of me were hit in the legs, and two were killed and thirteen wounded in the 1st Platoon. T/Sgt. Francis Kelly, who had received a battlefield commission that morning, was one of the wounded. I helped two of the wounded back to the road, one of whom had a large hole in his heel from which the blood was gushing. I applied a tourniquet and the bleeding stopped. There were jeeps waiting at the road to take the wounded to the aid station. The man with the heel wound was thirty-seven years old, one of the oldest men in the company, and he had three children. Despite the wound he was in good spirits. I suspect he was willing to pay this price to get off the front lines. None of the three ever came back to the company.

I followed the communication wire forward to locate the company passing through the area that had been shelled. Many of the shells had exploded on contact with the trees, throwing shell fragments out and downward. Limbs and wood fragments were scattered over the area and in places the ground looked like it had been plowed. Some of the shell fragments were large enough to sever the limbs or trunk of a man. The air was heavy with the sickening odor of cordite. On the way to rejoin the squad, which was digging in for the night, I passed four dead GIs.

Nickel and I dug in together alongside a large log we thought would help protect us from shrapnel. The digging was easy and the soil was

---

*Sgt. Kearny, S/Sgt. Daniel J. Rankin, and S/Sgt. Edmond A. Sorel were all hospitalized. None of the three ever returned to G Company.

well drained. We covered the hole with logs and dirt and collected pine boughs to make a soft bed. Rations for the next day were brought up and for the first time in three days we had bedrolls. We spread two shelter halves over our hole to keep out the rain. (A shelter half was a piece of lightweight canvas; two shelter halves fastened together made a pup tent. Two wool blankets rolled up inside a shelter half made a bedroll.) We never set up tents on the front lines as they were too conspicuous. Before we went to sleep, Nickel and I pulled two hours of guard duty. It was so dark we could only see a short distance and the constant dripping of the rain from the trees sounded like someone was moving in the woods. Otherwise it was a quiet night; there was no small arms fire and very little artillery.

Nov. 14, 1944. Nickel had his knees in my back most of the night, but other than that I had a good rest. We had stayed dry and our wet clothes, which we slept in, steamed dry during the night. A replacement in the squad went back with trench foot this morning. We ate a K ration for breakfast, rolled up our blankets, and left the bedrolls near the road. T/Sgt. Straw handed out some extra D-bars [Army chocolate ration] to those who wanted them. I never turned down food.

Easy and George Companies led the attack today. We moved up through F Company's positions and formed a skirmish line, crouching behind trees as we waited for orders to move ahead. I saw Curtis with F Company, but there was no time to ask him about Dixon, Erickson, and others.* Curtis was later killed in action, but I'm not sure where or when.

A replacement by the name of Henry Huckabee and I were standing behind a tree, which didn't provide protection for both of us, so I decided to move behind another tree. As I moved out a bullet struck my helmet, knocking it from my head. I hit the ground immediately, crawled behind the tree, and tried to locate the sniper. He must have cleared out, as we received no more fire from that area. The bullet had creased the top of my helmet without breaking through the metal. I wore that same dented helmet through the remainder of the war.†

Shortly after this incident, the skirmish line moved forward, firing our rifles as we advanced. Most of the time we fired from the hip as we

---

*Pfc. Robert L. Dixon and Pfc. Kenneth O. Erickson were both killed in action at Moncourt on Nov. 8.

†While we were preparing this work for publication Egger received a letter from his old G Company buddy, Hank Sosenko, who mentioned that he still remembered "that crease in your steel helmet."

could not see anything but trees. I did fire at a shadowy figure moving low to the ground through the brush, but I couldn't tell whether it was a man or a large animal. We made good progress in the morning and did not give the Germans a chance to set up a defensive position. We were far enough forward to stay in front of the German artillery and mortars.

We hadn't had a chance to clean our rifles for several days and the operating rod on several of the rifles, including mine, was sticking, so the spent shell casings were not ejecting. Every time I fired I had to hit the operating rod with my shovel handle to eject the cartridge.

There was considerable noise and confusion. Parts of the skirmish line would be held up and the rest would stop and wait to keep the line even. The line was continually bearing right or left so we could maintain contact with the road on our left. With the continual shifting of the skirmish line, some of our men ended up with the 3rd Squad, which was on our right next to the 2nd Platoon. Before the day was over some of us from the 3rd Platoon were with the 1st Platoon next to Easy Company.

I learned later in the day that shortly before noon a German machine gun across the road in the 101st Regiment area had wounded Kuchyt and Lt. Greup. T/Sgt. Bill Straw, the platoon sergeant, was killed.* Shortly thereafter the advance was halted for some reason, and German mortars started falling in the area. A dud landed within ten feet of Fonrose LeCrone (another of the replacements of November 10) and me. We lost no time in getting away from the spot for fear of a delayed explosion.

We spotted five German soldiers to our front near a road. Someone hollered at them to surrender, but it was evident that they had something else in mind as their rifles were slung over their shoulders and they were preparing to escape on bicycles. My rifle jammed and I only got off one shot before the bicycles disappeared behind the trees and brush.

Evidently we had moved too far to the right, since the skirmish line was told to bear left to find the road we were supposed to be following. After about twenty minutes we were halted and told to sit down and wait. Most of us took the opportunity to eat a ration. After about two hours of waiting and becoming chilled, we started moving forward again.

In the meantime, a patrol had been sent back to contact our reserve

---

*Pfc. Frank Kuchyt and 2nd Lt. Ernest Greup were both listed as seriously wounded; neither returned to G Company. T/Sgt. Williard S. Straw was shown as killed in action.

force. They found a large number of Germans to our rear that we were able to take by surprise. The battalion took over eighty prisoners that day, with George Company accounting for about half of them.

Other than that we met no opposition. After advancing about a quarter of a mile, we crossed a road and dug in on a knoll. The digging was easy and Huckabee and I soon had a large hole dug behind a log. Bedrolls were brought up and we had a good rest with only a few shells landing in our area during the night. Sgt. Robert Starcher from the 2nd Platoon had taken charge of the 3rd Platoon.

There were about 150 men left in E, F, and G Companies out of a normal complement of some 525 men.

━━━━━━━━━━━━━━━

OPERATIONAL BACKGROUND At this point Egger and his G Company comrades gained a badly needed respite from the difficult fighting they had been involved in for a week: November 15–20 the 2nd Battalion was in regimental reserve, though it continued to maintain defensive positions in the Foret de Bride et de Koecking on top the Dieuze Plateau.[11] [P.R.]

━━━━━━━━━━━━━━━

EGGER *Nov. 15, 1944.* Another battalion was to resume the attack this morning and we should have been able to sleep late, but the sound of machine guns and cannons at daylight brought us out of our foxholes with rifles ready. We thought the Germans had returned, but it was a tank unit attached to the 1st Battalion that had fired into our positions by mistake, wounding two men in F Company.

My neighbor in the adjacent foxhole was sitting near a warming fire, clad in long johns, boots, and a wool cap, heating coffee water and drying his trousers. This was my introduction to Stan Nachman, who had joined the company on November 10.

We were told that our battalion would rest here for a few days and reorganize. Those who thought they might have trench foot were told to report to the aid station. The medics treated my blisters and although my feet were red and swollen, their condition did not warrant a ticket to the hospital. When the toes started to turn black at the joints, it was time to become concerned. Nickel and one of the replacements were sent to the hospital.

There were seventy-five men left in G Company, twenty-five of whom were headquarters personnel. Twelve men—S/Sgt. Starcher, Stan Nachman, Junior Letterman, Henry Huckabee, Fonrose LeCrone, Oscar Stribling [pseudonym], Larry Treff, Vic Popa, Vern Olson, Charles Foster, Jim McCowan, and I—made up the 3rd Platoon. Nachman,

Letterman, Huckabee, LeCrone, Popa, Olson and McCowan had joined us in the replacement draft of November 10. Foster, Starcher, Stribling, and Treff had come over with the 26th Division. Foster, Stribling, and Treff were the only originals of the platoon left. There had been a total of twenty-one men in the squad since I had joined it nine days ago. Four had been killed, eight had been wounded, and five disabled from trench foot. I don't know what happened to the replacement I shared a foxhole with on the nights of the 11th and 12th. I inquired about him, but no one had seen him after the attack started on the 13th. No one knew his last name, so I wasn't able to check the company's casualty list.

We were able to build warming fires during the day and I dried four blankets, an overcoat, shoes, and my stockings. I got another rifle, as the stock of my original one had been broken by a bullet or shrapnel. I had never felt the impact. I also discovered a hole through the baggy part of my trouser leg, probably caused by a bullet or a shell fragment. Yesterday had been a day of near misses.

Nov. 16, 1944. On the less active days in my journal I am adding some information that may be of interest to the reader.

The squad, consisting of twelve men, was the smallest unit in an infantry division. There were three squads in a platoon and three rifle platoons and a weapons platoon in a rifle company. A rifle squad had eleven riflemen and one man with a Browning Automatic Rifle (BAR). The weapons platoon had light machine guns and 60mm mortars, how many I don't recall.★

A staff sergeant was in charge of a squad, with a buck sergeant for his assistant. The platoon was led by a first or second lieutenant, with a technical sergeant second in command. The platoon guide was a staff sergeant. A medic, or first-aid man, from the regimental medical detachment was assigned to each platoon, which also had a runner. Each company had a commanding officer, usually a captain; an executive officer, who was second in command; a first sergeant who was in charge of the company's support services and the administrative details; and four runners.

The support members of the company were the mess sergeant, a kitchen force of six, the supply sergeant and a helper, a weapons-repair specialist, two jeep drivers, a mailman, and an advance assistant to the

---

★The weapons platoon in a World War II rifle company normally was equipped with two .30 caliber and one .50 caliber machine guns, three 60mm mortars, and three bazookas.[12]

company clerk. The company clerk had the the safest job, since he stayed at regimental headquarters miles behind the front. There was also a communications sergeant, who carried the heavy radio pack. He and his assistant ran the wire for the sound-powered telephones after the platoons were in fixed positions. There were supposed to be forty men and an officer in a platoon and 187 men and six officers in a company of infantry.

A battalion was made up of a headquarters company, three rifle companies, and a heavy weapons company. The heavy weapons company had 81mm mortars and heavy machine guns.

A regiment had three battalions, a headquarters company, an anti-tank company, a service company, a cannon company, and a medical detachment. There were three regiments in a division plus a headquarters company, divisional artillery, a recon troop, a combat engineer battalion, a quartermaster company, an ordnance company, a signal company, and a military police platoon. Total manpower in a division was approximately 15,000.

During a battle or when holding a defensive position, a battalion would have two companies on line and one company in close reserve. The machine guns were attached to the attacking or holding companies and the mortars operated from positions just behind the riflemen.

While we were recuperating here in the woods, the other two battalions of the 328th Regiment were probably attacking.

I think some companies were called upon to attack more than others. This may have been because their leaders were more aggressive or more capable. In our battalion Fox Company seems to have been called upon most often in tough situations. This is reflected in the number of casualties they suffered, which was the highest in the 328th Regiment.

Our food supply was mostly C and K rations. After Christmas our kitchen crew took additional risks and provided us with more hot meals than they had previously. When we were attacking or when our positions were close to the enemy, we ate rations. As I recall, the longest interval between hot meals was about a week. Sometimes we would be on rations for a week, hot meals for one or two days, and rations for another week. It was difficult for my digestive system to adjust to the change between concentrated rations and the soft foods—such as dehydrated potatoes, canned fruit, and powdered eggs—our kitchen served. I frequently suffered from diarrhea due to these changes in diet.

My description of the field rations may not be entirely accurate as I am relying on recollections spanning thirty-seven years. The K and C rations were the mainstay of the infantry. The 10-in-1 ration was the most palatable, since it consisted of such items as canned bacon, potatoes, and eggs. This ration came in bulky containers and was used by the tankers and artillery, who had more motorized transportation than the infantry.

The K rations were packaged in red (breakfast), blue (lunch), or green (dinner) wax-coated cardboard boxes about the size of a pound butter carton. Breakfast consisted of a ham-and-egg mixture in an approximately five ounce can, fruit bar, coffee, sugar, and hard crackers. In the lunch ration were a can of cheese, lemonade, sugar, caramel candy, and crackers. A can of pork loaf was the main course of the dinner, with beef bouillon, crackers, and a chocolate bar. A package of accessories in each ration consisted of a can opener, toilet paper, three cigarettes, and matches. The wax cartons were easily ignited and made good kindling.

Six C ration cans made up the daily issue. Three of the cans contained crackers, jam, coffee or cocoa, sugar, can opener, toilet paper, and cigarettes. There was a variety of C rations: pork and beans, beans and frankfurters, hash, stew, beef and noodles, hamburger, and spaghetti and meat balls in a main-course can, five or six ounces in size. The large chunks of gristle commonly found in the stew made me wonder about war profiteering. C rations were better if you didn't have to carry them yourself, if you had a way to heat them, and if you had plenty of time to eat. K rations could be carried easily and eaten cold on the march.

The D-bar—a concentrated chocolate bar—supplemented the C and K rations. I usually kept two or three D-bars in my field jacket for emergencies. It was no wonder I thought so much about food and dreamed of my mother's cooking.

Our clothes were woolen and khaki colored. We had two-piece woolen underwear, wool stockings, and leather boots with overshoes. Our shirts and trousers were wool and the field jacket, which had four large pockets, was cotton. The steel helmet, which had a liner with a headband, was heavy. We had knee-length raincoats and wool overcoats. We were provided with wool gloves and scarfs. During the cold weather I wore one scarf over my head and ears and tied it underneath my chin.

Our M-1 rifles weighed nine pounds. Around our waist we wore a cartridge belt, to which was fastened a first aid kit, bayonet, canteen, cartridge pouches, and a small shovel. The shovel was hinged at the connection of the blade and handle and was eighteen inches long when folded. The weight of the belt was supported by canvas suspenders. A small field pack was used to carry rations and personal items.* A ban-

*In a letter dated Dec. 1 Egger told his parents: "We pack everything we own on us, which in my case consists of the clothes I wear, weapons and ammunition, a razor,

doleer of ammunition was carried over each shoulder, giving a rifleman about 160 rounds of ammunition. One or two grenades were fastened to the front rings of the suspenders.

FROM EGGER'S LETTER OF NOVEMBER 17

You surely must have been praying for me lately because I wouldn't be writing this letter if the Lord hadn't been watching over me. . . .

I have seen enough war and it wouldn't hurt my feelings if they quit anytime. A person doesn't realize or can't possibly imagine what it is like until they actually experience it. It seems like I dream of home almost every night. . . .

Nov. 17, 1944. The 3rd and 4th Platoons were taken by truck to Chateau Voué, where our kitchen served us coffee and steak sandwiches. I was able to shave for the first time in ten days and buy some candy bars. Some of the men got new clothes, but I did not qualify since mine were only eight days dirty.

I did some inquiring about Davidson's whereabouts, since he was not with the 4th Platoon. I was told he had taken some prisoners to the rear on the 14th and had not returned to the platoon. When I talked to him after he rejoined the company at Metz in December, he told me that while he was taking the prisoners back he encountered an armed unit of Germans who took him prisoner. He was released by a unit of the French army when they captured Strasbourg.*

During the past three days I had an opportunity to become acquainted with the men in our platoon. Men had come and gone so fast I had not learned the names of most of them, and I had only been with the squad two days before Moncourt.

Stan Nachman, who was of Polish descent, was a factory worker from Johnson City, New York. He was twenty-five years old, good natured, and intelligent. He and I became good friends. Henry Huckabee,

---

towel, fork, can opener and all my pockets full of junk. Still have the Bible you gave me."

---

*The morning report for Dec. 11 shows Pfc. William S. Davidson as having been liberated from German captivity at Strasbourg on Nov. 24.

twenty-seven, was a six-foot-three-inch farmer from Alabama. He never had much to say, but he was a good soldier. Fonrose LeCrone, a farmer from Illinois, was thirty-one, an old man by infantry standards, but he was in better physical condition than many men ten years younger. Oscar Stribling, the platoon runner, was twenty-two years old. Larry Treff, nineteen, was Jewish and from New York City. He had an abundance of courage and eventually became platoon sergeant of the 1st Platoon. Vic Popa, Vern Olson, and Jim McCowan were transfers from ASTP, as were Treff and I.

I found a hayloft in which to spread my blankets for the night. For a change we were not concerned about artillery. That night a bronchial condition caused me to cough so much that I lost my evening meal.

2 The Mud of Lorraine
November 18–December 2, 1944

OPERATIONAL BACKGROUND   On the south end of the Third Army line, where the 26th Division was engaged, the fiercest fighting in Patton's fall campaign in Lorraine had occurred in the first week. The capture of the Morhange and Dieuze (Foret de Bride et de Koecking) Plateaus, where Egger and the rest of the 328th Regiment had encountered such heavy going, had unhinged the main German line of resistance in the south. The next barrier would be the Saar River. This was the objective of the 26th Division's drive that resumed on November 19, after a brief halt for rest and regrouping (see Map 3). Fortunately for the men of the Yankee Division, the German line in this area was weakly held since the main enemy forces had withdrawn to the east side of the Saar River. Nevertheless, this screening force was manning well-prepared defenses. These included not only woods and the sturdy stone houses of Lorraine, but the old French fortifications of 1940, the Maginot Line.[1]

Pfc. Bruce Egger and his comrades of George Company, 2nd Battalion, 328th Infantry, were about to enter the second phase of the offensive that had begun so disastrously at Moncourt on November 8 and continued with the grueling advance through the Foret de Bride et de Koecking. Although the fighting would be less sanguinary over the next month, the weather conditions—the unremitting rains now interspersed with snow—would continue to make the lot of the foot soldier a miserable one. In this effort they would be joined on November 18 by 2nd Lt. Lee M. Otts, a son of Alabama who would find himself dismayed to be assigned to the Yankee Division. [P.R.]

Nov. 18, 1944.   G Company goes back on line and new replacement Lt. Otts is assigned to Easy Company.

EGGER   The trucks took us back to our positions in the morning. The villages we passed through were in ruins from the shelling and fighting, and the fields were pock-marked with shell holes and laced with

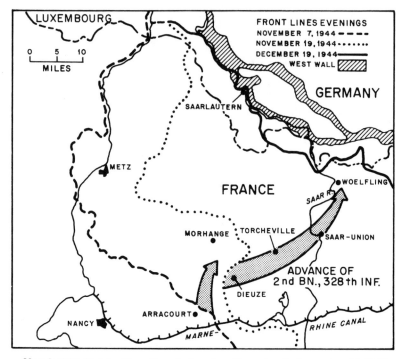

Map 3. 26th Division Operations in Lorraine, November 8–December 19, 1944

trenches and fortifications. I had seen an Army paper at Chateau Voué that said the Third Army was moving ahead against light resistance.

Stashin and Nickel rejoined the platoon today but were destined to go back for good three days later because of the condition of their feet. Very few of the men who were evacuated with frostbite or trench foot ever came back. Trench foot was caused by the feet being exposed to the wet and cold. Three or four days of exposure could cause the disease. The circulation is affected, and severe cases may result in gangrene. There was no way to keep our feet dry with the footgear the Army provided, and without bedding we could not dry and warm our feet at night. We never received proper footgear until the end of January, two weeks before we no longer needed it. I had a supply of heavy wool socks from home that I used instead of the lighter-weight wool stockings the Army issued.* My parents kept me supplied throughout the war, and I

---

*On Dec. 3 Egger wrote his parents: "I haven't any more heavy wool socks, if it hadn't been for those I did have I know very well I would be back in the hospital with trench foot." The 328th Infantry had lost over 500 men from trench foot and exposure

don't think my feet would have held up without them. My feet were much more sensitive to cold after the winter of '44–'45.

[We now pick up the account of 2nd Lt. Lee Otts, who having arrived the day before at the regimental train area of the 328th Infantry Regiment, on November 18 was assigned as a replacement platoon leader with Easy Company, 2nd Battalion.]

OTTS About an hour before daylight it seemed like all hell broke loose. We could hear guns firing and shells whistling over and falling. They sounded like they were right on top of us. For the first time, but far from the last, I was really scared.

When it got light enough to look around us, we saw what had been making all the noise and scaring us. All over the valley, camouflaged so we could see them only when they were fired, were our 240mm and 150mm "Long Tom" cannons. Most of the noise and bright flashes had been from them. There had been only two enemy shells that fell anywhere close to us, and they were strays meant for the artillery in the valley. We felt much better after we learned all this.

Across the valley was a small field with four field artillery liaison planes. As soon as the haze lifted the little planes took off and circled over us, directing the fire of our big guns. We soon learned to love these little planes—or "grasshoppers" as they were sometimes called—with the love we had for our mothers who used to keep the "bad men" away from us when we were children. The Germans did not love them, but they certainly respected their fire-directing ability. Usually when the "grasshoppers" were up, we didn't have to worry much about La Boche's artillery, for as soon as he fired they would spot him and he would be kaput.

Shortly after we finished our breakfast of C rations, we learned that we were joining the 328th Regiment of the 26th "Yankee" Division. That last part nearly killed [Lt. Law] Lamar and me, as we were staunch Alabamians. What would the people back home say?

There were 782 enlisted men and fourteen officers among the replacements going to the 328th that day. We all went to the 1st and 2nd Battalions, which had suffered the most losses.

Several of us had a long conversation with Lt. James Fagan, Executive Officer of E Company, who happened to be in the area that day.

---

during the first four days of the November offensive. For reasons nobody has been fully able to explain, the German troops did not seem to have suffered much from trench foot.[2]

He gave us several pointers he had picked up in battle. The one we took most to heart was that you never look like an officer—never have any bars or insignia showing, never wear officers' coats or overcoats, and do everything possible to look like an ordinary GI. The tale was that the Germans got bonuses or three-day passes for every officer they could prove they had killed. After this there was quite a bit of activity among the new officers, scraping the painted bars off their steel helmets or rubbing mud over them. We also decided we wouldn't wear our officers' trench coats.

Trucks came and carried the men off to their new battalions and finally came and took the officers to Regimental Headquarters. Here we were interviewed individually by the adjutant, and then assigned to a company. I was placed in Easy Company.

After the interviews and assignments we went into the Regimental CP for a short talk by the Regimental Commander, Colonel Ben R. Jacobs. Col. Jacobs had been wounded in the right arm only a few days before and still had his arm in a sling. He shook hands with us with his left hand. Col. Jacobs told us a little about the 328th and gave us a few battle pointers. One that I remember well was: "When in an attack, keep going in spite of hell until you reach your objective. If you stop and let the Heinies have time to zero their mortars and artillery on you, you're a dead duck." He wished us all the best of luck. We were beginning to realize we would probably need it.

A truck finally came and we started out to hunt for our various units. Since I was the only one from this group going to Easy Company, the driver dumped me off at the H Company CP, where I met Captain Arma E. Andon, Howe Company Commanding officer. He was quite a character, as I found out later, and I liked him at once.

After walking through the woods a little farther, I came upon a group of foxholes and was told when I inquired that I was in Easy Company's area. One of these foxholes turned out to be the Company CP, and there I found Captain Vaughn Swift, the Company CO. He had taken over when the former commanding officer had been killed.*

In the short two weeks that I was with Easy Company, I learned to love, admire, and respect Captain Swift more than any other man I had known in the Army. He was undoubtedly one of the best combat company commanders in the ETO. He was not a regular army man who had spent his life training for the battlefield, but just a quiet school teacher from Colorado. "Swifty," or "the old man," as we called him among ourselves, was just as calm and cool in the midst of an attack or a heavy

---

*Captain Clifford Lierman was killed in action on Nov. 13, 1944.

shelling as he must have been in the classroom. Whenever we were given an attack order, Swifty would give us our detailed instructions, tell us what was expected of each of us and what we could expect to happen, and then end up with, "But I'm not worried much about it." Nothing seemed to worry him. He just wasn't afraid of anything—at least he didn't show it. He was also one of the fairest and most impartial officers I have ever known. No one could ever say that Captain Swift didn't give him a square deal.

Easy Company had been one of the hardest hit companies. About 120 replacements joined it along with two other officers and myself. I soon found out that the replacements had all been in my replacement company. I knew more of his men than Captain Swift did.

Since it was getting late, I set about trying to find a place to sleep. I didn't want to dig by myself, so I found a couple of men I knew and pitched in to help them with their hole, making it big enough for the three of us. While two of us dug, the other hunted limbs and pieces of wood to put over the top to protect us from tree bursts. Night caught us before we had time to dig our hole very deep or get a good cover over it, but we were too tired to care very much; and, as everything was quiet and we were in reserve, we quit and went to bed.

Nov. 19, 1944. G Company receives replacements and new officers and Lt. Otts meets his platoon.

EGGER One hundred and fourteen replacements were assigned to the company, so we knew the battalion would be going to the front lines soon. I was always impressed by how clean and neat the replacements looked and how shiny smooth their faces were.

Captain Carrier, George Company Commanding Officer, was transferred to Service Company and Lt. Shipman, our Executive Officer, was transferred to Regimental Headquarters Company. Captain Gardner Goldsmith was our new CO; Lt. Jack Hargrove, a replacement, was our platoon leader; and Lt. Charles Walter, also a replacement, was Executive Officer.

I had got caught up on my letter writing the last few days. Receiving or not receiving a letter could make the difference in our day, and we all looked forward to mail call. I wrote every opportunity I had and my parents and relatives wrote to me regularly.

OTTS Just before daylight the next morning we received a pretty good shelling and I saw my first battle casualties. One man had been slightly wounded in the arm while going to wake up the new guard, and a shell had hit right in front of a foxhole, mortally wounding two of the veterans of the company. The men had been evacuated when I saw their hole, but the blood-soaked blankets and clothes, the riddled helmets and shoes, gave us some idea of what had happened.

After the excitement of the shelling subsided, I was assigned to the 2nd Platoon, which was down to six men. I faced the immediate task of becoming acquainted with the veterans and getting some organization in a platoon full of new replacements, many with only seventeen weeks in the Army before coming overseas.

The problem with the replacement system is that a lot more work and responsibility is thrown on the officers and non-coms, since they don't know the new men, their capabilities, or how responsible they are. Rather than taking a chance and giving important missions to untried men, the officers and non-coms have a tendency to do it themselves. This often resulted in the loss of key men. At the least it ended up with the best men being overworked.

The only experienced non-coms left were the platoon sergeant, T/Sgt. Frank Camerlin, who was back at the aid station for a few days with trench foot, and the platoon guide, S/Sgt. Batiste La Ninfa. The squad leaders—S/Sgt. Samuel "Fleazy" Hughes, S/Sgt. Willis Burhans, and S/Sgt. Robert E. Pennington, Jr.—had all been Pfcs. a week before. So had Sgt. Thane S. (T. S.) Warren, assistant squad leader of the lst Squad. I had to make two of the new replacements, Pvt. Dudley Winters and Pvt. Luther Ellison, acting sergeants and appoint them assistant leaders of the 2nd and 3rd Squads. Winters didn't talk very much but was always good natured, and all the men liked him. Ellison had achieved a sergeant's rating during a pre-war hitch in the Army so he really knew his soldiering. He had been a school teacher in Texas before joining up again when the war came.

La Ninfa was a quiet, conscientious fellow whose job as platoon guide was mainly to take care of receiving and distributing rations, ammunition, and PX supplies. He also attended to getting clothing and equipment from the supply sergeant to replace any that was worn out or lost. In an attack his job was to bring up the rear of the platoon and see that there was no straggling.

Fleazy Hughes was one of those devil-may-care fellows who was always the first to volunteer for patrol or to lead an attack. He wasn't afraid of anything and ruled his squad with an iron hand. He wasn't very big but no one questioned his authority. Burhans and Pennington were alike in that they were both young, both had been in ASTP, and were new to the Army and to their jobs as squad leaders. Although they didn't have the force Hughes did, they were well liked by the men and were good squad leaders.

I never knew how old T. S. Warren was. He was a little guy with a thick black beard above which his dark eyes twinkled. Warren had been a BAR man, and although as a sergeant he wasn't supposed to carry one he still wouldn't give it up. That was all right with me because I believed in every man choosing his own weapon as far as it was practicable. Later he fastened the pistol grip of a German burp gun to the forestock of his BAR so he could shoot it like a Tommy gun.

I spent that night in the foxhole with Captain Swift, who gave me some pointers on being a platoon leader and introduced me to the use of the EE-8-A field telephone in a combat area. We were connected into the battalion switchboard and heard several calls during the night between the companies and battalion headquarters.

The EE-8-A operates on two flashlight batteries and has a crank on the outside of the leather case that rings a bell on the other end of the line when turned. In a holding position such as we were in, where no action is expected, much of the battalion's business is transacted over field telephones.

In the intra-company communication system, we ordinarily used sound-powered telephones that required no batteries. All that was necessary was to talk over it and the sound of your voice was transmitted over the line. But without batteries there was nothing to power a bell, so someone had to sit with the phone close to his ear all the time. To call the other party to the phone we would whistle over it or, if maintaining silence was necessary, tap on the phone with a pencil or such.

Nov. 20, 1944. George and Easy Companies both reorganize and prepare to move out the next day.

EGGER By now I was feeling rested. The fires had to be extinguished at dusk, which came at about 1630, and there was nothing else to do but sleep. The wooded area where we had been since November 11 was called Foret de Bride et de Koecking. The local inhabitants would be finding bullets and shell fragments in the trees for another century.

S/Sgt. Starcher asked me if I would be an assistant squad leader, but I didn't want the responsibility. I had noticed that so far the non-coms hadn't fared too well.

The replacements were assigned to platoons today and we were told to be ready to move at any time. Treff had the first squad and T/5 Frank Richardson, one of the new replacements, was his assistant. Other members of the squad besides myself were Stan Nachman, Henry Huckabee, Alex Stoddard, and six replacements who arrived yesterday: Marshall Pearcy, Carmel Nutt, Tom Oakley, Lee Allen, and two new men I can't remember. Foster and Pvt. Daniel Dafoe (another new replacement) had the 2nd Squad* and Vern Olson and Jim McCowan led the 3rd Squad. Alex Stoddard had come over with the division and until today had been a runner at company headquarters. He had not gotten along with his superior and was sent to a rifle platoon.

I dreaded going into combat again. The past two weeks indicated that my chances of getting through the war unharmed were close to zero—though the odds of coming out of it alive were about four to one.

It started to rain in the evening.

OTTS 1st Lt. Leroy Lassiter [pseudonym] joined us this morning and was given the 1st Platoon. Lassiter had a high opinion of himself. I can see him now, cigarette in his hand, his carbine slung over his shoulder, rocking back on his heels as he explained to us some of the finer points of combat.

Most of the day was spent in organizing and equipping the company. Lt. Lassiter and I found an abandoned foxhole that had been dug under the trunk of a fallen tree, and as both of us were allergic to digging we decided to use it. We went to bed about 1630, all curled up to get our fifteen hours' sleep, but after a couple of hours we discovered that the hole was about six inches too short. Our legs got so cramped we thought we couldn't stand it any longer. We relieved the situation somewhat by putting our feet on the top edge of the hole, thereby almost standing on our heads. This helped a little but it also let a lot of cold air in. We managed to pull through the night but resolved to exert a little more energy and make our foxhole a little longer from then on.

OPERATIONAL BACKGROUND On November 19, while the 2nd Battalion of the 328th was still resting in the Foret de Bride et de Koecking atop the Dieuze Plateau, the 3rd Battalion had moved down to take the important crossroads town of Dieuze immediately to the south. Despite being checked in its initial attack, the 3rd Battalion was able to walk into town unopposed the next day, the German rear guard having left during the night.

The fall of this key junction opened up the area immediately to the east. On the night of November 20–21 the 3rd Battalion of the 101st Regiment made a forced march in the rain to seize the village of Torcheville. The 2nd Battalion of the 328th was rushed to that area to press forward with the advance that was now gathering momentum.[3] [P.R.]

---

*Pfcs. Lawrence Treff and Charles N. Foster were both promoted to staff sergeant on Nov. 25 to give them the rank appropriate for their new duties as squad leaders. Foster had been slightly wounded at Moncourt but had returned to duty on Nov. 12.

Nov. 21, 1944. The 2nd Battalion moves to the outskirts of Torcheville, where Lt. Otts wishes the tanks would be quieter.

EGGER We boarded trucks this morning and rode about ten miles. Our route took us through a small village that had been leveled by the recent fighting. Three destroyed American tanks were at the edge of the village and beyond the town were several burnt-out German vehicles. A dead, disemboweled German soldier lay in the ruins of a building near the road and a dog was sniffing among the rubble.

We de-trucked in a field and began the familiar process of hurry-up-and-wait. While we waited I built a small fire and cleaned my rifle. It had rained all day and I didn't want to be caught with a malfunctioning rifle again. After about two hours we started moving through the woods that the 101st Regiment had cleared yesterday. We had to travel cross-country because the Germans had mined the roads, felled trees across them, and had blown out the bridges. Late in the afternoon we came out of the woods and followed a small stream through a field. The ground was saturated and most of the time we were wading ankle deep in the water.

We dug foxholes in a muddy field just outside Torcheville, which the 101st had taken last night. Nutt and I hit water with the second shovelful. Even though our bedrolls had been brought up to us, we spent a miserable night because of the dampness and cold and the artillery and flares that lit the sky most of the night.

OTTS My platoon sergeant, T/Sgt. Francis Camerlin, came back to us, much to my relief. I didn't want to go into my first attack without a platoon sergeant. Camerlin had been with the YD for several years and had been running the platoon without an officer for some time. He was a big, strong, happy-go-lucky guy who was always talking and laughing. I told him right away that in the first attack I wanted him to handle everything and just let me go along for the ride.

The battalion loaded onto trucks before noon and we rode for about ten miles east to catch up with the progress of the battle. After unloading we walked about a mile and stopped to eat our lunch of K rations. After the break we continued for about another mile and then sat or stood along a path beside the woods for about two hours while a patrol, followed by the regimental and battalion commanders, went into Torcheville to look over the situation and to get orders from division.

Finally orders were issued and our company moved out across an open field and took up positions on top of a bald hill northeast of Torcheville. While crossing the open field, I picked up another combat tip from Sgt. Camerlin. I was walking beside the path that the others were making because it wasn't so muddy and the walking was easier. I asked Camerlin why he didn't walk out there with me. He replied that he was afraid of mines or booby traps and that as long as he stayed in the path made by the others he had nothing to worry about. I got back in the path plenty fast and immediately decided against any future "trail blazing" on my own unless I had to.

Captain Swift assigned platoon areas to us, and Camerlin and I assigned squad areas to each of the squad leaders; then they showed each man where he should dig his hole.

I soon found out that Camerlin was as lazy as I, or else he was allergic to digging a foxhole—he didn't even carry a shovel. There were several holes in the hill that the Germans had dug, and one real nice one that had a roof over it. It must have been their command post since the place was littered with gas masks, telephones, and papers. Remembering my training, I was afraid it might be booby-trapped, but Camerlin talked me into using it. We decided we would make it our CP.

Darkness came fast and I stumbled around through the dark for several hours trying to locate the Company CP, the rations, the blanket rolls, and trying to get the new password.

Whenever possible our blanket rolls were carried on trucks and brought up to us at night. Blanket rolls contained from two to four blankets, and to keep them dry we rolled them inside a shelter half. At first we also placed our personal articles inside the blanket rolls, but after fumbling in the dark trying to find our bedroll out of a stack of two hundred we gave up the idea and settled for the first roll we came to.

In the valley below us there were several of our tanks and TDs (tank destroyers). We were glad to have their support but didn't care much for the noise they made or the fires they built. We were afraid to speak in a normal tone or even light a cigarette for fear of bringing artillery fire in on us. But the tanks came roaring up, ground to a stop, and immediately built a large fire with ration boxes and gasoline. We were sure that all the noise and light would bring on an artillery barrage, but the night passed without incident.

Nov. 22, 1944. The 2nd Battalion takes Munster, where Egger and Otts are introduced to nebelwerfer fire.

EGGER The weather cleared during the night and our blankets were covered with frost in the morning. The walk and dampness yesterday had caused the blisters on my feet to bleed and become ulcerated. My platoon sergeant, Starcher, told 1st Sgt. Germain about my feet and I was told to stay and help with the bedrolls today.

The company moved out about 1000 to attack Munster, a small town not far from Torcheville. A tank battalion was attached to the division and some of the tanks accompanied the troops. I stayed in Torcheville with Lt. Walter, lst Sgt. Germain, the jeep drivers, and several replacements. The medics dressed the blisters on my heels.

At 1600, after Munster had been cleared, another man and I were taken there by jeep to pick out a place for G Company's CP. The Germans were shelling the road, so the jeep driver wasted no time. All the haystacks and many of the buildings in Munster were on fire. We took shelter in a barn, but the jeep driver decided the time was not right for the CP to move to Munster. I decided to stay and look for my squad. The other two went back to Torcheville when there was a break in the shelling. There was a soft drink bottling plant across the street, so I ran over and got a few bottles. The stuff didn't taste very good and gave me the cramps.

It was getting dark and I hadn't seen any of the company personnel, so I decided to eat a ration and spend the night in the barn. Most of the barn roof had been blown away and it was raining, but I burrowed into the hay and slept warm.

During the night I was introduced to nebelwerfers, which we called "screaming meemies." These were rockets that were fired simultaneously from a launcher and could be heard from the time they left the launching tubes.

OTTS Morning came at last, and all the platoon leaders went down to the pillbox that served as Company CP to eat breakfast and receive the attack order. We formed on each side of the road leading from Torcheville to Munster with Easy Company on the right, George on the left, and Fox following George. A platoon of four medium tanks accompanied us down the road. Our mission was to clear a wooded area and take the high ground on which the town of Munster stood, about four miles away.

The attack was to take place at 1100 hours, preceded by an artillery barrage from 1050 until 1100 to soften up any resistance. Something went wrong though, for the barrage began as the leading platoons of each company were beginning to enter the woods. Before we could get back out of range we suffered several wounded and killed in Easy and George Companies. Luckily my platoon was second in line and no one was hit.

Captain Swift kept the 300 radio hot calling the battalion and finally the artillery fire ceased. When we reached the woods we deployed—with the lst and 2nd Platoons on line and the 3rd in reserve. On the other side of the woods there was about a mile and a half of open, rolling hills between us and Munster. We left the woods and went over the top of the hill in front of us. When we got out where we could see the road, we found that our platoon was out there all by itself—the 1st Platoon had been held up, waiting for the tanks or something. I let a few hot words go over the radio about "where the hell is the 1st Platoon?" and got in reply, "Just keep your pants on." So we lay down in the muddy field with no cover at all to wait for the rest of the company, praying that the Germans wouldn't throw any shells at us.

The remainder of the company finally caught up and we started on again. When we were within fifty yards of an orchard that was surrounding the first buildings of the town, the Heinies decided that that was far enough. They cut loose with several 20mm guns that were positioned about a thousand yards to our right front. Also a burp gun and a light machine gun opened up from the orchard in front of us. We immediately hit the prone and for a moment were scared to move a muscle. By this time our tanks had pulled in between the 1st Platoon and us and were firing directly over our heads.

I think Captain Swift had become disgusted with our being pinned down so long, for he shouted over the radio, "Why haven't you gotten your platoon into town?" With that I saw no alternative other than to get moving so I got up, waved my arm, and shouted, "Let's get the hell out of here." The men got the idea, and we all tore for the top of the hill as fast as we could run while the tanks blazed away to give us cover.

When I reached the road, all out of breath, T/Sgt. Ruszezyk of the 1st Platoon called to me to come on into town, so I kept on running until I got past about four houses. Then I turned and saw that no one from my platoon was with me so I went back. Captain Swift had instructed Camerlin to stop the men and put them in defile on the left of the road until they could catch their breath and get reorganized.

Although we had been in one of the hottest spots, we had come through so far with only one casualty—a man had been wounded in the hand. The other platoons hadn't fared so well.

After a few minutes we were on the go again. Our platoon had been given the right side of our company's sector of the town, and we went from house to house, searching each one from attic to cellar for any Germans that might be hiding there. We knocked down locked doors or shot the locks off. We were pretty disorganized as the men were new to each other and no teams for house-to-house fighting had been picked. I just walked up the middle of the street pointing out to each group the house I wanted searched as they finished with one. Fortunately, we ran into no booby traps and very few Germans. We took four prisoners in the cellar of a cafe and bar. They were merely sitting there waiting for us and gave up without any resistance.

The Germans had left only a handful of men as a token force to delay us and inflict as many casualties as possible. As soon as we entered the town, they had retired to their cellars and appeared as innocent as lambs.

Our platoon was given a front of some two hundred yards in a semi-circle around one edge of the town bordering on the flooded rivers. We dug foxholes about twenty yards from the buildings and at intervals of about thirty yards all across our platoon front. The men not on guard duty in the holes were to stay in the buildings, where we hoped they would get a little rest and at least have a chance to warm up and dry out. My CP was in a kitchen that was the center room in one of the houses. This would make it the safest during a shelling.

We were still in the process of organizing the outposts and digging our foxholes when artillery and mortar shells began raining in on the town. The buildings shook and the windows rattled and broke. Men hit the ground and the floors where they lay without moving a muscle— chilled to the marrow with fear that the next shell might have their name on it. During a heavy barrage no one moved or spoke, but everyone prayed.

An 88 shell in flight has a peculiar whine all its own—more like the scream of a madwoman than anything else I can think of. You could hear them coming long before they hit. It was an often-discussed question as to whether you could hear the shell that hit you. Eighty-eights were mounted on tanks and were used as self-propelled and stationary field pieces. Mortar shells travel a good bit slower and make a swishing sound like when you pass telephone poles in a fast-moving automobile.

During this barrage our battalion got its first dose of nebelwerfers, or "screaming meemies," as they were nicknamed. The nebelwerfer was a German rocket shell. It was fired from tubes mounted in groups of six or twelve on the backs of trucks or on stationary mounts. They don't usually throw as much shrapnel as artillery or mortar shells, but the sound and concussion effect plays hell with morale.

The shelling finally let up for a while and we built a fire in our stove and made some coffee. There were several jars of preserves and some bread left by the civilians. We were glad to have something to supplement our K rations.

The shelling kept up at intervals all through the night. They seemed to know just when we were changing guard because they always sent in a barrage while the men were out of their holes. We changed the time for the guard to be relieved from on the hour to ten minutes past. This helped some, but we still took an awful beating.

About the middle of the night we had our first case of battle fatigue— in other words, the first man to crack mentally. His was the most violent case I was to see. A couple of men brought him to the CP and laid him on a mattress that was on the floor. For the rest of the night he lay there crying loudly, laughing, screaming, or just sobbing quietly. At times he would try to get up and run out, and it took several men to hold him down.

I think that such a case is the worst thing that can happen for morale. I know it certainly affected me plenty and made me wonder if I were going to crack. The man himself is not to blame; it is all in the way one is made inside. Some men crack up very quickly, others last longer, and still others never crack. I saw some of the bravest of men snap under the strain of too many days in combat.

We evacuated this soldier when morning came and never saw him again. I don't know if he got well or if he is still suffering the effects of that experience. I certainly hope he snapped out of it.

During one of the heaviest shellings just before daybreak I lost my first man killed in action. Three men were standing in a hallway preparing to go on guard when a shell landed in the hallway wounding all three of them. One man had part of the top of his head blown off, and although the medic reached him while he was still living there was nothing he could do for him. He died in a few minutes.

One of the wounded, a great big boy about nineteen, came into my CP and stood around for about twenty minutes before anyone noticed him. Finally, when asked why he was there, he replied that he had been wounded in the foot. He had a hole through his foot about the size of a man's thumb but had been so dazed by everything that he had just been standing on it with no thought of pain or of getting medical aid.

Nov. 23, 1944. George and Easy Companies spend Thanksgiving Day resting up in Munster amid sporadic shelling.

EGGER Today was Thanksgiving, but the festivities were not of the sort I was used to at home.

I found the 3rd Platoon in a house next door to the barn. We stayed at the house all day but pulled guard from foxholes in the backyard, which faced an open field and woods beyond. The losses to the battalion had been relatively heavy yesterday, but George Company only had five men wounded, including Richardson and McCowan from our platoon.*

Artillery shells landed in town all day, wounding a man from the 4th Platoon.

*T/5 Frank K. Richardson and Pvt. James R. McCowan were both listed as "slightly wounded" and hospitalized; neither returned to the company. The morning reports show that G Company lost three men killed and fourteen wounded in the period Nov. 21–24.

We killed a rabbit and chicken and cooked them together. We also had fresh eggs and milk. I got acquainted with Paul Scheufler and Ray Tompkins from the 3rd Squad, who had arrived in the replacement draft four days ago. They were both nineteen-year-old farm boys from Kansas. Nachman and Stribling were made assistant squad leaders of the 1st and 3rd Squads, respectively.

The house we were staying in was so crowded there was hardly room to stretch out on the floor, but it was dry and warm.

OTTS Morning finally came, and although the shelling and rain did not let up we felt much better just because it was daylight.

The morning passed uneventfully for our platoon, but the 1st Platoon had to evacuate six men with battle fatigue. They had all been sitting in a cellar and had more or less talked each other into a state of panic. Some of them were just smart enough to figure out that this was no place for them—you might even get hurt—so they decided to get out of it one way or another. There were several cases of fake battle fatigue, but there were also many genuine cases.

In another cellar in the 1st Platoon area the pin on a hand grenade was accidentally pulled and the grenade went off in a room full of men. Only one was wounded, but not very seriously. This somewhat diminished my opinion of the effectiveness of hand grenades.

This was Thanksgiving Day, but it seemed more like the Fourth of July. The rain and shelling continued and everyone sat tight. Our dinner was chicken and scrambled eggs. I don't think there were many chickens or eggs left in Munster. The beverage of choice was soda pop from a bottling plant next to the Battalion CP. Some of us who were lucky enough to have a farm boy in our group also had milk, as there were cows in almost every barn. The barns were built right onto the houses and the cows and chickens were frequently sticking their heads in the doors.

The night passed much as the one before had, with lots of shells and rain. The Heinies were really unloading their ammunition stores on us.

Nov. 24, 1944. The 2nd Battalion moves twelve miles through the rain and mud to Givrycourt.

EGGER When I came off guard at 0400 I went to a room on the second floor to sleep, since the downstairs was so crowded. A nebelwerfer landed outside, rattling the house and bouncing me off the floor. I decided it would be safer downstairs.

At 0500 we were alerted that we would be moving out to clear a wooded area near the town. I could have stayed at the Company CP because of my feet, but I chose to go with the platoon. A man in the 2nd Squad shot himself in the hand before we moved out.

It was dark and raining when we left. We walked about twelve miles today. Our objective was to clear the woods of the machine guns that had been firing at Munster, but the Germans had apparently pulled out the day before. About 1600 we emerged from the woods near Givrycourt and waited while a patrol went into town, which proved to be free of the enemy. In order to get to Givrycourt we had to wade a stream that was waist deep. I was afraid Pearcy might disappear, since he was only about five-foot-four.

This was the first time we had found civilians in a town. They seemed to be pleased to see us and gave us apples and warm milk. Our platoon stayed in a tavern in a room heated by a wood stove. For a change we did not have to pull guard duty and I had a good rest.

OTTS Fox and George Company pulled out early this morning to clear out the woods to the north of town. Easy Company stayed in Munster, but the morning was not without its excitement. A platoon of engineers was sent out to repair the bridge coming in from the west, but by some mix-up in orders they started working on the other bridge to the south. They had just gotten on the bridge when the Germans opened up with long range machine gun fire, wounding three men. They all dived into the ditches and the river and after about forty-five minutes of swimming or crawling on their stomachs up the flooded ditches they made it to the safety of the buildings along the road. They were a pretty beat-up bunch, suffering from shock and exposure if not from wounds.

A new team of engineers was sent up, and in no time they had thrown a Bailey bridge over the other small river. The enemy let us know they had that one zeroed in by bracketing it with a couple of 88 rounds.

The time came for us to take off for Givrycourt, with my platoon in the lead. The bridge and its approaches were about three hundred yards long and within perfect observation and range of everything the Heinies had. Then the road turned and ran parallel along the river for about three-fourths of a mile with no trees, bushes, or any kind of cover. We all prayed and held our breath across the open ground, but for some unknown reason we weren't fired upon. The Germans were unpredictable; you never knew what to expect.

We were to outpost the right side of the town so I moved my men into position, pointing out each squad's area without bothering to go into the town. Fox and George Companies had already searched the buildings.

The men set about digging two-man foxholes. It was raining as usual, so they improvised covers for them with whatever they could find. But they were far from leakproof; the water seeped in through the walls and the man on guard had to bail continually with his helmet. There was plenty of straw available and that helped make the holes warmer and drier.

We set up our Platoon CP in a barn and slept in an adjoining grain bin. They brought in another man who had cracked up. Nothing was hurting him; he just couldn't stop crying. We tried our best to reassure him that he was all right, but when we couldn't we just let him cry.

Nov. 25, 1944. The 2nd Battalion enjoys a belated Thanksgiving dinner and Lt. Otts makes friends with a local family.

EGGER Our clothes and equipment dried out during the night. The Germans were still shelling the area around the bridges between Givrycourt and Munster. G Company had to guard several outposts today. The duty was only two hours on and the rest of the day off, so we spent most of our free time around the stoves.

Our belated Thanksgiving dinner was brought to us by jeeps this afternoon. The meal of turkey, mashed potatoes, and coffee was cold. The kitchen crew was almost always several miles in the rear and was often subjected to artillery fire, but that shouldn't have prevented them from preparing a hot meal, especially when we could be reached so easily. My dinner didn't set very well on my stomach, as I had bronchial coughing spells that caused me to lose an occasional meal.

The ulcerated blisters on my feet were not improving and I was badly in need of a new pair of shoes. I was always impressed with how the rear echelon managed to be so well dressed. When a new supply of clothes arrived, the troops in the rear were closer to the supply and the infantry was always last in line.

Pearcy and I were on guard duty together tonight. We had a foxhole filled with straw and several blankets, so we were comfortable. It was cloudy, but there was a full moon and visibility was good.

OTTS The next morning the man who owned the barn came in and seemed very much surprised to find us in his grain bin. He was very nice, though, and offered us some apples.

I wrote home that this was the best day I had spent since we landed. The sun came out and we had a belated Thanksgiving dinner of turkey, potatoes, tomatoes, and rice pudding—more than anyone could eat. It was really welcome after eating C and K rations for so long.

I went to the house that adjoined the barn where we spent the night, and with the help of some of my men, got it across to the Frenchman that we wanted to use one of their rooms with a stove in it. My men were wet and I wanted to rotate them in a few at a time to dry out. The Frenchman told us we could use the room during the day, but they needed it at night. We built a roaring fire in the stove and dried out somewhat.

Somehow I made such a hit with the French family that they insisted I spend the night in the room, so Camerlin and I had a room all to ourselves. They even put clean sheets on the bed.

We spent about two hours that night talking with the family—after a fashion. I had a little GI French-English handbook and they had three other French-English books. The family consisted of an old man and woman, about sixty, one other man about thirty-five, and three other women from twenty-five to thirty-five, a girl of three, and a baby. The younger man's name was Guisse Michel and his wife was named Speider Jeanne. He had served with the French army in Indo-China. He showed us a large album of pictures of himself and his family. He even brought his uniform he had worn in Indo-China out of the closet to show us. I'll bet he looked good in it, because even in his peasant garb he looked every inch a soldier. They seemed pleased that we were interested in everything.

The old man brought out a bottle of wine and a bottle of schnapps and we drank toasts to each other and to President Roosevelt. It was wonderful being with them even if I couldn't understand them.

Nov. 26, 1944. Egger gets to observe a battle in progress, but Otts has a bad night.

EGGER   I was with an eight-man patrol that our platoon had sent to a farmhouse overlooking the town of Honskirch. We stayed there all day providing protection for artillery observers, who were in the barn. The artillery was providing support to the 1st Battalion and some attached tanks that were trying to take Honskirch. They were running into stiff opposition. It wasn't often that we had a good view of a military operation from a relatively safe place, about two or three miles from the fighting. Late in the afternoon the artillery threw in smoke shells so our 1st Battalion and the tanks could withdraw.

As we were returning by foot to Givrycourt we talked to some men from the 1st Battalion. They said the battalion had taken heavy losses.

The people at the farmhouse had been friendly to us, but it was difficult to know where their sympathies lay. We were only about fifteen miles from the German border and the people spoke both French and German. Lorraine had passed between France and Germany several times.

There was a young man between twenty-five and thirty at the farm. Some of us assumed he was the son of the family; others were not so sure and thought he might be a German soldier left to report our activities.

OTTS The next day we had to leave, and I thought the French family would all cry. They brought out cake, cookies, and wine and kept stuffing our pockets full of apples as we were leaving.

We outposted the far side of the woods between Givrycourt and Honskirch to protect the 1st Battalion, which had been forced to withdraw into the woods after having the hell knocked out of them trying to take Honskirch. Three of the lieutenants in the battalion who had come over with me were killed, and my old college buddy, Lt. Law Lamar, had a very narrow escape. A bullet had entered the front of his helmet and had gone through the steel helmet, helmet liner, and wool knit cap and just grazed his scalp, going out the back of the helmet. He had been standing in water up to his chest for several hours and was suffering from exposure.

That turned out to be a helluva night for all of us. When we first got up there someone out in front of us was screaming, "Help! Help! Can't anyone hear me? For God's sake help!" This went on all night. You can't imagine what it does to you to be sitting in a foxhole with the black night all around and someone yelling for help in a mournful voice.

I knew we had lots of wounded men out there, but the Germans had often used calls for help as a trick to ambush anyone going out to give aid. So I ordered the men to stay in their holes regardless of what the man yelled. The battalion was going to send a stretcher party out about midnight.

It was raining again, and as fast as we dug a hole it would fill up with water. Camerlin had stayed behind as his feet were hurting him, so La Ninfa and I were digging together. What with the wet foxholes, the cries of the wounded, and having to check the outposts every hour, we didn't sleep any that night. The sound-power phones were not working very well, so most of the time we had no communications with the outposts, the other platoons, or the Company CP. We dug three different holes— to keep warm by digging as much as to get the warmth they afforded. During the night about fifty men from the 1st Battalion infiltrated back through our lines. Some of them were not wounded but had been pinned down and couldn't move until after dark.

Nov. 27, 1944. G Company occupies Honskirch while Easy Company is pulled off line and returns to Givrycourt.

EGGER In the afternoon, G Company went into Honskirch without meeting any opposition. After watching the 1st Battalion yesterday, we were expecting the worst, but the Germans had withdrawn during the night. The town had been well fortified with trenches and barbed wire barriers in the orchard at the edge of the village. We saw a dead GI at the edge of the orchard and four disabled American tanks in the field in front of the fortifications. LeCrone and Starcher found two dead German soldiers in the church while they were looking for candles.

Honskirch had been heavily shelled and the people had lost a lot of their livestock. They seemed happy to see us and offered us schnapps to drink. On this occasion I would rather have had warm milk.

We stayed in a house that was much too small for a forty-man platoon and their equipment. It was difficult to move or stretch out to sleep without bumping someone. The men were tired and irritable and occasionally tempers flared. I nearly had a confrontation with Tom Roberts, a replacement who had joined us eight days before, but cooler heads intervened. LeCrone did some foraging and we had ham and eggs for supper; we had been expecting that we would have to eat C rations. LeCrone went to the barn after dark to try to milk what he thought was a cow but soon discovered it was an ox.

The barns in this part of the country are attached to the houses, which provides some additional warmth in the winter to the occupants of both. The homes seemed pretty clean but there was always a big pile of manure out in front.* I can only imagine the situation in the summer months. What bothered me most was that the barns were almost always above the well.

Tompkins and I were on guard together tonight; four on and four off.

OTTS Dawn came at last, and we gazed out upon what a few days before must have been a beautiful scene—rolling grassy hills leading up to a town perched on top of the highest slope. But now the earth was pockmarked with shell holes, and the dirt from the holes made the countryside black. American soldiers were lying dead all over the hills and valleys. Rifles and other equipment were strewn everywhere.

It was obvious that Honskirch had been hard to take as it was situated on top of a hill with nothing but a rolling meadow between the woods we were in and the town. There was no cover for our troops at all. I could picture what had happened. The Jerries had stayed quiet and let the two attacking companies get out in the open, almost to the city, before they opened up with all they had. The town looked very peaceful

---

*In a letter to Secretary of War Henry L. Stimson, Patton suggested that the Germans should be forced to keep Lorraine after the war "because I can imagine no greater burden than to be the owner of this nasty country where it rains every day and where the wealth of the people consists of assorted manure piles."[4]

and quiet now. Just a few plumes of smoke were going up from the fires our shells had started.

We waited around all morning expecting every minute to be relieved and sent back. In the meantime, they were having a little trouble back at the Company CP. A jeep had backed over a land mine, killing two men and wounding others who were standing nearby. It caught fire and the ammunition on the jeep exploded, sounding like a firefight. We thought maybe the CP was being attacked.

Finally sometime that afternoon we were relieved and went back to Givrycourt for rest and hot chow.

The whiskey ration came up that afternoon and was a welcome sight. Once a month each officer got a quart of Scotch, two quarts of champagne, a quart of cognac, and half a quart of gin. We always shared with our men, though, so there wasn't too much for anyone. This time the regiment had come upon several cases of wine and cognac, and we had a little more.

I took my quart of Scotch and Camerlin, Van Gilkirken, and I went calling on Guisse and his family. They were so glad to see us they almost cried. Van could speak French fluently, so with him as interpreter we talked a good bit. They tried our Scotch but said they preferred their schnapps.

Some other soldiers were in the room I had occupied, but Guisse and his family insisted that we stay with them. They fixed us a pallet on the floor upstairs. We enjoyed the night's sleep very much, as it was quite a relief to be quiet, warm, and dry.

Nov. 28, 1944. The 2nd Battalion moves back into reserve at Torcheville, where the men enjoy unaccustomed comfort.

EGGER G Company stayed in Honskirch all day. The guard duty was much lighter during the daylight hours. The weather had been better since Thanksgiving—several days of sunshine and some cloudy days, but no rain. It was good to be able to sleep inside, even if it was on a hard floor.

After dark this evening we walked to Givrycourt, where trucks were waiting for us. They took us back to Torcheville, where the squad found housing in a barn. Nachman, Huckabee, and I found some hay and made ourselves a comfortable bed, no hard floors.

OTTS We loaded onto trucks and rode back over the battleground of the last few days through Munster and into Torcheville. In Torcheville as soon as we were assigned to buildings the mad scramble began to collect stoves and stove pipes. Stoves were set up in all the rooms with the pipes running out the windows, doors, or just holes in the walls. The men became busy cleaning away the debris, boarding up broken windows and trying to make the place livable. It's surprising how much can be done in a short time by a bunch of GIs. They may be tired almost to dropping, but they will really hustle to rig up some of the comforts of home.

Nov. 29, 1944. Egger loses a perfectly good steak, and Otts gets neither the shower nor the movie he expected.

EGGER I had a good night's sleep with no interruption for guard duty. The kitchen had three hot meals for us today. Nachman was so sick with diarrhea and the stomach cramps that he didn't eat any meals today. I wrote some letters and sent some Christmas cards the Army had given us. We spent part of the day cleaning our weapons and equipment.

After going to bed I had a coughing spell and lost the steak I had eaten for the evening meal. Cigarette smoke aggravated the cough, but most of the men smoked so it was difficult to stay away from it.

OTTS We were looking forward to the showers we had been promised, but the equipment didn't arrive and we had to settle for sponge baths and clean clothes. That night everyone gathered in a barn for a picture show. Men were sitting all over the floor, the hay rack, and the rafters. After waiting about two hours for someone to show up with a projector and film, we got discouraged and went to bed.

Nov. 30, 1944. The 2nd Battalion moves up to Harskirchen and Otts' platoon is sent on to Viller, where he stakes out an attractive CP.

EGGER In the morning we were taken back to Honskirch by trucks and then we continued east by foot. Along the way we passed many trenches and gun emplacements. There were no signs of fighting, so the Germans must have withdrawn from this area before our troops arrived. We passed several canals and reservoirs on which there were some small boats. The walking had made my blisters throb and itch and caused my feet to swell.

Huckabee was the BAR man for the 1st Squad and I was made his assistant today. The Bar weighs about sixteen pounds and has a magazine that holds twenty rounds. Both sides tried to destroy the automatic weapons first with mortars or small arms. I had to carry twelve magazines of ammunition for the BAR besides my own rifle and rifle ammunition.

We entered Harskirchen in the afternoon. The Germans had blown up the bridge and our engineers were repairing it. Our platoon and part of the 4th Platoon stayed in a schoolhouse. We had been told by our officers that the people here were not to be trusted as we were close to the German border and many of the people might support the Germans.

The town had been damaged by German and American artillery. The people were busy repairing the damage, although the Germans were still shelling the place. Our platoon had the job of guarding the bridge over the canal and manning several other outposts.

OTTS Before dawn we loaded onto trucks and rode by a circuitous route for about fifteen miles to Honskirch. Then we went by foot another ten or fifteen miles to the town of Harskirchen. The mission of our battalion was to clear a road along the canal paralleling the river so an engineer unit could repair a damaged bridge over the canal. Although the Jerries were just across the river, they contented themselves with lobbing in a few mortar rounds on Fox Company while it was crossing the bridge on some planks that had been put there temporarily.

Captain Swift took our company to the east of town on the road to Saar-Union. We had just reached the junction of the little road leading off to the village of Viller, where my platoon was to set up an outpost, when we heard an explosion and machine gun fire.

An automobile with two civilians had been coming along the road from Saar-Union when it hit a mine, injuring the occupants. About half a dozen men from some cavalry group were standing around our building, and one of them went out to help. As he reached the injured men, the Heinies opened up on them with long range machine gun fire.

There was much debate over where the fire was coming from. Some said it was from the woods across the river, but the majority thought it came from a mill in Viller on our side of the river. The mill was a four-story concrete structure that sat right on the bank of the Saar River. Swifty told me that since it was my town to outpost, my platoon could clean it out and eliminate the machine gun and its crew.

I wasted several minutes trying to decide how to approach the mill, asking Captain Swift questions all the time. By dodging from building to building and trampling the flowers and fences of the people of the village, we finally surrounded the mill on three sides. After we had slipped and peeped around for several minutes, I suppose "Fleazy" Hughes got impatient; anyway he went tearing for the mill door with a couple of men from his squad right behind him. It turned out that the place was deserted.

It was getting late, so we began searching the houses and manning the outposts. Every home was occupied by civilians, and there were several pretty girls in the town. I made a mental note of the location of the girls as we went from house to house with the idea of having my CP in the house with the prettiest one. I decided that the Glock family residence would be an ideal location. They had a daughter, Madeleine, nineteen years old with blond hair and grey eyes, about five-feet-three inches tall. I can't say what her weight was, but it was just about perfect and all in the right places. I never saw her in anything except a dirty pair of slacks and a sweater, but I imagine that she would have been very pretty dressed up.

It was well after dark when we got all the men placed, the sound-powered phones running to each outpost, and the EE-8-A connected on the company line. Just before midnight shells started falling on Viller and the barrage kept up at intervals all night. The shells sounded as if they were coming from behind our lines, so Camerlin and I stayed on the phone trying to give azimuths and pleading with Swifty to stop those damn guns. He kept trying to reassure us that he had checked; the word he had was that our division artillery was not firing at all and that corps and army artillery were not firing in our vicinity.

Every one of us in Viller remained convinced that those were our own guns laying down the barrage. I am not saying we were right, but the next day I carried Swifty some fragments of shells with "fuse time" and "fuse setting" written on them in good old American. Fortunately, the town suffered very little property damage.

FROM EGGER'S LETTER OF DECEMBER 1

Everybody here lives in hope. Hopes the war will be over soon and that they will still be alive when it does end. Everybody talks about what he is going to do when he gets back to the States, about their children, wives and sweethearts, and you know that some of them won't be going back. Don't even know if you are going back yourself. . . .

I know what it's like to be hunted now, and be glad to see the end and beginning of each day and be glad you are alive.

Dec. 1, 1944. Egger enjoys life in Harskirchen, but Otts enjoys it even more in Viller.

EGGER Except for the guard duty, this was a good life compared to what we had been through during the last month. We had three hot meals a day and a dry place to sleep. We received ten dollars more in our pay today for being combat infantrymen.* Ten dollars a month that is, not a day, not much for all the hazards we put up with. Unless you gambled there was little use for money. Some of my pay was withheld for savings bonds and I sent most of the rest home every month.

OTTS Day finally came, the shelling stopped, and we began to get better organized. We had two rooms upstairs in the Glock house. Camerlin and I were in one room, and a couple of other men were in the other one with the telephones. The other bedroom was vacant, as the civilians would not go upstairs at all because of the shelling.

I found out by looking at pictures and letters and questioning Madeleine that she had an older brother fighting with the German army on the Russian front. The family didn't talk very much about him to us. It didn't seem to make any difference to the family that we were fighting on the opposite side.

Checking on my outposts during the day was a real pleasure. At each house the family would rush to the door, usher me in, and offer me cake, cookies, wine, and schnapps. The Esch family had a large house on the river near the mill, and as there were two cute girls in the family I made it a point to go back that night.

This was another time I was sorry that I hadn't studied French or German. Madeleine knew absolutely no English, and as I knew no French or German we couldn't carry on a very intelligent conversation. I had the French-English dictionary the Army had issued me, but all it was good for was to get medical aid, food, shelter, and to ask questions about enemy troop activities. As far as I was concerned it was of no help at all for romancing. If the Army ever puts out another French-English dictionary, I hope they add a few words suitable for use on a moonlit night with a beautiful mademoiselle at your side. I guess the Army had enough trouble with us and the French women without helping us any.

The whole family from the grandfather down to the little brother seemed to live in the one living room, so with nothing but dictionaries to talk with and with the whole family chaperoning me, I didn't get anywhere with my romancing. Madeleine and I just sat around the table with the kerosene lamp and tried to talk with our dictionaries by pointing to different articles around the house and giving the French and English for them. She was very smart and remembered much better than I did.

---

*A Pfc. was paid $64.50 a month, ten dollars of which was overseas pay. An additional ten dollars a month was paid to combat infantrymen for a total of $74.50. [Egger's note.]

I soon got tired of this and went calling on the Esch family. Their house was much nicer and larger than Madeleine's and their clothes and manners showed them to be a more well-to-do and better educated family. One of the young boys in the family had studied English in school and he helped the conversation along a bit. The two girls—Elsa, twenty-two, and Hilda, seventeen—were very pretty but I still liked Madeleine best.

Madeleine's family was very poor, and the house wasn't nearly as large and nice as the others. But whenever I mentioned the Eschs, Madeleine or her family spoke of them with disgust; it seemed by the language they used that the Eschs were friendly with the Germans, whom Madeleine's family did not like. This was confusing, with Madeleine's parents not even being able to speak French and her brother fighting for the Germans, but maybe they had never had a chance to learn and her brother might have been forced into the German army. Madeleine always tried to make it clear to me that she was a mademoiselle, but I noticed several letters around the house addressed to her as Fraulein Madeleine Glock. Probably her boyfriend just across the river with whom we would be exchanging shots in a few days had written them to her. In spite of all this we slept in their house, ate their food, drank their wine, and never worried about getting poison in our food or a knife in our backs while sleeping.

Dec. 2, 1944. Egger learns how easy it is to get sent to the rear, and Otts enjoys an active social life in Viller.

EGGER The supply sergeant finally got me a new pair of shoes today. The old ones wouldn't have lasted many more miles. We were getting plenty of rest, eating well, and keeping dry. Lee Allen, two replacements, and I were on guard tonight at the church, which was next to the bridge. A shell landed close enough to scare all of us, although no one was hurt. After we were relieved the two replacements went to the medics because of their nerves. They never came back to our company; perhaps they were sent to a rear echelon unit. I didn't realize it was so easy to get away from the front.

OTTS The Glocks invited Camerlin and me to have dinner with them. It would have been hard to turn down the invitation, but it was harder to eat the food. We somehow managed to force it down, however. We had some kind of hash mixture; I will never know what all was in it. It was very highly seasoned and I didn't like it but ate it anyway. Also we had some black bread that wasn't too palatable. They made their bread in dome-shaped loaves that were black and hard. It seemed to us that if you dropped a loaf on the floor it would probably go right on through.

Somehow we managed to get through the meal, and with our fingers crossed we told them how much we enjoyed it. We gave them some C and K rations and some D-bars and chewing gum, for which they were most profuse in their thanks. That afternoon while Madeleine was washing dishes and cleaning up the kitchen and I was sitting on a table watching her, the Germans threw in a few mortar shells. One of them hit the roof just outside the kitchen window. The explosion and fragments broke all the panes of glass in the window and punctured several pots, pans, and a big water container in the kitchen and the pantry. Fragments were whistling by my ears on both sides, but luckily neither Madeleine nor I received a scratch.

While we were cleaning up the debris, Madeleine cut her finger on a piece of glass she was picking up. I sent for my platoon medic, who came running in, all out of breath. His look of disgust when he discovered that instead of someone having an arm or leg blown off all he had to treat was a cut finger soon changed to one of amusement.

The Glock house had no modern plumbing. Water was obtained from a pump in front of the house. I don't believe I saw a bathtub or inside toilet in the whole village. This was not uncommon; I saw very few throughout rural France.

The small town of Schopperten was across the Saar River, some two miles away. After receiving reports of considerable enemy activity in the vicinity, the battalion commander decided we would give the Jerries in that area a taste of real fire power. Division artillery was alerted and a platoon of antiaircraft half-tracks was brought up into Viller.

At the appointed hour we let go with the 155mm and 105mm artillery, our 81mm and 60mm mortars, the half-tracks with their .50 caliber machine guns and 37mm cannons, and with our own heavy and light machine guns. A few of the townspeople of Viller came out to see the show, but most of them headed for the cellar because they knew our barrage would provoke a response. As expected, we received a few shells in return, but not as many as we had expected and very little damage was done.

Later in the day, when things had cooled off a bit, Madeleine and her mother made about eight apple pies. They were really delicious, and we made pigs of ourselves.

3 Transition: From Lorraine to Metz

December 3–19, 1944

OPERATIONAL BACKGROUND   Prior to the launching of the offensive in Lorraine on November 8, General Patton had declared that the Third Army would reach the West Wall, the line of fortifications on the border of Germany some forty miles away, "in not to exceed D plus 2 days."[1] When the offensive was suspended on December 20, however, the battered American forces were still somewhat short of that objective in several areas.

Despite the stubborn German resistance, by November 30 the 26th Division had closed to the line of the Saar River and was preparing to breach it. While the 328th Infantry was retained as a screening force centered on Harskirchen a couple of miles west of the Saar, on December 1 the 101st Infantry, assisted by elements of the 4th Armored Division, crossed the river and launched an assault on the small manufacturing town (pop. 3,000) of Saar-Union (see Map 3). Because this was a key point on the way to the highly industrialized Saar Basin, the Germans put up strong resistance and Saar-Union was not secured until December 4.[2]

On December 5 the 328th, on the left flank of the 26th Division, crossed the Saar and swung north in a clean-up operation that was to register the greatest gains the Yankee Division had made since the beginning of the Lorraine Campaign.[3] [P.R.]

Dec. 3, 1944.   G Company remains in reserve in Harskirchen, where 2nd Lt. Lee Otts joins it.

EGGER   We attended services conducted by our chaplain in the village church this morning. Except for the windows, the church had suffered little damage from the shelling.

Harskirchen was shelled periodically by the Germans. The heaviest barrages were at night and when we were changing guard. I wondered how they knew when the changing of the guard took place. Perhaps they had communicated with informers in town.* We ran from building to building when going to and from guard duty. A shell landed in a building across the street from the schoolhouse where we were staying and killed two men in an antiaircraft unit last night.

OTTS Today was Sunday and we all went to church. The church was pretty well torn up, but the service was very impressive. The dirty, unshaven men were standing among the ruins of a once beautiful church with the sun pouring in through the holes in the ceiling.

Two of the Tech Sergeants of Easy Company received battlefield commissions, so Lt. Lassiter and I were transferred to George Company today. In a letter home I wrote, "I hate to leave Easy Company as I am just beginning to know all my men, and this is by far the best company in the battalion." I later decided that no other platoon could equal the 2nd Platoon of George Company and no company could equal George. But for catching more than its share of hell and coming through victorious every time, my hat is always off to Easy Company.

It was almost dark when Lassiter and I got into Harskirchen with all our gear and reported to the Company CP, which was in a former beer hall. Captain E. Gardner Goldsmith, "Goldie," was the company commander. He was one of the old members of the 26th Division and had been on the regimental staff for a while.

Goldsmith, who was in his middle twenties and single, was about six-feet-four or five inches tall and weighed around two hundred pounds. He was a likable fellow, made friends quickly, and had a very good sense of humor. He should have been a Southerner, though, for besides myself I imagine he must have been the laziest man in the outfit. He wasn't just downright lazy like I was, but he just didn't want to exert himself any more than he had to. A Northerner may think it an insult to be called lazy, but we Southerners brag about our laziness.

The first sergeant of the company was Ed Germain, who was also one of the old hands in the 26th. Germain was about six feet tall, slim and dark with brown eyes and close-cropped black hair. He was an excellent first sergeant who handled his job exceptionally well.

---

*Like the French army in 1914, the Americans found numerous German informants in Lorraine. But much of the problem arose from an appalling lack of security by U.S. troops. Not only did the GIs themselves tend to be too noisy in the front lines, but their officers were notoriously talkative over the radio about tactical objectives and careless in their communications at the traffic control points along the routes where troops were moving.[4]

The communications sergeant was Rocco Clemente. "Rocky," as he was called, was not an old Yankee Division man but had joined the outfit along with several other ASTP transfers while still in the States. Rocco was about five-feet-seven, of medium build and with the dark Italian look. Everyone liked him and I soon counted him as one of my closest friends.

The other platoon leaders were Lt. Charles N. Walter and Lt. Chester J. Hargrove. Both of them had come over as replacements and had joined the regiment shortly before I did. Lt. Walter—Walt as we called him—was quiet and very serious. He had a good sense of humor, but was very serious about everything. Jack Hargrove was probably the best friend I had while overseas. He stood about five-feet-ten, was around twenty-six years old, and had sandy blond hair, blue eyes, and wore glasses.

I didn't get to know Jack well until he took over the company after the Bulge, but I had heard the men talk about him. Everyone thought very highly of him and wanted to be in his platoon.

I was not overly impressed with Jack at first. He had been a PX officer for three years, and I thought he was probably suited for the job. But I know now of no other officer with as much courage, coolness under fire, and leadership ability, personality, knowledge of human nature, and ability to get along with the men. He ranks along with Captain Swift as being the two top combat officers I have ever known.

Jack and Walt were both unmarried, so that left Lassiter the only married officer in the company. I was the youngest, twenty-two, and the only second lieutenant.

Captain Goldsmith had one of his runners take me over to where my platoon was billeted and I met the men I was to spend many hours with—happy hours and sad, carefree and dangerous.

My platoon sergeant was T/Sgt. Benoit Bergeron, an old YD man from Massachusetts. Benny, who was of French Canadian descent, was quiet and very thoughtful. He had plenty of courage but was not foolhardy like some of the men were. He did his job well but took no unnecessary chances. He was very capable and had run the platoon by himself for some time but lacked self-assurance and didn't like the responsibility of platoon leader. Captain Goldsmith tried for a long time to get Benny to try for a battlefield commission, but he didn't want one.

For the next 3½ months Benny and I shared the same foxhole almost every night. It is strange that you can spend so much time with a person and not learn very much about his family or home life—I guess I did most of the talking, though.

My platoon guide, S/Sgt. Alfred Bruno, was not with the platoon when I got there. The men told me I would never forget him once I had met him, and they were absolutely right. Bruno had been out on an observation post with Lt. Hargrove just across the river from Saar-Union, and even before I met him some of the men who were with him brought back tales of how Bruno with only a .45 in his hip pocket and a wool knit cap on his head had walked across a blown out bridge to contact elements of the 104th Regiment fighting in Saar-Union.

Bruno lived and fought on nervous energy. I don't know whether it was just plain guts or whether he had just built up his nerves to take it, but he wasn't afraid of the devil himself. There was nothing that Bruno wouldn't do, or at least try. He was in his early thirties, loud, always talking and laughing, but he could be very serious at times, although you always thought you saw a smile in the corners of his eyes even during his serious moments. Like Benny, he was one of the old hands with the 26th Division. Bruno was from Springfield, Massachusetts, where he had been a cab driver. I can picture him in his cab, caught in a traffic jam with his head out the window and a cap perched jauntily on it, blowing his horn and shouting at the other drivers.

The first squad leader was S/Sgt. John Austin from Mt. Vernon, Washington. John was about twenty with rosy cheeks and blond hair. He had been in ASTP and joined the division shortly before it sailed. Although young, he was very capable. The second squad leader was S/Sgt. Dave Smith. Smitty was in his middle thirties and on occasions had a difficult time keeping up with the younger men.

S/Sgt. George Van Winkle, who was about twenty-six and married, was leader of the third squad.* He was the first man I remember meeting when I reported to the second platoon. Van was one of the best liked and most capable non-coms I have ever known even though he had not been in the Army very long. Van was always concerned very much with the comfort and safety of the men under him. He never thought of himself until every man had been taken care of.

The three assistant squad leaders were Idelson, Seeney, and Hedgpath. Sgt. George Idelson was from Brooklyn. He was about twenty, had been to college a year or so, and was liked by all the men in the platoon. He received more Christmas boxes from home than anyone else and always had something for us to eat. Dave Seeney and Vern Hedgpath were both in their late twenties and were serious, tough, and quite capable.

---

*Austin, Smith, and Van Winkle were Pfcs. who were acting staff sergeants at the time. The latter two had arrived in the replacement draft of Nov. 19.

My platoon runner and right-hand man was Pfc. Donald Thompson of St. Joseph, Missouri. Tommy had a great dry wit and kept us laughing all the time. Whenever spirits were low, he would come out with some crack and we would be laughing again.*

Dec. 4, 1944. George Company is in reserve at Harskirchen one last day.

EGGER American airplanes were strafing and bombing an area several miles ahead of us all day. In the afternoon there was an intense firefight a mile or so to our left. We heard that the 101st and 104th Regiments were trying to take Saar-Union. Treff, Nachman, a replacement named Wendell Wolfenbarger, and several others were sent on patrol near Saar-Union this afternoon. They came back loaded down with jars of canned fruit. We were moving out the next morning, so we gorged ourselves on the canned goods.

OTTS After meeting all the men, I went back out to Viller that night to see Madeleine. The whole family was still sitting around in the living room; but, on the pretense of going to get a drink of water, Madeleine and I went into the kitchen and stole a few kisses. I really wished that I could speak French or German so I could have told her how wonderful I thought she was. I think she knew, though.

Dec. 5, 1944. Saar-Union having fallen to the 101st and 104th Regiments, the 328th crosses the Saar River and sweeps northward.

EGGER We left for Saar-Union before daylight. I had diarrhea, which was undoubtly caused by eating too much fruit. My stomach had not been accustomed to soft foods, especially canned berries.

We passed through the northern outskirts of Saar-Union and waited in a wooded area until daylight. We then cleared the woods to a railroad but met no opposition. There were signs of heavy fighting in this area, including a number of dead American soldiers. I walked past three in one foxhole with a heavy machine gun and tank tracks a few feet away. I tried to figure out what had happened and decided they had probably set up the machine gun to provide support for the attacking infantrymen. The Germans had then counter-attacked with tanks, and the German infantry, using the tanks as protection, had shot the three

---

*Idelson, Seeney, and Hedgpath were also still Pfcs. The latter two and Thompson were also replacements from the draft of Nov. 19.

GIs. Perhaps I had heard their machine gun and the return fire yesterday.

We followed the railroad to a small village that was deserted. We then moved on to a small town [Keskastel] near Saarbuckhein, which was occupied by a few civilians but, to our relief, no German soldiers. The Germans must have retreated to new positions. We stayed in town overnight and set up some outposts along the railroad.

I was made assistant squad leader of the 3rd Squad tonight.* Some of the replacements who arrived after Moncourt had already become noncoms and my observations of them made me feel that I could do as well. I hated to leave my friends in the 1st Squad. The members of 3rd Squad when I joined them were Vern Olson, now a buck sergeant and the squad leader, Jasper Fockler, Fonrose LeCrone, Walt Lee, Wilbur Munns, Tom Roberts, Oscar Stribling, Ray Tompkins, and Paul Scheufler. Stribling had been assistant squad leader for a short time, but his performance had not been good. In college I wrote an essay entitled "The Coward." This essay was about the Striblings of this world.

OTTS   At about 0200 the battalion moved out from Harskirchen to an assembly area on the northern side of Saar-Union. Just at daylight we all took off. My platoon led the advance for George Company. I sent two scouts out ahead and followed about thirty yards behind them with my runner and the rest of the platoon.

There was about a three- or four-hundred-yard stretch of flat, grassy land without a bush or tree in sight from the railroad out to the woods. It was really nerve-wracking to walk slowly across that field just at daylight, not knowing when a hidden machine gun in the woods would start sweeping the ground and us with no place to take cover. But we made it without drawing any fire and spent most of the rest of the day combing the woods. All we netted for our efforts were a few German stragglers.

We found several dead Americans and Germans, the result of a combat patrol sent out the night before. Several of the dead Germans had pieces of American equipment, and it made us mad to think of how they probably got it.

We marched on through Schopperten and got to moving so fast that we ran off my map, and I had no idea where we were going. From Schopperten we went down a long narrow road through a swamp. We

---

*On Dec. 18 Pfc. Egger was promoted to sergeant, the rank to which he was entitled by virtue of his new position as assistant squad leader.

soon left the road and followed a railroad track into the station about a mile outside of Keskastel.

Some civilians at the station told us there was a German in one of the warehouse sheds and that he wanted to surrender. I had to call to Benny to find out what they were talking about. Bruno was there too, so I let him (I won't say "sent" because you didn't send Bruno anywhere; you just let him go—he was always ready and eager) and another man go to the shed and take the prisoner. We took him into town with us where we met Captain Goldsmith and the other platoons.

We spent the night in nice quarters in Keskastel. The people there were wonderful to us. Everywhere we went they were standing in front of their houses handing out apples, cookies, and wine. It continued to rain.

Dec. 6, 1944.   The 328th continues the chase northeastward, with the 2nd Battalion in reserve.

EGGER   We walked all day trying to catch up with the Germans. The country was rolling, so we had a few hills to climb but we were on roads, which was easier than traveling cross-country. The leader of the column set a stiff pace and we had very few rest stops. We passed through a large town in the late afternoon, walked several miles beyond, and dug in for the night on the reverse slope of a hill facing the Germans.

It had rained most of the day and the ground was soggy. The rain started falling again while we were digging our foxholes. Olson and I had straw for our hole and two blankets, but the blankets were wet by morning, so we didn't have a very comfortable night.

We all sampled canned snails that Alex Stoddard had found in some German rations. They tasted just as slimy as they looked.

OTTS   We would all have liked to stay in Keskastel longer but had to move out that morning. The 2nd Battalion was in reserve and we spent most of the day sitting on the top of a big hill just on the edge of a large forest watching the movements of the forward elements. Everything was very wet, so we built some fires to dry out and heat our C and K rations.*

Late in the afternoon we moved down the hill through the town of Germingen, deep in the valley and up another valley into the village of

---

*The reader will note that Egger's and Otts' accounts for Dec. 6 differ markedly. It appears from the 2nd Battalion history, *Handcar White*, that Otts' is the more accurate, but the editor has made no effort to reconcile the two narratives.

Kalhausen—that is, all the battalion except G Company moved. We outposted the town and dug in on a bare hill. We were very bitter about this at first, preferring more comfortable quarters in town, but it turned out we were the luckiest after all. All that evening and early the next morning the Germans shelled the hell out of Kalhausen with 88s and mortars, and all we received were two or three stray shells.

Dec. 7, 1944. Finding it had advanced beyond its sector, the 2nd Battalion has to pull back to near Weidesheim.

EGGER We stayed in some buildings along the railroad most of the day waiting for orders to move to a forested area. An occasional 88 landed near our position. E Company had moved through the woods but couldn't take the town just beyond [Weidesheim]. We moved to the timbered area in the evening and dug in. Olson and I dug a shallow hole (the water table was high) and made a covering of evergreen boughs. But this only held out the water for a short time, so we spent another wet night.

During the night, Olson, Fockler, and I were sent on a patrol to the edge of Weidesheim to make contact with the 3rd Battalion. We didn't find anybody, friend or foe, so we returned to our position. It was so dark I don't know how we found our way back. The shelling was heavy in our area during the night, but there were no casualties in our platoon.

OTTS It turned out that Kalhausen belonged in somebody else's sector, so the next morning we headed back toward Germingen. We made several rest stops. At one of them, while we were standing around on a bare hill, I counted eleven 88 shells that hit in our vicinity, and every one was a dud. They just plopped in the soft mud without going off. We had a good time joking about the German 4-F's in the munitions factories goofing off.

While Easy Company was attacking Weidesheim we were huddled in a little group of buildings by the railroad tracks, trying to keep out of the weather and warm up. Soon George Company moved into the woods on a hill overlooking Weidesheim, where E Company was encountering some resistance. There were about ten battalion headquarters officers in a group just standing around talking and looking at the maps when an 88 shell hit about ten yards from us. The group scattered amazingly fast; some ran behind trees and others hit the ground. Luckily no one was hurt, but I noticed that there were no large gatherings after that.

Just before dark we began to dig our holes for the night. Just as we started to dig, the 88s and mortar shells started coming in as thick as hailstones. My hole was only about four inches deep then, so we all just lay flat on the ground and prayed. After two or three casualties I considered ordering the men to fall back from our position until the shelling ceased and then come back, but I had no way of getting the order to everyone; besides, the shells were falling almost as thick behind us.

The shelling finally let up a little, and we dug like hell to finish our holes before another barrage started. Not only did we need deep holes, but we needed heavy covers over them to protect us from the tree bursts. There was intermittent shelling all night with a heavier barrage just at daylight.

Dec. 8, 1944. The 2nd Battalion occupies Weidesheim.

EGGER We pulled back to the buildings along the railroad and were able to dry our clothes. E Company took Weidesheim in the morning, meeting little opposition, and we moved into the town in the afternoon. I noticed that one of the German prisoners E Company had taken was wearing American military shoes. I wondered if he had taken them from a prisoner or off a corpse.

We spent the night in one of the barracks of a concentration camp whose occupants had been moved out by the Germans ahead of our arrival. Perhaps these people had been used to dig the trenches and emplacements the Germans had been using. The buildings were drafty but dry and had bunks with straw mattresses.

OTTS Easy Company moved into Weidesheim early in the morning and found a few German stragglers. The rest of the battalion followed later that day. Our company took over a couple of nice buildings, and we started cleaning them up for a pleasant stay. Then the battalion brass decided they needed the same buildings, so we moved across town to a German concentration camp. We busied ourselves cleaning them out and gathering up stoves and coal.

The concentration camp buildings were made of wood, with several branch buildings and kitchens, dining halls, and a laundry. The whole thing was surrounded by a high barbed wire fence. The bunks were made of wood with no springs but had straw-filled mattresses. Most of us had been lying around on our bunks for a while when someone discovered that the mattresses were full of bed bugs, so we had to take them all outside. We set up a perimeter defense around the camp and dug holes for the sentries.

That day Easy Company captured a German soldier in a 1938 Chevrolet truck who had blithely driven through a thick mine field and right into Weidesheim to deliver hot food to his troops. The astounding part of the incident was that none of the mines had detonated.

That night I met with an officer from each of the other companies plus one from battalion headquarters, and we organized a roving patrol to check on our local security throughout the night. I stopped by Easy Company CP for a while and chatted with Captain Swift and the other men. Swifty was very pleased with his Chevrolet truck and a German pistol he had taken from a prisoner.

Dec. 9, 1944.   The 2nd Battalion advances nine miles through the old Maginot Line to the town of Woelfling.

EGGER   Everyone was scratching from the lice we picked up from sleeping in the barracks. Shortly after daylight we moved out through some woods and across open rolling fields. We were passing through the Maginot Line, where there were many abandoned forts and pillboxes.

Accompanied by tanks, we entered Woelfling in the afternoon as the Germans were leaving the other end of town. Several men from H Company, who had been ahead of us, ran towards us shouting that the Germans were counterattacking. Some of the squad panicked and ran into the cellars of the houses along the street, but Olson and I routed them out. I picked up a discarded bazooka and with Munns and Lee went to the edge of town where we found Lt. Hargrove, S/Sgt. Starcher, Pearcy, and Stoddard, who also had a bazooka.

Starcher placed us behind a stone monument facing down the road. The other men were behind a house and were at right angles to the road. A German half-track outside town was firing its machine gun at us. We fired back, but it was outside a rifle's effective range. The monument we were huddled behind provided protection from the bullets, but I was afraid that a tank would blow the monument and us away with a round from its 88mm cannon.

The Germans occupied the high bluffs to the north overlooking Woelfling and it wasn't long before mortar shells began to fall around us. I hollered to Starcher that we weren't in a very good position. He agreed and had us move across the road to where he was located. Instead of coming toward town, the half-track turned and went away from us, ending the threat of a counterattack.

G Company moved to the west end of town, where we started to dig in on a hill above the road. While we were digging, artillery and mortar shells, probably from the bluffs overlooking the town, began to rain down on us. The shells sank some into the soft ground before they exploded or we would have suffered more casualties than we did. Munns and Roberts from the 3rd Squad were wounded and evacuated.

Wolfenbarger was hit by a piece of spent shrapnel, which bruised him slightly.*

Captain Goldsmith, the Company CO, decided we were too exposed to observation by the Germans so we moved to a draw, set up an outpost, and later in the evening moved to a building. It had been a long day.

OTTS   The next morning, accompanied by tanks, we set off northward on a muddy nine-mile march past dilapidated forts of the Maginot Line to a town called Woelfling. Lt. Lassiter took his platoon and led the company into town. My platoon followed his at about one hundred yards. On the way Lassiter tripped over a fence and broke his finger.†

We had been in town only a short time when someone sent up the alarm that tanks were coming from the woods. Woelfling was in a shallow valley with a road leading straight out of town to the woods, about a mile to the northeast where the tanks had been seen moving around. The Battalion CO and all his staff began running around like mad, trying to get all the bazookas concentrated on the road and some mines put out. The tanks didn't attack, but we began setting up a defense just in case.

We were on the back side of town, which was located on a hill that was in direct line with the woods where the Heinies were. We had just started placing our men and digging foxholes when enemy tanks and field pieces in the woods started cutting loose with point-blank direct fire. The town was in a valley and couldn't be reached with direct fire, but the hill we were on was behind the town in a direct line and only about 1½ miles from the woods. They were picking us off with 88s just like a sniper would with a rifle. We finally got the Company Commander and Battalion CO to let us move off the hill into the valley beside the creek.

It was raining as usual and my sergeants and I spent the night checking on the outposts and rotating a-squad-at-a-time into a building where we had a room and a stove where they could get dry and warm. I don't remember sleeping at all that night, but I guess I did a little.

---

*The G Company morning reports show Pfc. Wilbur L. Munns as "slightly wounded" and Pfc. Thomas L. Roberts as "seriously wounded." Both were hospitalized. Munns returned to duty with G Company on May 21, 1945, but there is no further record of Roberts.

†Lt. Lassiter was shown on the morning report as "seriously injured in action" and hospitalized. He returned to duty on Dec. 18.

Dec. 10, 1944. George Company has a close call with some tanks in a wood outside Woefling.

EGGER Pearcy and I went on guard at 0200. Our foxhole was full of straw and each of us had a blanket, so we managed to keep dry despite the snowstorm.

The battalion left early in the morning with George Company in the lead. The 3rd Platoon reached the edge of the woods without encountering any Germans, so we signaled for the rest of the company to come up, but an enemy tank hidden in the woods opened fire on us with its cannon and machine gun. At the same time mortars began to fall in the area. Popa said he could see the turret of the tank, so a bazooka was brought up and Popa fired three rounds at it.* The tank was partially hidden by an embankment and Popa was unable to hit it. Orders came from Captain Goldsmith for us to withdraw.

Olson, Popa, and I were the last ones to leave. As we began to make our way out of the woods the tank started firing again. A shell knocked down a tree near us, filling the air with splinters, one of which hit Olson in the side. We hit the ground, facing in the direction of the tank. Machine gun bullets with an occasional tracer mixed in were landing in front of me. I was surprised at how slowly the tracers seemed to travel, but then I realized there were five bullets between each tracer. The tracers sputtered and went out in the damp leaves at my side. I could hear the engine of the tank and could see the turret, cannon, and machine gun. We managed to crawl out of the line of fire and out of the woods and withdrew to Woelfling.

Foster had been shot in the arm and Sgt. Henry Bilendy from the 4th Platoon had been killed.† Olson was bruised by the sliver and Scheufler had a bullet hole through his canteen and a wet leg.

We spent the night in a house and had no guard duty. It was good to take my clothes off and sleep the night through without interruption. The lice seemed to be thriving and multiplying on my blood. They were more active at night and I could feel them scurrying across my body.

A rumor was circulating today that the 87th Division would be relieving us soon.

OTTS The next day the attack plan was for Easy and Fox Companies to advance down each side of the road to the woods, and for G Company

---

*Sgt. Victor M. Popa was awarded the Bronze Star for this action.

†S/Sgt. Charles N. Foster was listed as "slightly wounded" on Dec. 10 and was hospitalized. He never rejoined the company.

to be in reserve. We were supposed to come up to the right side of the woods to protect the battalion's right flank. We liked the idea of being in reserve, but something got messed up; the other two companies didn't jump off and we weren't notified. We assembled in the draw on the right of town, moved up it a short distance, and halted. Then I took my platoon forward to the woods for reconnaissance. We ran into a little edge of timber about twenty feet wide, and then came to a cut about twelve feet deep at the bottom of which was a road.

I sent two scouts across the road and was getting ready to follow with the platoon when a truck with about fifteen Jerries came racing by and turned up another road to go deeper into the woods. They didn't see us, and we were so taken by surprise that we didn't have a chance to fire at them.

We crossed on over the road and into the woods. Since there were no Germans in sight, I sent a runner back to tell the CO to send the rest of the company up. Hargrove got his platoon up and Walter got about half of his across the road when a Heinie tank pulled up into the cut and started firing down the road and into the woods around us. The tank had the road so well covered that no more men could get across it and into the woods and we couldn't get back.

The tank was really spraying the woods with its machine guns and getting tree bursts all around with its cannon. The Heinies also threw in several mortar rounds for good measure. But all the German infantrymen we saw were about a half-dozen with automatic weapons clustered around the tank. The woods were shallow at this point and not far away was a large three-story house. Germans were all around it, walking around casually with no helmets or weapons. They must not have known that we were in the woods. We could not go to our rear because of the tanks firing down the road. To our right was a bare hill in plain view of the Heinies in the house, and to the left was the thick woods and the whole German army for all we knew.

With no idea of what to do and with self-preservation foremost in our minds we started digging like hell. Soon a couple of men in the 3rd Platoon took a bazooka and fired enough rounds at the tank to make it back up some. We all took off running as fast as we could, carrying our equipment and wounded across the road and back down the draw toward Woelfling.

We hadn't been back in town for more than a half-hour when the Battalion CO, Major Medbourn, called me in to the Battalion CP and I told him what had happened to us. He told me he wanted me to take a patrol back into the woods and see if we had knocked out the tanks. Three tanks had been seen in that vicinity and all our artillery had been firing on them. He said that a TOT had been laid on that sector and that the field artillery forward observer had reported all the tanks knocked out. (TOT means "time on target"—all artillery, from the battalion's mortars to division and corps heavy artillery, were zeroed in on a certain spot and fired simultaneously.)

I wasn't at all eager about the patrol, but there was nothing I could do. Back at the platoon I called for volunteers, but the narrow escape we had just had in those woods was still too fresh in the men's mind and I couldn't get the twelve men I needed. Then Bennie and Bruno sent me off and talked to the guys privately. I don't know what they told them, but in a few minutes I had more volunteers than I could use. It was almost dark when we set out. I instructed the patrol that if we were fired upon it was every man for himself and to get the hell out of there as fast as they could. We were in a reconnaissance patrol and didn't want to engage in a fire fight.

We got back up to the road cut, and I sent Bruno and a couple of other men across the road first. Just as they reached the other side, we heard a tank start its motor and two others began strafing with their machine guns. I waited for Bruno and the others and then we started running like hell. As soon as we got over the crest we were safe from the machine gun fire and the tracers were whizzing harmlessly overhead. I was pretty hot in several ways when I got back to the Battalion CP and really let the CO know what I thought of his TOT—at least as much as a 2nd lieutenant can tell off a major without getting dressed down.

Dec. 11, 1944. The 2nd Battalion tries again to clear the woods outside Woelfling.

EGGER We started toward the woods this morning accompanied by a tank. A German tank sent an 88 through it before we got there. Only one of the four-man crew escaped. The tank burst into flames and the ammunition for the machine gun and cannon exploded. We pulled back to Woelfling again and set up an outpost at the edge of town. The battalion seemed tentative about attacking and just seemed to want to maintain contact with the enemy, which was fine with us.

It rained all night and our foxholes filled with water. Each of us spent half the night on guard. As Nachman and I were returning from guard I fell in a creek and really got wet.

OTTS At 1000 the next morning we tried again, only this time Easy and Fox Companies attacked and we stayed in reserve. We pulled into our same draw on the right and watched the attack. This time we had tank and artillery support. The German tanks were still in the woods. They were dug in so that only their turrets showed and every time our tanks or tank destroyers topped the crest of the hill in front of them our tanks were silhouetted against the skyline like ducks in a shooting gallery. One of our TDs came to the top of the hill to try to get a shot at the enemy tanks, but Jerry was quicker. He sent an 88 shell through the TD from front to back, and the shell came screaming on down the valley above us. The TD caught fire and the ammunition in it made quite a racket going off. It burned far into the night.

E and F Companies got only part of the way into the woods so George Company outposted Woelfling between the town and the woods.

Dec. 12, 1944. After nudging across the border into Germany, the 328th Infantry is relieved amid much noise and confusion.

EGGER The Germans had pulled back from their previous positions and in the late afternoon we were able to move through the wooded area, down the railroad tracks, and into another woods. The Germans were about two hundred yards from us across an opening at the edge of the woods. By the time we had moved into position it was dark and had started to rain. The ground was rocky and we were trying to be quiet as we dug so as not to give away our location. Occasionally the Germans, employing their usual harassment tactics, would drop a mortar in our general area and fire a machine gun overhead.

A unit of the 87th Division relieved us at 2000. The division had never been in combat and the men talked and banged their equipment as they moved into position. I could not get out of there fast enough as I was sure the Germans would hear them and throw in a barrage of mortars and artillery. The relief was carried out without incident and we walked back to Woelfling and spent the night in a barn loft.

OTTS Yesterday a regiment of the new 87th Division had relieved the 104th Infantry, which was on our right flank, so this morning we expected fresh troops to take over for us also. But the relieving forces didn't show up and an attack was ordered for 1330 hours.

Easy and Fox Companies again led the way and advanced without much opposition across the highway and to the next hill, where they dug in on the reverse slope. We were still in reserve, a couple hundred yards or so behind the other companies. It was raining hard and almost dark when we set up our defense.

German automatic weapons and our light machine guns were firing intermittently, but it was useless to try to dig in. As fast as we dug a hole it would fill up with water, just like in the sand near the ocean; we couldn't bail the holes out with our helmets fast enough. Benny and I sat propped up against a tree beside the little swimming pool we had dug and watched the tracers flying through the trees above us.

It was the darkest and coldest night I had ever spent. Since we had been expecting to be relieved, we didn't have any blankets so we just sat around huddled up in our rain coats with our teeth chattering and cursing the rain, the Heinies, and the delay in being relieved.

Sometime that day Able Company had sent a patrol across the German border, making them the first unit in the 26th Division to set foot on German soil in World War II. We may have been mistaken, but it was common talk among us that the only reason we weren't relieved sooner was that some of the divisional brass wanted to have it announced in the Boston papers, "YD Crosses German Border." As far as we were concerned, we would just as soon have been just close to the border. It seemed to us that it would have been much easier to effect a relief while we were in the town of Woelfling, and not under fire, than in the drenched foxholes in the pitch black of night and in very close proximity to the enemy.

So we sat there and shivered in the rain and darkness while contact patrols were sent back to try to lead the relieving company up to us. Finally, just before midnight, they arrived—fresh and green. We had been afraid to talk above a whisper for fear of bringing a mortar or 88 barrage in on us, but they came up talking loudly, wanting to know where their foxholes were, shining flashlights, and making quite a racket in general.

I had only about fifteen men left in my platoon, and the new platoon leader had forty, so naturally there weren't enough holes. I told him we weren't using foxholes anyway, wished him luck, and then cleared out.

I'll never know why the Germans didn't throw a heavy barrage of 88s in on us. They could have really messed things up. We had run maybe one jeep a day down the road we were taking out, and it would go at top speed, but now the road was full of 87th Division vehicles, bumper to bumper from the town to the woods. We shrugged it off with a few remarks of "They'll learn" and forgot about them.

When we got back into Woelfling we took over a few houses and started filling our empty stomachs and getting some much needed rest. The house I was in with about a squad of men plus my headquarters group was occupied by an elderly couple. They were always in our way, the old woman wringing her hands and crying, "Alles kaput," meaning "All is finished" or "This is the end." We weren't deliberately harming her property, but whenever someone spilled something on the floor or set a hot canteen cup on her table she would wring her hands and cry, "Alles kaput!" We were in no mood to pacify her so we would say "Alles kaput" right back at her and try to make her see that we were not hurting her house nearly as much as the German shells had. They had torn up most of the houses in the town, but she didn't seem to realize how lucky she was.

I didn't have much patience with the German-speaking, so-called French anyway, especially when they made it plain that they would rather have the Germans than us. We hadn't asked to come over there, and as long as we were fighting their war for them I thought they could at least make us comfortable when we had a chance to get indoors.

AFTER ACTION SUMMARY. The men of G Company probably couldn't have cared less, but that last woods they saw ahead of them, the Obergailbach Woods, was in Germany. Able Company of the Ist Battalion had advanced six hundred meters inside the German borders before pulling back.[5] Thus the 328th Infantry, the last of the Yankee Division regiments to be relieved, was the only one to penetrate into enemy territory.

The Lorraine Campaign had been an old-style, bitterly fought infantry battle. In the thirty-five days since the opening of the offensive on November 8, the 26th Division had advanced only forty-five miles. The tenacity of the German resistance was reflected in the division's casualty list—661 killed, 2,154 wounded, and 613 missing.[6] Additional thousands of GIs of the Yankee Division had been evacuated because of trench foot, exposure, and fatigue.

George Company's losses were probably proportionate to the division as a whole. In a few days it would receive seventy-seven new replacements, making a total of 270 men, not including officers, who had joined its ranks since the opening of the offensive. Probably about half of these replaced actual battle casualties; the rest of the losses had been from trench foot and the other weather-related ailments.

But for now it was all over. The 26th Division was headed back to Metz for an extended period of rest, refitting, and training after sixty-seven grueling days of combat. With the Army scraping the bottom of its manpower pool, General Patton had ordered that five percent of all non-divisional personnel were to be converted into riflemen. On December 18 the battered Yankee Division would receive some 2,500 of these "five percenter" replacements, who were slated to undergo thirty days of intensive infantry training at Metz with the rest of the 26th.[7] [P.R.]

Dec. 13, 1944. G Company pulls back to the Weidesheim area.

EGGER We stayed in Woelfling until afternoon and then walked nine miles back to Weidesheim, where we talked with some GIs from the 87th. I'm afraid some of our men spun some tall tales. I could remember similar stories the returning wounded had told me in the replacement depots. Now some of them rang true while others obviously fell into the category of "snow jobs."

The kitchen had a hot meal waiting for us at Weideshiem. We heard that we would be going back for a long rest, which put everybody in good spirits. We slept in a wooded area but were far enough to the rear that there was no need to dig foxholes. Pearcy and Stoddard had stolen some C rations from the kitchen and they called me over to share with them. In retrospect I don't know why we were eating rations after a hot meal. We were always hungry, but I don't know whether it was because we burned so many calories or if it was a means of relieving tension. The men were constantly foraging for food in towns and lifting rations from other outfits. Any unit except your own platoon was fair game, so a smart soldier kept his rations and possessions with him at all times.

OTTS The next day we moved back over the route we had come and spent the night in some woods near Weidesheim. We were so elated over being out of the combat zone that we didn't mind sleeping in the woods very much. We even pitched tents after a fashion for the first time since I had joined the outfit.

Dec. 14, 1944. The 328th Infantry Regiment is sent back to Metz for rest and refitting.

EGGER Our blankets were covered with frost by morning and I had slept cold. The trucks to take us to Metz arrived shortly after breakfast. There were no covers on the trucks and we had orders that we were not to wrap ourselves in blankets, so we knew we were in for a cold ride of fifty miles. Covers on the trucks would have hindered our lookout for enemy aircraft and being wrapped in blankets would have got in the way if we had to pile out in case of an air attack. Stribling was the only man who didn't comply and he soon caught hell from Starcher.

The route of travel took us through the Foret de Bride et de Koecking. It seemed like more than a month since we had fought through these woods. The quiet there now was a welcome contrast to the noise and confusion of that time. Dead German soldiers, scattered among the debris of battle, were visible from the road.

Before we reached Metz I had an attack of stomach cramps and diarrhea that usually came when I changed from a diet of rations to cooked food. The truck wouldn't stop and I wasn't able to get back to the tailgate in time. If the smell bothered anyone, they were too polite to mention it.

We were quartered on the third floor of a former French Officer Cadet School barracks. My first priority was to heat some water so I could clean myself up and wash my underwear. The latrine was on the first floor, so I had to sprint down the stairs several times during the night.

OTTS The next morning we assembled on a hill outside Weidesheim, had a hot meal, and loaded on trucks for the fifty-mile ride to Metz, where we arrived about noon and were quartered in former French OCS barracks. They were very nice, though dirty and with several broken windows. But at least they were warm and dry.

Dec. 15, 1944. The men of G Company relax at Metz.

EGGER Metz, France, was an ancient city with a population of about 100,000. The main city had been taken on November 22, but some of the forts had held out until December 13.

We had a physical inspection in the morning and it didn't take long for the doctor to discover that we were lousy. We were allowed to take showers (what luxury!), our first since November 5, were sprayed with DDT powder, given a shot for typhus, and issued clean underwear.

We slept on the floor, each man with a small area where he could sack out and store his equipment and weapons. The building was steam-heated. That afternoon the officers left us alone and we rested.

A gradual attrition had cut the 3rd Platoon to twenty-four men. We had all been together since at least November 19 and had become more of a cohesive unit. Vernon Olson, our squad leader, was a big Swede from South Dakota. Walt Lee from St. Louis was a devout converted Catholic. He was twenty-eight years old, married with two children, and was a very good soldier with leadership abilities. Jasper Fockler, from Michigan, was twenty-four and had a younger brother in E Company. At every opportunity they were checking on each other's welfare. Other members of the 3rd Squad were Fonrose LeCrone, Ray Tompkins, Paul Scheufler, and Oscar Stribling.

Members of the 1st Squad were Larry Treff (squad leader), Stan Nachman, Marshall Pearcy, Alex Stoddard, Henry Huckabee, Tom Oakley, Lee Allen, and Wendell Wolfenbarger, who was from Missouri and had a cousin, Opal, I had known in Boise. All that was left of the 2nd Squad were the squad leader, Dan Dafoe, Albert Evans, Junior Letterman, and Francis Gormley, the assistant squad leader. 1st Lt. Chester Hargrove of Portland, Oregon, was platoon leader, T/Sgt. Bob

---

THE 1ST AND 3RD SQUADS, 3RD PLATOON, SINCE NOVEMBER 19

1st Squad	3rd Squad
S/Sgt. Lawrence Treff, Ldr.	S/Sgt. Vernon Olson, Ldr.
T/5 Richardson, Asst., WIA 11/22	Pvt. McCowan, Asst., WIA 11/22
Sgt. Stanley Nachman, Asst. 11/23	Sgt. Bruce Egger, Asst. 12/5
Pfc. Lee Allen	Pfc. Jasper Fockler
Pfc. Bruce Egger (until 12/5)	Pfc. Fonrose LeCrone
Pfc. Henry Huckabee	Pfc. Walter Lee
Pvt. Carmel Nutt, to hosp. 11/23	Pfc. Wilbur Munns, WIA 12/9
Pfc. Thomas Oakley	Pfc. Thomas Roberts, WIA 12/9
Pfc. Marshall Pearcy	Pfc. Paul Scheufler
Pfc. Alex Stoddard	Pfc. Oscar Stribling
Pvt. Wendell Wolfenbarger	Pfc. Raymond Tompkins
2 unidentified men lost to duty	2 unidentified men lost to duty

---

Starcher was platoon sergeant, S/Sgt. Vic Popa was platoon guide, and Pfc. Roger Dumais, better known as "Frenchy," was the runner. Two of these 3rd Platoon veterans would be killed, twelve wounded, two would be disabled with frozen feet, and one would be taken prisoner after being wounded.

OTTS Our battalion was given an abandoned apartment building across the street for the officers. G Company officers had two bedrooms and an adjoining living room. Jack, Walt, and I spent most of the day plundering the adjacent buildings for furnishings. We had just about everything we needed when the regiment put a big "Off Limits" sign on each of the other buildings.

Dec. 16–17, 1944. The 328th receives replacements and starts a training program.

EGGER I recovered from diarrhea and DDT took care of the lice. A training program was started on the 16th, which naturally drew complaints from all of us. There were the usual close order drill, discussion of combat experiences, and hikes to keep us in condition.

The 328th had received a number of five-percenters as replacements the regiment would train. General Patton had decreed that five percent of the non-combatants would be transferred to the infantry and given infantry training before going into combat. We had heard that the regiment would be in Metz from three to eight weeks for that purpose.

I talked to McCammon, who had been with me in Company B, 387th Regiment, at Fort Leonard Wood and San Luis Opisbo. He had joined F Company at Arracourt. I also visited with Giovinazzo of F Company and he told me that Dixon and Erickson had been killed at Moncourt. He said that twenty-one of the twenty-five replacements who joined F Company with him in late October had been wounded or killed.

FROM EGGER'S LETTER OF DECEMBER 16

. . . Can't say where I am or what I am doing but it beats what we had been doing. . . .

I sure learned what it was to have prayers answered during the last two weeks. Had a few exciting scrapes and I know prayer pulled us through. . . .

My feet are in better shape now and I feel pretty good, rheumatism bothers when I have to sleep on the wet ground, which hasn't been very often. . . .

We had a movie for entertainment in the evening. LeCrone found a case of C rations we really didn't need since we were being served three hot meals a day, but that didn't keep us from sharing in the loot.

This morning I went to the church service, which was conducted by the Protestant chaplain. There were far more in attendance than the room could hold and men were standing in the hallway.

There was no training on Sunday. Some of the guys went to town but I thought there would be time enough to see the city since we would be there three to eight weeks.

OTTS It was rumored that we were to be in Metz for eight weeks. A training schedule was set up and we began receiving new replacements—men from ordinance, field artillery, antiaircraft, and the quartermaster. Most of them were pretty bitter about being transferred to the infantry—I can't say that I blamed them—but some of them were glad to get away from the "chicken" and "spit and polish" of the rear echelon outfits. Most of these men made excellent infantrymen, although we were able to give them only about one day's training. My platoon was down to some fifteen men so I was given about twenty-five of the "five-percenters." The ones I remember are Fred Gilluly, Bobby Phipps, and Phil Sarro.

December 16 went down as a red letter day on my calendar—I had my first bath since November 1 and my first shave in several weeks. We all lined up and went through the hot showers. Each group had three minutes to get forty-six days' dirt off, but usually they let us stay a little longer. We took off all our clothes on the way down to the showers and were issued clean clothes as we came out. In the infantry we never bothered to wash clothes—we just kept on the same ones for a month or two until we got a shower then peeled off everything and were issued new ones. The bath really worked wonders on our morale. In every letter I had previously written home I had started with "still no bath, still no bed, and still no mail."

Sunday morning I went to church in the OCS chapel and afterwards Lt. Zera and I went into Metz. (Zera was a former Tech Sergeant with the 4th Platoon who had recently received a field commission.) There were several rumors of pro-German civilians who had been sniping at the division that had been there before us. The sniping ceased a few days after we got there because whenever one of our men was shot at he would get some of his buddies and take the building apart. Nevertheless, we carried our weapons into town with us.

We went by the officers' clothing PX and I ran into Law Lamar, who proudly showed me the hole in his helmet made by the bullet that had grazed his scalp. He and another lieutenant that I knew from our replacement draft had a jeep, so we toured part of Metz. Almost everything was closed up, but there were a few bars open. There was nothing to drink but very weak and stale beer—no wine, cognac, or champagne.

Lamar and I started checking up on the other twelve officers who had joined the regiment with us. We found that only six of us were left, and two of those were the ones who had gone to the heavy weapons companies.

We had a wonderful setup in Metz and enjoyed ourselves immensely. The comfortable quarters with real beds, an inside toilet, a table and chairs, and Jack's little radio made it almost seem like home. A barber shop was set up and I had my first haircut in a couple of months. I really felt slicked up with a bath, shave, haircut, and a clean uniform.

This was the first chance I had really to become acquainted with the other officers of G Company, as we had always been with our separate platoons. Captain Goldsmith, Walt, Jack, and I got together in our room one afternoon and while talking over old times in the States and listening to the radio we drank seven bottles of wine. It was totally relaxing to be able to sit and talk without having to keep an ear open for shells coming in. We were certainly looking forward to our eight weeks' rest, but Hitler upset our plans.

Dec. 18, 1944. The 328th Infantry continues its stay in Metz amid rumors that it will be moving out soon.

EGGER I received notice today that my promotion to sergeant was official. My pay was now one hundred dollars a month. I had a bond withheld each month and had the Army send all but twenty dollars to my parents, who banked it for me. During combat I never spent even that much, so I would send additional money home periodically.

Frenchy, our platoon runner [Pfc. Roger Dumais], who had been with us since November 19, was a French Canadian from Maine. Since he could speak French he was useful as an interpreter. He was very dapper and managed to keep his mustache well groomed throughout the war. He was a good runner and was still performing that job when the war ended.

The PX rations we got today included a candy bar, fruit juice, and cookies.

There was a rumor going around today that the 26th Division had been alerted. I often wondered if some of these rumors were deliberately leaked to help prepare the troops to accept the reality of the situation when the rumor turned out to be true. Of course not all rumors were true, but this one was.

Dec. 19, 1944. G Company, placed on a twenty-four-hour alert to move north, quickly absorbs its new replacements.

EGGER We resumed training in the morning. The rumor about the unit being alerted continued to circulate.

Captain Goldsmith called the officers and the non-coms together in the evening and told us that a large force of Germans had broken through the First Army's sector to the north. This was the beginning of the Battle of the Bulge, as it was later called. It appeared that the 26th might soon be sent there. The Captain tried to soften the news by saying that there might not be anything to the report or that it might be exaggerated. We knew it was true, however, when rations were distributed and the seventy-seven replacements G Company had received were assigned to squads later in the evening. The new men joining the 3rd Squad were Harley Packer [pseudonym], Ed Sturgis, Ralph Coolidge [pseudonym], and George Schmitt. The 1st Squad received Bob Adis, Bill DeSoto, Sol Rubin, Bob Lees, and another man whose name I didn't note. The new men in the 2nd Squad were Harold Schroaf, W. C. Lundy, Tom Montgomery, Rufies Morgan, Tony Messina, Frank Santarsiero, and Rene Poirier.

I was not happy about going into combat again, although I knew the time had to come eventually and it would keep on happening until the war ended. Nobody complained, but there was a noticeable change in the mood of the men. Although we had looked forward to spending Christmas here, we knew that the Army had to use us because we were rested and at full strength while the units to the north had been badly battered.

OTTS We were notified around midnight on the 19th that the division had been placed on a three-hour alert. I wrote in my diary that night, "Division on three hour alert. Will probably move out to get the hell knocked out of us." How true that was!

We all cursed and griped, but it couldn't be helped. Something had to be done and quickly to stop the German counter-offensive, and we were one of the few divisions the Third Army could get moving on such short notice.

4 Into the Bulge
December 20, 1944–January 8, 1945

OPERATIONAL BACKGROUND   The rumor going around on December 18 that the 26th Division had been alerted for a move was an example of how rapidly rumors can circulate in such an environment, since the decision to send the Yankee Division to Luxembourg had only been made that same morning. This had come in response to a military crisis of the first magnitude.

In mid-December of 1944 the Allies were confident that the stubborn German resistance encountered that fall was bound to crack and that a major break-through would soon occur. On the far northeastern corner of the Allied line Montgomery's British and Canadian 21st Army Group had penetrated into the southern reaches of Holland. On Montgomery's right, facing eastward, elements of the Ninth and First U.S. Armies had captured the key German city of Aachen and were launching assaults on the West Wall (Siegfried Line) in that area, seeking to break through into the Ruhr. And in the northeastern corner of France, Patton's Third Army was across the Saar River and probing the West Wall on the borders of Germany.

South of Aachen and north of Lorraine, in the triangular corner where France, Luxembourg, and Belgium abut, is the Ardennes, an area of deep gorges and rugged, wooded ridges that lay in the First Army sector. Although this had been the main invasion route used by the Germans in their stunningly successful assault on France in 1940, the Allies saw it as a quiet backwater where they could rest worn-out divisions and train new ones. Nor was there much fear in the Allied camp that the Germans were capable of a serious counter-blow anywhere. Accordingly, the eighty-five mile front of the Ardennes was held by only four divisions, about one-third the force considered desirable for a sector of that size.

But it was precisely in this militarily forbidding area that the Germans in the early hours of Saturday, December 16, 1944, launched a powerful counter-offensive that was to develop into what has gone down in history as the Battle of the Bulge. The German attack in the Ardennes was made on a front of roughly sixty miles with eighteen divisions, five of them panzer units (see Map 4). On the extreme northern flank, where the American line was more

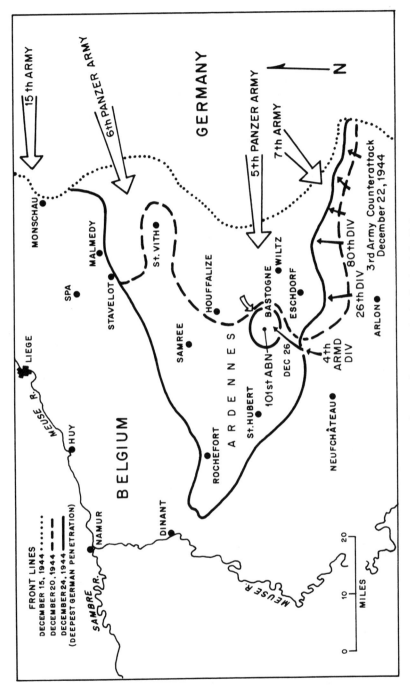

Map 4. Initial German Successes in the Battle of the Bulge

strongly held, the enemy made little progress. But a few miles to the south the Sixth SS Panzer Army overwhelmed and quickly outflanked the 106th and 28th Divisions. Two regiments of the raw 106th were all but wiped out, but several of their encircled units loom large in the history of the campaign because of their stubborn defense of vital crossroads that seriously disrupted the German timetable. In the center Manteuffel's Fifth Panzer Army had more trouble with the U.S. 7th Armored Division but by December 18 had opened a gap twelve miles wide through which three panzer divisions were driving. On the southern flank the battle-tested 4th U.S. Division yielded little ground to the four assaulting divisions of Brandenburger's Seventh Infantry Army, whose task it was to establish a flank screen.

The American forces had been surprised and overwhelmed, but things were not going all that well for the enemy either. The northern and southern shoulders of the bulge were holding, and although the Germans were making deep penetrations in the center, they were well behind schedule because of scattered stubborn resistance that was denying them the key road networks they had counted on. This was particularly true at the vital crossroads town of Bastogne, where straggling survivors from the 28th Division and a hastily dispatched combat command of the 10th Armored were joined on the night of December 18–19 by the 101st Airborne Division. Though Bastogne was soon encircled, these disparate American forces managed to thwart the German efforts to capture that critical road junction.[1]

In the meantime, the Allied High Command had reacted quickly. Eisenhower had immediately dispatched two armored divisions into the Ardennes, the 7th from Simpson's Ninth Army and the 10th from the Third Army.[2] The next day (December 17th) he followed this up by committing his entire strategic reserve, the 82nd and 101st Airborne Divisions, the latter moving into Bastogne just before the Germans closed the trap.[3]

When Patton and Bradley met with Eisenhower on the 19th, Ike began by declaring, "The present situation is to be regarded as one of opportunity for us and not of disaster." They would plug the holes in the north and hit the southern flank of the Bulge, initially in the direction of Bastogne, he said. When could such an attack be launched?[4] Patton replied that he could move the 4th Armored and the 26th and 80th Infantry Divisions to the Ardennes and be prepared to attack on the 22nd. This, he says in his memoirs, "created a ripple of excitement."[5]

Since part of the Patton legend rests upon this feat of disengaging from one battle and turning ninety degrees into another one so quickly, it should be noted that, to his credit, Patton had foreseen the necessity for this move and much of the staff-work for that complicated maneuver had already been done.[6] Indeed, by December 19, when he made the promise, the 4th Armored and the 80th Divisions were already on their way and the Yankee Division had been alerted to be prepared to move out the next day. These units would be asigned to the new III Corps, whose headquarters staff was then in Metz.[7] [P.R.]

━━━━━━━━━━━━━━━━━━━━━━━━

Dec. 20, 1944. The Yankee Division moves north to the vicinity of the Belgium-Luxembourg border.

EGGER At 1100 we packed ourselves into open trucks and trailers. It was a bitter cold, foggy day with frost hanging from the trees and power lines. The roads were congested with military traffic, which was all moving north. The convoy traveled all day at a slow pace, passing through Longwy, France, and reaching Arlon, Belgium, in the evening. This area seemed to be untouched by the war, as the city and stores were bedecked with decorations and Christmas trees. The scenes made me homesick for a moment and envious of those who could be in that warm home atmosphere for the holidays.

The column of vehicles stopped for a few minutes in Arlon and then moved a few miles beyond to a steep wooded hill near the Belgium-Luxembourg border. We had traveled about sixty miles in six hours. The ground was sandy so the digging was easy. The artillery sounded like it was a long way off, but no one knew the location of the Germans and the foxholes could have been needed before morning.

OTTS Just before noon on December 20, we loaded onto vehicles— long trailer rigs and 2½-ton trucks and jeeps—and headed north. The roads were jammed with trucks, bumper to bumper all the way. The 4th Armored, and probably another division besides the 26th, were all going the same way at the same time.

We drove as fast as possible, not stopping for anything except when the traffic got too congested. We ate our K rations while we moved, and there were no stops for nature's calls. We had to stand or sit on the rear of the truck and just let go. The scenery was awesomely beautiful; it would have been a lovely trip if we hadn't been so crowded, uncomfortable, and nervous over what lay before us.

Whenever we slowed up in a small town we would barter with the civilians for bread and wine. The long loaves of French bread were much better than our K ration crackers. On one five-minute stop in a small town, Bruno, running true to form, hopped off the truck and sauntered up to a house where two pretty girls were standing on the porch. They invited him in, or he invited himself in, and gave him cake and wine. The trucks pulled out while he was still in the house and we were all shouting for him as loudly as we could. He missed our truck but caught one behind us and joined us on the next stop.

We went over some of the steepest mountains I had ever seen and really went whizzing around the curves, far too close to the edge to suit me.

Just before dark we reached Arlon, Belgium, and stopped for about an hour. We didn't get off the trucks but enjoyed seeing the first city that reminded us of home since we had left the States. The streets were crowded with shoppers and people going home from work. The store windows were lighted and decorated with Christmas trees and everything had a holiday look about it. It really made us homesick. We all wanted to unload and stay right there.

It began to snow while we were in Arlon, and the wind was freezing cold. We moved about seven miles farther to a steep wooded hill near the village of Eischen on the Belgium-Luxembourg line and dug in for the night. All we knew of our mission was that we were to strike at the southern flank of the German counter-attack.

Dec. 21, 1944. While the rest of the 2nd Battalion plays a waiting game, Otts' platoon is sent forward to occupy the town of Beckerich.

EGGER We spent the day waiting while mechanized patrols were trying to locate the Germans. The cloudy weather had grounded the Air Corps. Mail was distributed and we were served hot meals.

T/Sgt. Starcher transferred to the Battalion Patrol. He was a good non-com but recently he seemed to be dissatisfied as a platoon sergeant and had become irritable and difficult to please. T/Sgt. Pete Ruffin [pseudonym], who had been wounded at Moncourt and had just re-joined the company, was the new platoon sergeant. The piece of shrapnel that had nicked him had left an ugly, livid scar extending across his forehead. Ruffin, a twenty-seven-year-old Virginian, was a big burly man, large enough to enforce his orders. This was the least of the problems we were to have with him.

Stewart Rorer, who had been wounded at Moncourt, also returned to the company and was assigned to the 1st Squad of the 3rd Platoon. The track of the shrapnel that had wounded him was visible across his right cheek and ear. Treff, Stoddard, and Stribling were the only men Ruffin and Rorer recognized in the platoon.

Captain Goldsmith was evacuated today because of sickness and Lt. Hargrove replaced him as G Company CO.* 1st Lt. Charles Walter was the new leader of the 3rd Platoon.

---

*Captain E. Gardner Goldsmith returned on Dec. 27 and resumed his duties as company commander.

Big snow flakes started falling in the evening. I was not particularly dreaming of a white Christmas this year.

OTTS   We spent the day in the woods, cleaning our weapons and getting our equipment in order. Our gas masks were brought up from Service Company and reissued.

About the middle of the afternoon I was called to the Battalion CP in Eischen and told that I was to take my platoon about six miles forward to Beckerich to hold the town and the two bridges on roads leading into town from the north. I struggled back up the hill and informed my men of the move. While we were getting ready, I heard a rifle shot and some-one crying, "Medic!" One of my men had shot himself in the foot. He said it was an accident, and no one knew whether it was or not. A couple of days later the same thing happened to a man in the 3rd Platoon.* It was not unusual for somebody to "accidentally" shoot himself in the hand or foot before almost every big push. These "accidents" became so frequent that an order was put out requiring a court martial investigation of every such "accident."† I'll bet there wasn't a man in the outfit who didn't think about shooting himself at some time or other during combat.

About 1800 we slid down the hill and started down a path marked on my map. We went a couple of miles or so to the 1st Battalion CP, which was in an isolated farmhouse. There I told the CO what my mission was, and he furnished me with a guide to take me on to Beckerich.

The moon was bright and the woods and fields were really beautiful with the light blanket of snow over everything. We passed through a dark forest of spruce that provided a comforting feeling of concealment while at the same time arousing sinister forebodings that a German might be lurking behind each tree.

I was much surprised on reaching Beckerich to find Lt. Law Lamar and his platoon from Charlie Company there. I wasn't expecting any American troops at all, and certainly not my friend Lamar. They were in an upstairs room of an old theater building. I told him I had come to relieve him, but he decided not to leave before morning; so we all bed-

---

*G Company rarely identified the self-inflicted wounded as such. The man Otts is apparently referring to was shown on the morning report of Dec. 22 as "slightly wounded (non-battle)." The incident involving the man from the 3rd Platoon was not actually a self-inflicted wound, as explained by Egger in his entry of Dec. 22 below.

†After visiting a hospital on Feb. 4 and finding several GIs with apparent self-inflicted wounds, General Patton put out an order that such men be court martialed. As Patton himself obliquely admits, it is not evident that this eliminated the problem.[8]

ded down in the stable and hayloft. Lamar explained to me the general setup—there were two bridges on separate roads coming into town from the north. The bridges were heavily mined and there was a non-com with about six men at each bridge with orders to let our retreating troops across in case of a counter-attack, but when the first German vehicle or infantryman approached to blow the bridge and run like hell.

OPERATIONAL BACKGROUND The III Corps attack set for December 22 had the limited objective of relieving the besieged American troops at Bastogne; it should not, Eisenhower emphasized, be allowed to spread into a general counteroffensive. Once the vital road net of which Bastogne was the center had been secured, it could be utilized for a Third Army drive north-ward to St. Vith in the larger Allied offensive.

The three attacking American divisions—the 4th Armored, the 26th, and the 80th—were accordingly deployed on a narrow axis north of Arlon, Belgium. The task of cutting through to Bastogne was assigned to the vet-eran 4th Armored, which was to drive up the Arlon-Bastogne road while the 26th and 80th Divisions were to secure its right flank. There they would be without benefit of adequate roads and would have to advance mostly cross-country. Their first main objective would be the crossroads town of Eschdorf, where they would be able to pick up a major road.

The 26th Division was in the center, with the 4th Armored somewhere off on the left—there was a dense woods between them—and the 80th on the right. Nobody in the Allied camp knew either the whereabouts or the strength of the enemy on this south flank of the Bulge. Accordingly, the first order of business, as Egger points out, was to make contact.[9] [P.R.]

Dec. 22, 1944. The 328th Regiment moves north in search of the enemy.

EGGER A light snow was falling at daylight as we prepared to leave. We were issued gas masks because the Germans dressed in American uniforms who had infiltrated the lines of the First Army did not have any. Since they were not normally worn by our troops but were stored far to the rear, the Germans had not captured any of our masks.

I carried an extra pair of drawers, two undershirts, a sweater, four pairs of heavy wool stockings, a scarf, and a pair of gloves in my pack.

All day we slogged on through the snow and slush, which became deeper as we traveled north. We had no destination other than to walk until the 1st Battalion, which was in the lead, contacted the enemy. About a third of the troops, mostly replacements, could not keep up.

After two hours of walking some of the guys began to discard their overcoats and overshoes to lighten their load. My overshoes were hurting my feet so I took them off and buckled them to my suspenders and I tied my overcoat to my pack.

In the afternoon we walked through Redange, Luxembourg, where the people greeted us with coffee, cookies, and apples, which we gratefully accepted and consumed on the move.

We had just passed through the village of Grosbous when gunfire to our front indicated that the 1st Battalion had made contact with the Germans.[10] The 2nd Battalion went back to Grosbous and the companies set up defensive positions around town.

The sky was clearing and it was evident that we were going to be in for a cold night without bedrolls. I congratulated myself for keeping my overcoat. Stragglers came in for several hours after dark. Olson and I dug a shallow hole and filled it with straw from a nearby barn, but it provided little protection from the cold and wind.

Oakley from the 1st Squad shot himself in the foot during the night. After he returned in February he told me that it was an accident and if it had been deliberate he would have made sure the wound was so serious he would not have to return. Knowing how conscientious he was, I never doubted him.*

OTTS   The rest of the regiment passed through us early in the morning, so we quit worrying about the enemy and relaxed all day in Beckerich. All the shops were open as before the war, and we enjoyed the long loaves of French bread, hot out of the ovens of the bakery. Also a little bar was open. They had some wonderful cherry brandy and better beer than we had had in Metz. The bartender could speak English, and we spent some time talking with him. Late afternoon approached, and we were still there with no orders to move. We thought perhaps they had forgotten about us and certainly hoped so, but no such luck!

We left Beckerich on trucks about 1600 that evening to catch up with our battalion. We reached regimental headquarters about 2200 and sat

---

*In 1987 Tom Oakley informed Egger what actually had happened that night. Oakley was sharing a foxhole with another soldier who accidently shot him in the foot. The other GI, afraid he would get into trouble for the incident, asked Oakley to cover up for him, which he did. While he was in the hospital Oakley decided that when he returned to the company he would ask his buddy to set the record straight, but the man was killed in action during his absence. Tom Oakley always believed that the accident was carried on his record as a self-inflicted wound until he learned from Egger in 1987 that the morning report for Dec. 23 had shown him as "slightly wounded in action." He returned to duty on Feb. 13, 1945.

around on our trucks in the rain and freezing cold for about three hours before we received orders to move on and were given a jeep to guide us. I had stumbled from building to building in the darkness trying to find someone to tell me where to go, but they were too engrossed with more important matters to worry about a lost platoon. We finally joined our company and helped in organizing the defense.

Dec. 23, 1944. The 2nd Battalion becomes "Task Force Hamilton" and moves forward to the vicinity of Eschdorf.

EGGER During the early morning I heard bombers flying toward the east. I may have slept an hour or two but spent most of the night on guard duty and moving around trying to keep warm. I saw a flight of American bombers returning from a mission shortly after dawn. One plane was on fire but was still in formation as the flight passed from our view.

The cold had caused a number of frostbite cases in the company, including Bob Adis from the 1st Squad. They were evacuated. Despite what they were told some of the men must not have taken care of their feet. Bill DeSoto of the 1st Squad came down sick and was also evacuated.*

Alton Moores, a replacement from ordnance, joined the squad this morning, giving us thirteen men.

The platoon gathered in a barn and Lt. Walter passed along the information he had just received. The 2nd Battalion was to be part of a task force commanded by Lt. Col. Paul Hamilton of the 26th Division staff. It included a unit of tanks, tank destroyers, assault guns, and engineers. Our immediate objective was to seize the high ground around the town of Eschdorf, which was twelve miles to our northeast, and establish a bridgehead across the Sure River.

We left by trucks at 1100 and circled around through the 104th Regiment near Grosbous and unloaded when we started receiving fire from the tanks on the high ground beyond. The assault guns took care of the tanks and we marched up the road with E Company in the lead. About dusk we stopped at Weishof, a cluster of buildings about two miles from Eschdorf. George Company dug in at the edge of the woods on the high ground to the rear of E Company. Bedrolls were distributed and we slept warm despite the freezing temperatures. The Germans were close

---

*Pfc. William DeSoto returned to duty on Jan. 14, 1945; Pvt. Robert E. Adis on May 7, 1945.

so we were on guard duty half the night. I slept with my shoes on; I didn't want to waste valuable time in case the Germans attacked.

OTTS Task Force Hamilton set out around 1100 the morning of December 23 and proceeded to near Grosbous where we de-trucked and stood around for several hours on the road that led up the mountain. Easy Company had met some resistance from enemy tanks and couldn't make any headway so they dug in near a group of buildings called Weishof, not quite two miles from Eschdorf. The other two companies dug in on the high ground in the rear.

It had been snowing all day and there was then a blanket about eight or ten inches deep with a coating of ice under it. The snow had to be cleared away and the ice penetrated before we could start digging our foxholes. We slept with our canteens in our foxholes next to us to keep the water from freezing and bursting them. The holes were more comfortable than they had been before the snow—at least they were not full of water. Two men with eight blankets could sleep very comfortably; the only difficulty was getting the eight blankets. We would put one shelter half and our raincoat with about three blankets below us and the other five blankets and another shelter half (if we had one) over us. It was much warmer in the holes than on the outside, so we hated to get out of them.

At that time I was wearing a suit of summer underwear, two suits of heavy long wool underwear, two pairs of wool pants, a wool shirt, a wool sweater, a field jacket, a combat jacket, two pairs of wool socks, combat boots, gloves, a wool knit cap, and a steel helmet. I didn't like to wear an overcoat as it was too bulky and hard to handle.

Dec. 24, 1944. Task Force Hamilton moves into position to attack Eschdorf on Christmas Eve.

EGGER Moores tossed his boots outside his foxhole last night and they were frozen solid this morning.

F Company took the lead in the morning, but they only moved about a quarter of a mile before running into trouble. George Company outposted the right flank again. We couldn't see what was going on, but we could hear the mortars, artillery, and small arms fire. My view of the war was usually confined to a very small area, so the details and strategies of many actions were not known to me until I talked to other people afterwards or later read *Handcar White*, the 2nd Battalion history.

When Fox Company went over the hill toward Hierheck they were silhouetted against the sky, making them perfect targets for the enemy machine gunners. Our tanks were receiving fire from a camouflaged 88 in the yard of a farmhouse. The Germans were so well dug in that our artillery had little effect and the battle was at a standstill for several hours.

Giovinazzo and another man from F Company crawled forward and with bazookas knocked out the 88 and a tank sitting behind the farmhouse. H Company mortars went to work on the foxholes, breaking up the resistance so the riflemen could rush them. E and F Companies then took Hierheck. Our artillery and mortar fire had knocked out several tanks and killed many of the Germans, who were wearing white camouflage suits.

I have never understood why Giovinazzo was not decorated for his action. A lot of guys received medals for less.

E and F Companies dug in facing Eschdorf and G Company remained in position behind Hierheck. There was a lone house at the edge of the road where we could go every four hours to get warm and heat our frozen C rations. A disabled German tank, four dead Germans, and a dead GI were scattered around the area near the house.

I had come off guard at 2100 and was preparing to get some sleep when we received orders to get ready to move; the task force was attacking Eschdorf at 0100.

OTTS Fox Company led the advance in the morning with G Company still in reserve. I think the reason was that Captain Goldsmith had become sick again and Lt. Hargrove had taken charge of the company. Since this operation was so important, I suppose they were afraid to have an inexperienced lieutenant leading the attack.

G Company moved out northward and took positions around a house between Weishof and Hierheck. It was on top of a hill in a little patch of woods with perfect observation of Hierheck as E and F Companies, supported by tanks, fought for possession of the buildings and the high ground. It was like watching a movie; I spent most of the day standing on the edge of the woods watching the progress of the battle through my field glasses.

Two Fox Company men were able to crawl forward and knock out an enemy anti-tank gun and a tank, and after a mortar barrage their buddies rushed the dug-in Germans and took a number of prisoners. The Jerries came out of their holes with their hands up and our men would simply point back down the road to our rear, where they went running with their hands held above their heads—no one was even sent to guard them.

Easy and Fox Companies dug in in an arching line around the north side of town facing Eschdorf while G Company remained in reserve on the hill south of Hierheck. It was Christmas Eve, and we sat around on the floor in our house, each man with his own thoughts of home and dreading what Christmas Day might bring. I had dozed off for about an hour when we were awakened and told to "saddle up" and hit the road.

Dec. 25, 1944. The 2nd Battalion gets badly bloodied in the fight for Eschdorf.

EGGER This was the coldest night we had experienced to date. At 2400 we moved up the road to Hierheck. A burning building lit up the area and a number of dead Germans could be seen along the road. E and F Companies' attack at 0100 was stalled by machine gun fire, so they pulled back to reorganize. A new assault was ordered for 0400.

We waited six hours at Hierheck for orders to move up. I kept jogging back and forth on the road trying to keep warm. Several of the men in my squad wanted to lie down in the snow to sleep but I kept prodding them to get up and move. A German machine gun kept firing overhead.

According to the 2nd Battalion history, *Handcar White*, the assault guns and the remaining tanks were to move within five hundred yards of Eschdorf while Easy Company took the high ground around the crossroads to the right of town and Fox Company moved around Eschdorf to dig in on the far side. Then George Company was to enter the town with tanks and clear it. We were not told any of the above or anything else except that we were supposed to have taken F Company's place, but they moved out before we could relieve them.

E and F Companies found the town and adjacent area teeming with German infantry and tanks and a lot of their men were taken prisoner, wounded, and killed. By daylight the Germans had machine gun coverage at the entrance to Eschdorf so the companies could not withdraw.

At 0630 G Company tried to enter the town by way of the open hill to the left of the road. In our brown overcoats against the white snow, we made perfect targets for the German machine guns and were immediately pinned down. Dafoe was shot in the arm and Doc, our medic, was hit in the leg.* The medic attached to the 1st Platoon, Louis Potts, was killed.

A wounded man from the 4th Platoon kept crying, "Mother, Mother!

---

*Sgt. Daniel D. Dafoe was listed as "slightly wounded in action" near Eschdorf on Dec. 25. He returned to duty on Mar. 14, 1945. "Doc" appears to have been T/5 George Jetzke, who was listed as "slightly wounded in action" near Eschdorf on Dec. 25.

Help me!" as he struggled to rise. Another burst from the machine gun silenced him. That beseeching plea on that clear, cold Christmas morning will remain with me for the rest of my life.

George Company pulled back and built up the line in front of Hierheck. Although cross fire still came from the flanks, we were able to hold off several attempts by the German troops to reoccupy their positions near the road that would have cut off the other companies completely.

Just before dark our planes dropped smoke bombs to help the remnants of Easy and Fox Companies withdraw. Survivors straggled out all night, mostly in groups of two, three, or four.

Lee Allen shot an old man who was wandering around during the night. Fortunately, the wound was not serious.

OTTS At 0100 on Christmas morning G Company moved up to the south side of Hierheck. We were in reserve to provide support for Fox and Easy Companies, who were supposed to take Eschdorf, three-quarters of a mile away. We learned later that the assaulting companies had run into a withering cross fire from the Germans on the hill in front of Eschdorf and had to pull back to regroup. They tried again at 0400, this time with support from the armor.

The plan, as later recounted in *Handcar White*, was for Easy Company to advance into the east side of town while Fox Company circled around to the rear. Both units ran into a buzzsaw of opposition and suffered heavy losses in killed, wounded, and captured. The remnants of one platoon from F Company managed to hide out in a barn for thirty hours. Much the same thing happened to my old friend, Captain Swift, and thirty of his E Company men, except that Swiftie crawled out through machine gun and small arms fire and made it to the rear to bring some tanks back. He found two of them but the one he was riding on heading back to Eschdorf was hit broadside by a round from an 88 and the entire crew killed. Swift was thrown twenty feet away but didn't suffer so much as a scratch. The other tank disappeared, so Swift made his way back into town and holed up in some buildings with his 3rd Platoon, where the 1st Battalion of the 104th Infantry found him on the morning of December 26.

While George Company didn't catch as much hell as Easy and Fox, we spent anything but an enjoyable Christmas Day. We left our house on the hill just before midnight on Christmas Eve and marched in single file down the road until our forward elements were almost to Hierheck. We then stretched out prone in a frozen ditch beside the road, where we remained for 6½ hours. Every few minutes machine gun bullets would come zinging down the road and across the flat, snow-covered fields on both sides of us, so we were afraid to stand up and had to crawl back and forth up the ditch. I made the trip up and down the length of my platoon on my stomach and hands and knees several times, trying to keep the men awake and moving around. As long as we kicked our feet together and flexed our hands and fingers I knew we wouldn't freeze. The men were so tired and sleepy, though, that several had to be evacuated before daylight with frozen hands and feet and frostbitten faces.

There was an old stable beside the road near the rear of my platoon, and my sergeants and I were kept busy trying to see that all the men didn't get inside at one time and that after one man had been there a while he would leave so another could come in and get warm. There was no fire, but the building blocked out some of the wind and made us think we were warmer anyway. It seemed cruel to chase a man back out into the cold, but we didn't want to take a chance of losing all the men at once if the building was hit by a shell. Nor did we know at what moment we might be put into action with very little notice.

After stumbling several times over something in the center of one room of the building and saying "Pardon me" because I thought it was a sleeping GI, I decided to investigate. Some of the men said it was a log and that they had been sitting on it. I turned on my flashlight and discovered it was a dead German, frozen stiff with his mouth open and his eyes rolled back. I also noticed that there was a 155mm dud on the other side of the room. Dead Germans didn't bother us too much until we started thinking about sitting on them.

About an hour before daylight Lt. Hargrove sent for me to join him at a house in Hierheck that was being used as the Battalion CP. The task force commander, Lt. Col. Hamilton, and all the battalion officers were there. It was really good to get into a warm room, but the elation soon disappeared when I saw the serious, worried look on the faces of the brass and heard what was happening to Easy and Fox Companies.

Colonel Hamilton was really in a sweat; he didn't know whether to gamble everything by throwing in his reserve company or to try to get the two companies in Eschdorf back out. He kept General Paul, the division commander, on the phone most of the morning telling him what was going on and remarking, "I guess I'll send George Company up." Jack and I stood there with our fingers crossed, hoping something would happen so George Company wouldn't have to join in the attack.

At daylight G Company moved forward and set up a semi-circular defense atop the crest of the hill and across the road leading into Eschdorf. Before we even got the men placed in position or started digging holes the Germans counter-attacked, and we were kept busy for a while. Several times during the day they would attack to try to take the road, which would have cut off the other companies completely.

We lost several men that day who would not have been hit if they had been given any infantry training. One of my men was killed while standing up firing when he should have been lying flat in the snow. I saw him and yelled at him to get down, but he couldn't hear me above the noise and before anyone could get to him to pull him down a bullet hit him right in the forehead.

We were really having a hot day, sweating out being sent into Eschdorf every time Colonel Hamilton would tell General Paul, "I guess I'll send George Company up," and rushing our men from one sector to another to stop the German counter-attacks. One of our P-47s came over low and some of the new men stood up and fired at it with their rifles.

The 1st Platoon medic, Pfc. Louis Potts, was killed while attending to a wounded man. He had already dressed one man's wounds and had moved to another when a German picked him off, killing him instantly. Potts was small in stature but what he lacked in size he made up in courage and determination to do his very best to help the wounded, regardless of personal danger. He was liked by all who knew him, and it really made the men mad for the Heinies to shoot a medic who carried no weapon and displayed the red cross very plainly on his arm band.

We set up a permimeter defense for the night and rotated a few men at a time inside to get warm and eat their K rations. That night we had the first instance I know of when a man flatly refused to obey an order. One of the machine gunners in the weapons platoon was told by his section leader and then by his platoon sergeant to remain in his hole by his gun. Instead he came inside the building and, on being ordered to go back, flatly refused. This was reported to Hargrove, who was still the acting CO, and later to battalion and regiment. They decided that the best thing to do was to court martial him because if a thing like that should go unpunished it might lead to more cases of the same type. Some weeks later the court martial board gave him a five-year suspended sentence and sent him back to us. He was later killed at Saarlautern. Sending men back to their unit with a suspended sentence was the best thing to do; some of the men would have taken five years in prison if they could have gotten away from the front for good.

Dec. 26, 1944. The battered 2nd Battalion pulls back into reserve.

EGGER A battalion from the 104th Regiment occupied Eschdorf in the morning.[11] The 2nd Battalion moved back to Grevils-Bresil about 1000. The 3rd Platoon stayed in a house at the edge of the village. The owner spoke good English and said that he used to live in Chicago.

Giovinazzo told me that McCammon had been captured by the Germans yesterday and that E and F Companies had lost more than half their men, captured, wounded, or killed.

We had our Christmas dinner today: turkey, dehydrated potatoes, gravy, sweet potatoes, and cranberries. In contrast to our Thanksgiving dinner, this meal was hot.

I was able to heat some water, wash, and shave. It was good to receive a letter from home today. I had a bed in a haymow and guard duty was light.

OTTS   During the night a number of the survivors from Easy and Fox Companies were able to make it back through our lines. Early that morning sixteen of my men rode on tanks with the battalion patrol into Eschdorf, from which the Germans had withdrawn during the night. A group of F Company men who had survived by hiding in a cellar on the far side of town was discovered by a unit of the 104th Infantry, but otherwise the place was deserted except for the dead and wounded and a few civilians. Guns and equipment were strewn everywhere, with dead American and German soldiers lying in the streets, in doorways, and hanging out of tanks.

Later that morning we trudged wearily down the road to the town of Grevils-Bresil. Although we were glad to be leaving Eschdorf, there was no laughing or singing. We were all too stunned and haunted by what we had been through.

On reaching Grevils-Bresil we were told that since we were in Luxembourg, not France, we could not just move in and take over any house we wanted. We must first get permission from the mayor of the town and then each officer must make an inventory of the damage already done to the buildings his men were to occupy. The officer would then be held personally responsible for any damage done by his men. The higher-ups would really have preferred for us to stay in the woods and fields all the time, but some officer had enough guts to tell the big brass that his men needed to be in buildings and "by damn they would be in buildings."

My platoon took over a two-story house and shed. I went around with my notebook and counted the bullet holes in the doors and the broken windowpanes. It seemed rather foolish, but orders were orders.

For light at night we used bottles full of gasoline or kerosene with a rag stuck in the neck. They smoked a lot but gave a good bit of light. One night about a dozen men were sitting around in the living room when someone knocked the bottle-lamp off the table; it broke, and gasoline flames spread all over the room. Pfc. Bobbie Phipps and one or two others jumped through the window and the other men ran out the door. I could visualize myself paying for a house, but the men managed to put the fire out with blankets before much damage had been done.

There were three bedrooms in the house, and Bennie and I stayed in one that was only large enough for the bed. The other staff sergeants and Thompson had the other beds except that Van Winkle wouldn't leave his squad and slept in the shed with them.

That night we had our Christmas dinner of turkey and dressing. It was really wonderful even if it was a day late.

Dec. 27, 1944. The 2nd Battalion continues in reserve.

EGGER We were all happy to be in reserve again and to have a chance to rest, although E and F Companies had done the dirty work that earned the battalion a period of recuperation.

One of the replacements in my squad, George Schmitt, went back yesterday with frostbitten feet. Frank Gormley had taken Dafoe's place as leader of the 2nd Squad. Captain Goldsmith had returned from the hospital and Lt. Hargrove rejoined the platoon yesterday.

I got caught up on my letter writing and found out that the officers really did censor our mail. Lt. Hargrove called me aside and scolded me for mentioning Dixon's death in a letter to my parents. He was right; we had been told not to mention the death of individuals by name, since the next of kin in the States might not receive the correct information from the recipients of our letters.

I have often wondered what the officers thought as they read their men's outgoing mail. Perhaps the letters revealed more of the man's character than daily contact did. I had reason to suspect that his letters home might at least indicate that a man was beginning to suffer from the stress of battle and was a candidate for battle fatigue. In a letter to my parents in January of '45 I mentioned how nervous and tired I was and how few of the pre-Moncourt men were left in the platoon. A week later I received a three-day pass to Longwy, France.

I never let it bother me that an officer was reading my mail, but I took care to avoid mentioning restricted subjects. In a letter to my parents I mentioned our location and that part was cut out with a razor blade. My folks knew what division I was in and could generally follow our location by reading the newspaper. A letter I wrote to Uncle Rob complaining about our inadequate footwear was cut to pieces.

OTTS Our whiskey ration came in today and I sat around on the floor of our living room and gave toasts with champagne in canteen cups.

Idelson was one of the few men I remember who enjoyed mixing gin with the lemonade powder from C rations, but we all drank it.

I also went over to the Company CP and had a few drinks with the other officers. Captain Goldsmith had returned, still weak but smiling as usual. He had been sick for a month or more with dysentery—the "GIs" or "runs" as we called it—and would sometimes get so weak he would be forced to go back for a day or two to get some medicine. In the meantime, Lt. Zera of the weapons platoon had been hospitalized with jaundice a week ago and Walter had been evacuated with pneumonia yesterday, so that left only Goldsmith, Lassiter, Hargrove, and me as officers in G Company.

FROM EGGER'S LETTER OF DECEMBER 27

There was no Christmas for me this year, it will have to be postponed for another year or two. I just couldn't get that Christmas spirit, and who could when there is anything but peace and good will toward fellow men over here.

. . . I am afraid this war is far from being over. It's going to be a long tough grind and I know I'll need your prayers to see it through.

. . . I spent a miserable Christmas Eve, as I was up all night, but I can't complain because more than one man spent a more miserable time and I consider myself lucky to be alive.

. . . This weather isn't cold compared to what it is at home, but when you have to sleep out in it you really notice it, especially if you don't have any bedroll, which doesn't happen very often. My feet are the only part of me that really gets very cold, the Army doesn't seem to have learned how to dress in winter weather. . . .

I had been sick for several days with a bad cold, cough, and headache but was feeling better. If you ran a temperature of 101 or over the medics would send you back to the hospital for a checkup and probably a few days rest in a quiet place with a nice bed and clean sheets. I never could get my temperature up above a hundred though. I even carried a thermometer around in my pocket for three days, checking my temperature several times a day so if it ever got to 101 I would be sure to know it. I don't think I was trying to run away but certainly would have liked to have a few days rest and quiet.

I rode ten miles on the back of a 2½-ton truck to a shower point for my second bath while in the ETO. I had had one just eleven days before so I really didn't need one but didn't want to pass up anything. The trip on the open truck was very cold, and with the cold I already had it was wonder I didn't develop pneumonia on the way back after the hot shower. That day I swore off baths in the winter and decided to wait until summer for my next one.

Dec. 28, 1944. G Company remains in reserve in Grevils-Bresil.

EGGER Today Billy Cross, 1st Platoon of George Company, was awarded the Distinguished Service Cross—the second highest medal for bravery—for action at Moncourt. The 2nd Battalion had a parade in his honor but we were a ragged looking outfit and could hardly keep in step. I think there was a definite lack of enthusiasm among the men for the parade, but this was not out of lack of respect for Billy's deeds.

Task Force Hamilton was disbanded today. Before he returned to divisional headquarters Colonel Hamilton gave the non-coms a lecture on leadership. We received our Combat Infantry Badges today. Most of us mailed them home.[12]

FROM EGGER'S LETTER OF DECEMBER 28

I have been in combat only about two months, but I am so weary of it all. My feet are beginning to suffer from so much walking. Sometimes I feel awful discouraged when I think of what the future holds and the long bitter months ahead. I can make it with the help of the Lord, but not otherwise. I am glad so many people are praying for me because I sure need them.

The infantry man sure takes a beating in this war both physically and mentally. Nobody knows what combat is like until he has fought in the infantry. The infantry suffers the biggest number of casualties too, and to my notion they get the least praise. . . .

Pray for me, so I'll have courage and strength for whatever is ahead.

OTTS Today there was a formation for the presentation of the Distinguished Service Cross to S/Sgt. Melvin Cross of the 1st Platoon. There were two war correspondents present—a man and a woman.

We had a meeting of all officers and non-coms down through the staff sergeants at which Lt. Col. Hamilton and some other officers talked to us. He congratulated us on the job we had done at Eschdorf but told us that we had only begun to fight. The Germans must be pushed out of Luxembourg, across the Rhine, and on across Germany until we met the Russians.

If it hadn't been for the fighting, that would have been one of the most beautiful Christmases I had ever spent. I had never seen such a white Christmas nor such beautiful country. The rolling hills, the snow-covered fields and mountains, and the tall, majestic pines and firs really made it a Christmas I'll never forget in spite of the fighting.

It was wonderful to be in Grevils-Bresil—everything was so quiet and peaceful; the snow was white and not pock-marked and blackened by shells or reddened by blood. The sun shone brightly every day, and although we didn't laugh and joke as much as usual we felt much better inside for just being alive.

Latrine rumors were running wild, but the one I liked best and kept passing on was that our battalion was going to be sent to Paris to be MPs.

Dec. 29, 1944. The rest in Grevils-Bresil continues.

EGGER Surprisingly, we had been left pretty much to ourselves during this rest period. The battalion usually started a training program after a day's rest, but all they did was set up a range where we could sight in our weapons if we wished. I fired a clip through my rifle and was satisfied with its and my performance.

The sounds of war had moved farther to the north.

The Red Cross clubmobile made an appearance today and as usual I overate and had a stomachache.

OTTS Today a Red Cross clubmobile with three girls rolled up and parked in the field beside our Company CP. We were all glad to have the coffee and doughnuts but more glad to see the American girls and hear the American jive. I was in the clubmobile playing the record player when an old friend, Cox Webb of Demopolis, Alabama, walked up to the window for coffee and doughnuts. He thought he recognized me and asked one of the men if that wasn't Lee Otts. When he called me from the rear of the truck I didn't recognize him at first, he had lost so much weight and looked older. He was a quartermaster truck driver and had come to move our battalion.

I had saved a quart of my Scotch, so Cox and I went up to my tiny room and drank it while talking of friends back in the States. It was really a wonderful night, and I went to bed about twelve with a rich glow and feeling very happy about everything.

It didn't last long, though. At 0200 the company runner, Sgt. Bill Van Norman, came and woke me up to tell me that the CO had called a meeting of the platoon leaders. I knew only too well what that meant—move out. I dreaded those meetings and would have given almost anything to be able to go to bed at night knowing that I would not have to get up and get orders to push on.

We all met in the Company CP. While Captain Goldsmith described our route to us, we marked our maps and took notes on which trucks each of us would have for our platoons and in what order in the company we would be. We were to go to Kaundorf to be in mobile divisional reserve, ready at a moment's notice to be loaded on trucks and thrown in wherever needed.

Dec. 30, 1944. The 2nd Battalion, still in reserve, moves forward to the vicinity of Kaundorf.

EGGER We rode in trucks about ten miles today to get closer to the action. We crossed the Sure River and went through Kaundorf, which had been badly torn up by shelling. There were a lot of dead Germans in and near the town. The trucks let us off a mile beyond Kaundorf and we set up positions in the woods. We were in the Ardennes, a forested region of high plateaux in southeastern Belgium, Luxembourg, and northern France.

OTTS This morning we loaded on trucks and rode to Kaundorf, Luxembourg. Captain Goldsmith took over a big two-story house on the north edge of town for our Company CP. My platoon had the mission of guarding a road to the northwest of town, so we dug holes along the road for bazooka and riflemen. We rotated men to these outposts every two hours while the rest of us stayed in a concrete and brick shed beside the road about three hundred yards from the Company CP. We had a makeshift stove, but at night we had a hard time keeping sparks from going up the chimney and giving away our position.

December 31, 1944. The 2nd Battalion continues in reserve near Kaundorf.

EGGER We were about a mile from the front lines. Occasionally small arms fire could be heard and a stray bullet whined overhead. There were five dead Germans near our positions. Their faces were starting to turn black, so they had probably been dead for four or five days. Paul Scheufler was collecting straw for his foxhole this morning and uncovered a dead German inside the stack. Fortunately the cold slowed the decomposition of the dead so there was no stench of decaying flesh.

We alternated our time between the positions in the woods and the farmhouse where the Company CP was located. About half of the company could be housed at one time. Two hot meals were brought up by jeep.

The weather moderated today and we had blankets, so we spent a comfortable and uneventful New Year's Eve in foxholes.

OTTS On New Year's Eve we were alerted several times, got packed up and met at the Company CP but never pulled out. We could hear the continuous rumble of guns and the crashing of shells at the front about three miles to the north, and occasionally we would get a barrage of heavy artillery and "screaming meemies" in Kaundorf.

New Year's Eve was fairly quiet. The kitchen had set up and we got a hot meal. The cooks and jeep drivers always kidded me a lot when we had a hot meal. They called me the number one "chow hound" in the company and were always talking about taking my mess kit back to Service Company and having "side boards" put on it.

One of the jeep drivers I remember well was Pfc. Leonard LaFlam, commonly known as "Bananas," a reference to both the size of his nose and his comic behavior. He kept us in stitches laughing at him whenever he was around. He always drove his jeep as if an 88 shell were right behind him and he didn't want it to catch up. This must have worked for him, since he made it through the war without a scratch.

I had intended staying awake to help usher in the new year but fell asleep about 2230. All of the corps—and I guess the army—artillery fired a salute to and at the Germans from one minute past twelve to 0030.

Jan. 1 and 2, 1945. The 2nd Battalion continues in reserve at Kaundorf.

EGGER The duty here was like a vacation as we had time to keep clean, shave, write letters, and sit around the campfire and talk. Our holes were lined with straw and we could take blankets with us on guard duty.

I made an attempt to visit every foxhole of the squad each day to talk to the men. Since I still had friends in the 1st Squad I tried to see each day, I was acquainted with most of the guys in the platoon.

I never observed any loners on the front lines; the men automatically paired up. The buddy system worked very well; it provided additional security—two sets of eyes and ears working together were better than one—and it provided additional warmth in a foxhole because the two bodies warmed each other. Actually, we were a team, and sharing the adversities of the elements and combat brought us together and created a bond.

OTTS We had turkey and ham for our New Year's dinner. I took some cocoa powder that came in the C rations and mixed it with snow to make ice cream, after a fashion. It was pretty good. I guess all of us together cleared a large space of snow around the house.

I had had the "GIs" or "runs" for several days. As I had on three suits of underwear and two pairs of pants and had to go in a hurry, it took some quick unbuttoning. Every so often I would have to leave the fire, jump up, and run out in the snow. It was about knee-deep, and with the wind blowing all over your bare behind the experience made you long for the dear old USA and indoor plumbing. Afterwards I would grab all my pants and underwear with both hands and run back inside to the fire before beginning the long job of buttoning up.

As a kind of retaliation for our New Year's Eve barrage, Jerry sent in quite a few rounds of artillery and nebelwerfers on January 2. I went over to the wooded area across the road where the convoy trucks were hidden and saw Cox Webb and some of the other drivers huddled around a small fire. Cox said he didn't like the screaming meemies a damned bit and wished he was back in Paris. He gave me an extra cloth cap, the kind the tankers and truck drivers wear under their helmets. It came over my ears and buckled under my chin with a flap across the back to keep the snow off my neck. It certainly beat a wool knit cap and was to prove to be one of my most valuable pieces of wearing apparel.

Jan. 3, 1945. The 2nd Battalion is still in divisional reserve.

EGGER Lt. Hargrove took sick yesterday morning and was hospitalized. Since Lt. Walters had gone to the hospital on the 26th, G Company was now operating with only three officers—Captain Goldsmith, Lt. Lassiter, and Lt. Otts.

Today was payday. There is not as much gambling here as there was at the replacement depots; the fellows send most of their pay home.

Some replacement orders for clothing were sent up today; this usually is an indication that we will be moving soon.

OTTS Jerry was in the habit of throwing in an occasional barrage just to keep us on our toes. Today one of these random artillery rounds landed in the road beside one of our outposts and a fragment wounded

S/Sgt. Van Winkle in the arm. Although he was not too seriously hurt, he had to be evacuated. I knew I would miss him as he was an excellent non-com.*

The only other excitement was that a Bofors 40mm antiaircraft gun crew came up and dug in the gun in the field beside our Company CP. We cleaned our weapons, restocked our ammunition supply, picked new bazooka and BAR teams, and got our equipment in working order.

The table of equipment (TE) called for the platoon leader to be armed with a carbine, but I also carried my personal pistol. Since we were seldom up to authorized strength in men, we usually carried more equipment than the TE called for. My platoon sometimes had two bazookas rather than one and as many as six BARs instead of the allotted three. The assistant squad leader was the rifle grenadier of each squad. He had a grenade adapter on his rifle and carried a bag full of grenades, both anti-tank and anti-personnel.

The average infantryman is weighted down with equipment and gear. A combat soldier will wear about the same amount of clothing as I did and also probably an overcoat and overshoes. Then he adds a steel helmet, a rifle weighing nine pounds, about two hundred rounds of ammunition weighing about ten pounds, a canteen full of water, a shovel or pick, and a bayonet. And when the squad is understrength almost every rifleman is an assistant BAR or bazooka man and must carry either 120 rounds of BAR or three rounds of bazooka ammo.

None of the men in my platoon wore packs. We started a rule that if you couldn't wear it or put it in your pocket you threw it away, but it was still up to the individual. If a man wanted to carry a pack it was all right with us; we just advised the new men not to. Most of the men in other platoons and companies wore packs, but we got along fine without them.

Pack or no pack, the average infantryman had the pockets of his combat jacket crammed with K or C rations, shaving articles, pictures, cigarettes, candy, dry socks, writing paper and pens, and mess kit with spoon and fork. He would have his raincoat folded over the back of his belt or wear it to help keep warm. Also, if we were doubtful as to whether the trucks would be able to bring up blankets at night, he would carry from two to four blankets and a shelter half slung over his shoulder. Any time we had to make a foot march of more than just a few miles the roadside would be strewn with blankets, overcoats, overshoes, and gas masks. A truck would follow along behind us the next day, collect the equipment, and reissue it to us.

---

*S/Sgt. George E. Van Winkle returned to duty on Feb. 10.

━━━━━━━━━━━━━━━━━━━━━━━━━━━━━━━

OPERATIONAL BACKGROUND The initial limited objective of the III Corps attack against the south flank of the Bulge had been that of breaking through to the beleaguered American troops in Bastogne. This had been accomplished at 1645 on the afternoon of December 26, when advanced elements of the 4th Armored Division made contact with an engineer unit of the 101st Airborne Division.

From the first, however, Eisenhower, Bradley, and Patton had all agreed that as soon as the military situation allowed, a major offensive should be launched against the waist of the Bulge from both north and south in order to entrap the Germans remaining in the western portion of the salient. The date of the attack depended on when General Hodges' First Army would have all the gaps in the north plugged and be sufficiently revitalized to be able to go over to the offensive. In late December the attack was set for January 3. The plan was for Patton's Third Army, driving from the south, to link up with the First Army at the important road junction of Houffalize, which commanded the only good road by which seven German armored divisions could withdraw from the western portions of the Bulge.

Hodges' assault got off on schedule, though the Third Army, which was closer to the objective than was the First, waited until January 4 to launch its offensive. The Third Army attack toward Houffalize was assigned to VIII Corps, which would thrust in a northeasterly direction from west of Bastogne. III Corps, of which the 26th Division was a part, was to wipe out the salient left on the south flank by the penetration to Bastogne and then wheel eastward [see Map 5].[13] [P.R.]

━━━━━━━━━━━━━━━━━━━━━━━━━━━━━━━

Jan. 4–5, 1945. G Company goes on line and repulses a German attack.

EGGER Lt. Lassiter, who had transferred from E Company in early December and was now the leader of the 3rd Platoon in the absence of Lt. Hargrove, called us together in the afternoon and told us we would be relieving a unit of the 3rd Battalion tonight. I had never heard such a negative briefing; it sounded like we were going into an impossible situation. Going back on line was tough enough without his embellishing the facts. I came to believe that Lassiter immobilized himself with his briefings, since he never accompanied the platoon to the front. It seems he always had an excuse to stay at the Company CP. He was not held in high regard by the men in the platoon and we were hoping that Lt. Hargrove would get back soon.

Shortly after midnight we moved out on foot. It was a clear, cold

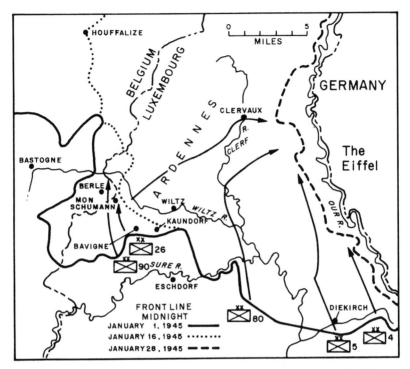

Map 5. Third Army Counter-offensive in the Ardennes, January 3–28, 1945

night with the temperature at zero or lower. The combination of moon-light and snow provided better night visibility than we usually had.

We stopped for a few minutes at Mon Schumann crossroads, or "88 Junction" as we were later to call it. The shells of four buildings stood at the edge of the road junction. I noticed several dead GIs at the edge of the road. A guide took us to a densely wooded area near Mon Schumann, where we relieved L Company of the 3rd Battalion.

Alton Moores and I took a foxhole near a small road extending from the main road into the woods towards the German position. The fox-holes were roomy and deep.

Just before we had arrived our predecessors had shot up a German patrol that had been travelling on the road past the foxhole Moores and I occupied. None of the patrol had escaped; there were four bodies on the ground near our position and two other Germans had been taken prisoner. For some reason the face of one of the dead men had been clubbed out of shape, probably by the butt of a rifle.

In the early morning before daylight Moores noticed that one of the presumed dead Germans moved when he stumbled over the body. The man had lain in the snow, in sub-zero weather, playing possum for four hours. We checked the three remaining bodies and found one live one who had been shot in the stomach. It looked like we were facing some tough troops.

Since we had no blankets and we were anticipating trouble, no one slept. A barrage of mortars and artillery arrived at daylight and we were alert when the Germans attacked a few minutes later. They were talking in loud voices as they approached our positions. I was surprised, as they usually exhibited more stealth. German machine guns started firing in our direction and our platoon returned the fire. The bullets were clipping branches and needles from the trees and singing overhead. Moores and I could not see the enemy, as our vision was blocked by the dense stand of trees. This made us feel uneasy; we wanted to help but did not want to leave the road unobserved. I shouted and asked our fellows if they needed any help and they said they could handle the situation.

In twenty minutes the firing died down and we assumed that the Germans had withdrawn, although no one wanted to expose himself to find out. I left Moores in the foxhole and started checking on the welfare of the men in the 3rd Squad. I got a favorable response from everybody except Walt Lee and Packer, who did not answer.

I crawled on my stomach to their foxhole where I found Lee, his body riddled with bullets.* He was sprawled backward in an almost upright position over the earth embankment at the rear of the hole. He had not been wearing his overcoat and his field jacket was in tatters with the padding exposed where the bullets had torn through his body. Packer, who was lying face down in the bottom of the foxhole, didn't answer when I spoke to him nor make any movement when I tossed frozen clods of dirt on his back. I didn't want to crawl over the embankment into the hole because we were not certain that the Germans had withdrawn. Although I could see no wounds, I assumed that Packer was dead so I crawled back to my foxhole. In the 2nd Squad Evans and Santarsiero had been wounded by small arms fire.†

The enemy made no more threats and we stayed in or close to our foxholes all day. Shortly after dusk I was surprised to find Packer walking around the area. He was not wounded but we sent him to the aid station because he was shaken up and incoherent.

---

*The G Company morning report listed Pfc. Walter V. Lee, Jr., as killed in action near Mon Schumann on Jan. 5.

†Pfc. Albert Evans and Pvt. Frank Santarsiero were both listed as slightly wounded in action near Mon Schumann on Jan. 5. Evans returned to duty on Jan. 21 and Santarsiero came back to G Company in June.

Several days later Packer told me that during the attack a machine gun crew had been concentrating on their position. Lee and Packer shot the crew of three, but in return Lee was shot in the arm. He stood up and took off his overcoat and Packer started to dress the wound. Lee joked about having a million dollar wound and that the war was over for him when a burst from a machine gun caught him in the chest, driving him against the back wall of the foxhole. Packer dropped to the ground as the machine gun continued to fire at Lee. German machine gun crews often worked in pairs, alternating fire and movement in order to keep us pinned down. Lee and Packer had not noticed the second crew. Packer said he passed out and did not hear me or feel the clods. When he came to he was afraid to call for help or leave the foxhole until dusk. After hearing this I felt that I should have taken more risks and crawled into the hole to check on his condition.

Stan Nachman of the 1st Squad told me that he and Stew Rorer had shot ten Germans in the chest and stomach during the attack that morning. They had approached upright and in single file without any attempt to protect themselves. Nachman said they seemed to be drunk or drugged, as they just kept coming and stepping over their fallen comrades. This was not characteristic of the Germans. The tactics used on Lee and Packer were more typical.

A German soldier, dressed in white, surrendered in the evening. He had come from the vicinity of Packer's foxhole and we strongly suspected that he was a member of the crew that had killed Lee. He told us that he was a Pole and had been forced to fight with the Germans. He may have been a German who could speak Polish and thought things might go easier for him if he claimed to be Polish.

Able Company of the 1st Battalion relieved us at 2000 and we walked about a mile to the rear where our Company CP was located. Upon our arrival at the command post we had to stand and wait for half an hour in a snow storm while they decided where to put us.

I shouted at Lt. Lassiter, "You've had all day to find a place for us to stay, how about getting on the stick and moving your men in out of the cold!"

"Sergeant," he said, "you're getting hysterical. Calm down before I have to slap your face."

I was still rational enough to realize that non-coms do not win confrontations with officers, so I calmed down. It was not long before the platoon was billeted in a barn for the night.

OTTS Our few days of resting and keeping our fingers crossed soon came to an end. Just before midnight on January 4 we moved up the road to the north through the completely demolished town of Nothum and stopped at an isolated farmhouse about a mile or so from Mon Schumann, where we waited for Lt. Thomas, CO of L Company, to lead us to our positions. Lt. Thomas was an Indian and an excellent combat officer.

We were led into position along a path leading to the right front of Mon Schumann crossroads. There was only one building left standing in the little village, and it was full of shell holes. The cellar served as Battalion CP and the first floor was the battalion aid station.

We took over foxholes from the L Company men so we didn't have to dig any ourselves. The holes were fairly large with a nice covering of logs, dirt, and snow over them.

Captain Goldsmith went back to the Battalion CP to find out what the score was, and Lt. Lassiter came and sat in the foxhole with me.

When daylight came we had a chance to look over our surroundings. We were in a forest of small fir trees. The branches were covered with snow and the trees were so close together that we could not see more than ten or twelve feet in any direction. It was really a beautiful spot, but rather frightening since we couldn't tell when a Heinie might pop out of the woods right into our foxhole. My hole must have been a German messenger center or something of the kind as there were about twelve bicycles on top and all around it.

The 3rd Platoon was on our right. While they were eating a cold K ration breakfast someone noticed a large number of Germans moving quietly up through the trees to begin a counterattack. S/Sgt. Larry Treff and his 1st Squad opened fire on them, mowing down some three dozen and breaking up the attack before it ever got started. One BAR man said he literally had a field day; he claimed to have killed fifteen himself. Two men were kept busy passing him ammunition, and he just fired until his BAR got so hot he couldn't hold it.

About this time Lt. Lassiter went back to the Battalion CP "to direct mortar and artillery fire," where he stayed all day, leaving me as the only officer with the company.

We really had a big day. As if visibility wasn't bad enough already, it started snowing and continued most of the day. Everyone was afraid to get too deep in his hole or turn his head for fear some Heinie might jump out of the bushes on him. We moved from hole to hole, whispering to each other and firing at every noise or every bush that shook.

The woods extended only about thirty yards to our front. The Heinies rolled an 88 field gun into the clearing about six hundred yards away and started banging away at us with point blank fire. We crawled up to the edge of the clearing and tried to knock off the gunners without giving away our position too much. We got one of them and caused them to back up for a while but it wasn't long before they were peppering away at us again.

We really didn't have a dull moment all day; if we weren't worrying about the field pieces or a tank, we would have an infantry counterattack to stop. The woods were full of dead Germans at the end of the day, and the company suffered several casualties. No one in the 2nd Platoon was killed, but several were wounded, including S/Sgt. Austin, who caught a piece of shrapnel in the hand. S/Sgt. Bruno had to be evacuated because of battle fatigue.*

About 2100 we marched quietly two miles back down the road to a group of buildings, where we spent the night in a barn, happy to get away from Mon Schumann for a while.

Jan. 6, 1945. G Company pulls back into battalion reserve.

EGGER George Company walked a mile or so back to the high ground in front of Mercher-Dunkrodt, where the 2nd Battalion HQ was located. The snow was about a foot deep and it made the walking difficult.

Since the snow had insulated the ground and there was only a light crust of frost, the digging was easy. Olson and I dug a deep foxhole and were able to cover it with shelter halves, which kept out the intermittent snow that fell all day. I preferred this dry cold weather over the drenching rains and the mud we had suffered through in November. Although we suffered some discomfort from the cold, we managed to stay dry.

We only had a few outposts to man so the guard duty was light. Two hot meals were brought up each day. Lt. Lassiter was here long enough to chew out two men for not wearing their helmets; there was no praise for yesterday's accomplishments. I wondered why he had not showed his face at the front yesterday.

OTTS The next day we climbed the high hill to our rear and took up positions on the reverse slope. As soon as we got there Captain Goldsmith and Lt. Lassiter went back down to the Battalion CP, and I was left in charge of the company again.

We were in a pretty nice spot on the reverse side of a steep hill where

*S/Sgt. John V. Austin was listed as "slightly wounded" near Mon Schumann on Jan. 5 and hospitalized. He returned to duty on Mar. 14. S/Sgt. Alfred Bruno is shown on the G Company morning report as having been hospitalized because of illness on Jan. 10 and returning on the 15th.

the enemy's artillery and mortars would have a hard time reaching us, even if they knew we were there. The rocky terrain made digging a bit difficult, but we finally got our holes dug and covered them with cord-wood some obliging person had left stacked around. I had an EE-8-A phone in my hole connected to battalion and spent most of the night listening to Capt. "Ham" Andon of Howe Company directing mortar fire.

Jan. 7, 1945. G Company remains in battalion reserve near Nothum.

EGGER Larry Treff was promoted to platoon sergeant of the 1st Platoon today. He was twenty years old and had risen from Pfc. to Tech Sergeant in two months. Some of the men resented this and thought he was a bit cocky, but most of us considered him intelligent, courageous, and a good leader. Nachman replaced Treff as leader of the 1st Squad, with Wolfenbarger as his assistant.

Olson took out a patrol last night and Poirier of the 2nd Squad was wounded.*

Sturgis and Coolidge were supposed to have relieved Moores and me on guard tonight but only Sturgis showed. Sturgis told me that Coolidge said he was not going to pull guard tonight. I walked to Coolidge's foxhole and asked him if he was sick. He said "No, I'm not sick but I'm not going to stand guard tonight." I unslung my rifle and told him to get out of the hole and move out. He didn't argue and I walked behind him to the outpost. I talked to Olson about the situation and he told Coolidge that if it happened again we would take the matter up with Lt. Lassiter.

OTTS We spent the day in our positions on the hillside and the kitchen sent us up a hot meal. Just before we were to pull out that night one of the 1st Platoon men accidentally shot himself in the foot, and T/Sgt. Treff and my medic, T/4 Arvil Lamb, volunteered to stay with him that night until we could send a jeep after him the next day.

Jan. 8, 1945. G Company pulls back to divisional reserve at Kaundorf.

EGGER The 101st Engineers relieved us at 0200 and we walked the five miles back to our former positions at Kaundorf. Along the way we saw the glow from a burning tank and could hear the exploding ammo.

---

*Pvt. Rene Poirier was listed as slightly wounded in action near Nothum on Jan. 7. He returned to duty on Feb. 14.

The cooks had a hot breakfast waiting for us when we arrived. We had only one outpost to man, so the rest of the squad spent much of their time sitting around the campfire or sleeping.

Packer came back today and I talked to him about his experiences of January 5, which had destroyed his effectiveness as an infantryman. He had only known Walt Lee since December 19, but Lee, who was brave and confident, had provided Packer with moral support and a sense of security. Packer had been married for eighteen months and had not seen his wife since July. She had been due to give birth two weeks ago and he had not heard from home for almost a month. Since he had just transferred from the artillery, he was afraid it would take a long time for his mail to catch up with him.

He had another problem, which we all shared, in that he feared he would be killed. He was not able to control his fear, particularly after Lee died. I felt sorry for him, as did the other men. The men in the platoon generally showed a compassion toward those whose nerves gave out on them. Packer told me he would never forget the sounds of the bullets hitting Lee and the last gurgling breaths he drew.

Soon after this the Red Cross notified Packer of the birth of his son, and then he began to worry that he might never see him. The war was even tougher on married men that it was on the rest of us.

OTTS We left after midnight and spent most of the night climbing up and down hills and trudging across snow-covered fields. Several times I thought we were lost, but Captain Goldsmith must have known where we were going; anyway, we ended up in Kaundorf shortly before morning and took over some buildings.

Most of the day was spent in reorganizing my platoon. I had lost Van Winkle and Austin, two of my squad leaders, and my runner, Don Thompson, had to go to the aid station today because of frostbitten feet.* Pfc. Fred Gilluly became the platoon runner. Sgt. George Idelson took command of the 1st Squad and Sgt. Vernon Hedgpath took over the 3rd. Sgt. Dave Smith continued to head the 2nd Squad. T/4 Philip Sarro, Sgt. David Seeney, and Pfc. Simon Yonut were their assistants.† Some of the other men had to be swapped around to balance the squads. I had only twenty-one men left in the platoon.

---

*Pfc. Donald D. Thompson returned to duty on Jan. 12.

*Idelson was promoted to staff sergeant on Jan. 10 and Hedgpath on the 15th; Yonut was appointed sergeant on Jan. 10.

5 Victory in the Ardennes
January 8–27, 1945

OPERATIONAL BACKGROUND   In the III Corps sector the offensive launched on January 4 against the German salient southeast of Bastogne had encountered such stiff resistance and made so little progress that the attack had been temporarily suspended on January 6. The 26th Division had maintained defensive positions while the veteran 90th Division, then assembling in the corps area, prepared to attack on its left. With the 90th assuming the main effort to eliminate the enemy pocket, the renewed thrust got underway on January 9 (see Map 5).[1] [P.R.]

Jan. 9, 1945.   G Company moves back on line near Mon Schumann Crossroads.

EGGER   Fockler went to the aid station yesterday morning with frozen feet, and Stribling had been missing since January 5. He had fallen behind that night as we were walking to the rear.

We were told this morning to be ready to move on line in the afternoon. As we were moving from the woods to the road on which the companies of the battalion were strung out in a long column, an 88 shell made a direct hit on a lieutenant standing in the road. George Company filed past the lieutenant, who had been an artillery observer, and the column halted for a few minutes when I was right next to the remains. I scanned the scene quickly and looked away. All that was left were a mound of bloody flesh and intestines, a blotch of crimson snow and two feet encased in overshoes. Maybe it was a better death than some had to endure, as it was quick, perhaps painless, and unexpected.

The column took off at a fast pace and the usual one-third of the men fell behind. We took over some old positions in a dense stand of hardwoods about a quarter of a mile from Mon Schumann crossroads. I made some improvements in my foxhole before the bedrolls were brought up.

OTTS This afternoon we moved back up to Mon Schumann and took up positions along the road to the right of the buildings. We made the move in the daytime so we couldn't go straight up the four-mile stretch that ran from Kaundorf through Nothum to Mon Schumann but had to go a round-about way, up and down steep hills that covered several miles.

When we reached our positions Lt. Lassiter jumped into a foxhole and turned his ankle. He was evacuated and did not rejoin the company as long as I was with it.*

When the men had been placed in position, Captain Goldsmith told me that he was going up to the Battalion CP and that I should take over. I told him he was going to have another case of battle fatigue on his hands and lose his last lieutenant if I was left alone in command of the company much longer. He just laughed, told me I would be all right, and took off.

Although the Battalion CP was only a quarter of a mile away, I didn't see him again for four days. I am pretty sure he was doing right, since the reserve company's CO is supposed to stay with the battalion commander at times, but I did not like the responsibility of having the whole company with no one to turn to for advice. I was only a 2nd lieutenant and just twenty-two years old.

Jan. 10, 1945. G Company remains on line at Mon Schumann.

EGGER The 104th Regiment was to our right on the high ground overlooking Wiltz. Occasionally we could hear an exchange of small arms fire but there were no big battles. We were on the uphill side of the road to Mon Schumann. The 3rd Squad covered a front of about forty yards. Olson and LeCrone shared a foxhole, Sturgis, Moores, and Packer were together, Tompkins and Scheufler were seldom separated, Coolidge had paired up with a man from the 2nd Squad and I had a foxhole to myself. We were in a support position so we could move about and look the area over.

There was a considerable amount of American equipment scattered about and three or four dead GIs partially covered with snow on the lower side of the road. They were from the 28th Division, one of the units overrun by the Germans in the December 16 breakthrough. The shoulder patch of the 28th was a red keystone. The men called it the "Bloody Bucket" because the division had lost so many men.

---

*1st Lt. Leroy Lassiter was listed as "slightly injured in action near Mon Schumann (injury unknown)" on Jan. 10 and hospitalized. He never returned to G Company.

Pearcy, Stoddard, Allen, and Nachman dug the German dead out of the snow and went through their pockets looking for rings, watches, or other valuables. The Germans carried letters from home and photographs of sweethearts, wives, and children, just as we did. The pastime did not appeal to me. Besides, I didn't think it would go well if we were taken prisoner with our pockets full of loot. I'm sure that rifling the dead for valuables was a common practice by both sides when the occasion permitted.

The good news was that Lt. Lassiter had been evacuated yesterday because he was ill. I think a large yellow stripe somewhere on his body was one of the symptoms of his illness. We never saw him again. I wondered if Captain Goldsmith had discovered something about Lt. Lassiter that the men had known from the beginning.

The 1st Battalion and F Company had attacked toward Wiltz this morning from positions at Mon Schumann crossroads. They made good progress and reached the ridge overlooking Wiltz, but the companies were scattered over a large area so they pulled back and set up a defensive line for the night.

Tompkins, LeCrone, Huckabee, Stoddard, and I volunteered to help carry out the wounded. We walked to the aid station at Mon Schumann, where Marvin Busby and two other cooks from George Company joined us. We were taken to where the attacking companies were bedding down and setting up a line of defense.

At 1900 a guide requested eight men to carry out two litter-cases. We took the litters and blankets for the wounded with us. The night was clear and the moon shining on the snow provided us with good light to travel by. On the way up we passed an American tank which had thrown a track. Our route took us across several clearings and out on a ridge covered with young spruce and pine so thick that it was difficult to travel. The guide lost his way and we wandered around for about twenty minutes before he found his platoon.

Two wounded men had been lying on the ground without blankets since late afternoon and were suffering from cold and shock. A medic had administered first aid and had stopped the bleeding of a man who had lost a leg. The other man, whom the cooks and I carried, had been shot in the ribs and it was difficult for him to talk.

It was hard work carrying the litters through the tangle of trees and brush and over the rough, steep terrain. The guide carried a rifle and I had brought one, since I did not want the group to be without some protection. The rifle was slung over my back but the barrel kept getting caught in the trees, so I asked the guide if he would carry it for me. Well, no, he did not want to carry it, so I gave him the choice of trading places with me. He chose to carry my rifle.

The trip was rough on the wounded and occasionally our man would groan and ask us to be more careful. Most of his complaints were about his cold feet. Despite the cold, my wool shirt was soaked with sweat.

After we had delivered the men to the aid station I discovered that the guide had thrown away my rifle because it was too heavy. I figured I could whip him so I took his rifle and told him he would have to figure out a way to get another. We returned to our foxholes about midnight. I never knew what happened to the two wounded men.

OTTS   Rocco Clemente, the communications sergeant, and I set up the Company CP in one of the foxholes. Soon Ed Germain arrived sporting a brand new set of second lieutenant's bars, and we widened our hole to let him in too. He had received a field commission and had been back to division for a few days to take care of the formalities. Rocco soon replaced Germain as 1st Sergeant.*

T/Sgt. Treff came by to visit us, making it necessary for one person to be outside as the foxhole was made for two and it was impossible for four to get in it. I was about fifteen yards behind the hole answering a call of nature when the Jerries threw in one of their barrages. I don't know whether I hit the ground first or not, but I dived head first into the hole on top of Treff, Rocco, and Germain with my pants and underwear down below my knees. They didn't stop laughing at me for an hour.

Elements of the 104th Regiment were engaged in a fire fight over on our right almost every day. The objective we were trying to gain by all this bitter fighting was the high ground overlooking the Wiltz River and the town of Wiltz, Luxembourg.

We furnished men from our company and battalion to act as stretcher bearers for the other battalions, and one night there were as many as a hundred men with stretchers bringing wounded back to our aid station. Jeeps were kept busy all night carrying the wounded farther back.

One of my men who went on the stretcher-bearing detail, a T/4—I won't mention his name; his conscience should hurt him enough without having his name brought to the public's attention—slipped off and went to Longwy and Arlon, Belgium, and then to Paris, spending several days in each city. He then joined the 35th Division, where he was discovered and sent back to us after having been a deserter for several weeks. We could have had him court martialed and shot or imprisoned but let him off with just a bust in rank to private.

---

*1st Sgt. Edward L. Germain was commissioned a 2nd Lieutenant effective Jan. 7. S/Sgt. Rocco F. Clemente became acting first sergeant on Jan. 20 and was permanently promoted to that rank on Mar. 10.

I overheard him telling some of the men of all the wonderful times he had in Paris while we were enduring periodic shelling in our frozen foxholes. It really burned me up, and none of the men would have anything to do with him. I don't think it is any disgrace for a man to crack up under the mental strain, but to desert your company and fellow soldiers in combat is the worst thing a man can do.

Jan. 11, 1945. G Company remains on line at Mon Schumann Crossroads getting pounded by German artillery.

EGGER The frequency of the shelling increased today, especially near meal time. The jeeps carrying our meals would dash up, leave the containers of hot food and coffee, two containers of hot water—one soapy, one clear to wash and rinse our mess kits in—load the containers from the previous meal, and speed four miles back to the kitchen. A few men at a time would run down to the road, fill their mess kits, and run back to the foxholes, eat the meal before it froze, and then dash back and wash the mess kits. It was not a very relaxing way to enjoy our food. This went on twice daily. If we wanted lunch we heated a ration.

The kitchen was taking more risks to provide us hot meals than they had in November. In the bitter cold weather, hot meals were important for the morale and nutrition of the troops.

Junior Letterman, who had been with the platoon since November 9, was hit in the hand and a few minutes later Harold Schroaf, also from the 2nd Squad, was wounded. Both were able to walk to the aid station at Mon Schumann. Alex Stoddard's leg was broken by shrapnel and I helped carry him up the road until we met a jeep.* He was suffering from the pain but did his best to hide it. Only Letterman later came back to G Company.

1st Sergeant Germain received a battlefield commission and became our platoon leader.

Bob Lees of the 1st Squad went back with frostbite today. He came back to the company in June.

OTTS About every half-hour during the day and at intervals during the night the Jerries would throw a barrage of from 200 hundred to 250 rounds of artillery, mortars, and nebelwerfers into our area. The sound

---

*Pfc. Junior L. Letterman, Pvt. Harold L. Schroaf, and Pfc. Alex Stoddard, Jr., were all listed as slightly wounded in action at Mon Schumann on Jan. 11 and hospitalized. Letterman returned to duty on May 16; neither of the others ever returned to G Company.

of exploding shells was deafening and the ground shook all around. We could hear the rocket bombs coming for miles away and they made a terrible racket when they crashed in the road and woods around us. The bombs did not throw much shrapnel, but the concussion was terrific—enough to kill a man if he were too close.

The snow all around was black from the exploding shells and the ground was littered with tree limbs. We were suffering several casualties a day, and the percentage of combat fatigue was running high. A couple of men shot their fingers off—anything to get out of that hell.

Jan. 12, 1945. G Company continues to take casualties from the German shelling.

EGGER The Germans increased the shelling again today. We had heard they were running short of ammunition, but you couldn't tell it from the amount of metal they were dumping on us. The interval between barrages was so short we hardly had time to get out of the foxholes to relieve ourselves. There was nothing to do but roll up in a blanket and keep warm.

The trees increased the hazards of the shelling as the rounds that struck the branches would explode in the air (tree bursts) and shower shrapnel downward and out, while a shell hitting the ground propelled fragments up and out. The pieces of shrapnel were jagged and made a whistling sound as they whirled through the air.

We could not move much because of the constant shelling, so I slept except when I had sentry duty. Moores, Sturgis, and Packer had the only foxhole with a log cover. If axes and saws had been available we could have provided the same protection for the other foxholes. The Germans were so close we could hear the mortars pop as they hit the firing mechanism in the mortar tubes. Then in a few seconds we could hear the shells whispering as they dropped from the sky to land near our positions.

Pearcy went back with frostbite yesterday evening.* I was not surprised—now that Stoddard had been wounded. They had been good buddies and I suspected that Pearcy had been toughing it out with his feet for some time because he didn't want to let Stoddard down.

Treff took a patrol out in the afternoon but they did not make contact with the enemy. Lee Allen came back with a beautiful gold pocket watch he had taken from a dead German soldier.

---

*Pfc. Marshall H. Pearcy was listed as "slightly injured in action" near Mon Schumann on Jan. 11. He never returned to G Company.

OTTS Whenever possible, if we were in a stable position, I always tried to go by each man's hole at least twice a day just to see how he was and either cheer him up or let him cheer me up. I had the whole company to look after instead of just one platoon.

One of the platoons was down at the right of my hole about a quarter of a mile away in a concrete shed sitting in an open field. I had to run up and down the road, dodging shells to get to them. About the last day I got tired of running so was walking slowly along while 50mm mortar shells were falling all around. I had seen so much big stuff lately that I was scoffing at the "baby" mortars when a fragment hit me in the seat of the pants; that speeded me up considerably, and I ran to my hole almost overcome with joy at the prospect of getting a purple heart. I started taking off my pants and underwear and was very much disappointed to find that the mortar fragment had gotten lost somewhere in the maze of clothing. There wasn't a single scratch on me.

Germain had been an excellent first sergeant, but being a platoon leader was a bit new to him and the responsibility came at the wrong time. I don't think he wandered more than ten yards from our foxhole the three days he was there.

We had some of the cooks with us to use as stretcher bearers. They spent the first day and night in the shed with our right flank platoon but didn't like it there so moved down to the battalion aid station. It proved to be an unlucky move because a shell landed right in the aid station, killing one of them and seriously wounding several others.

Jan. 13, 1945.   German artillery continues to pound G Company.

EGGER The Germans started pounding us with mortars at daylight and kept it up all day. Fortunately, some of the shells were duds—one hit the top of a tree directly over Pete Ruffin's foxhole. A particularly heavy barrage hit us about 1500, knocking over a tall tree that fell across three of the foxholes, including mine. My foxhole was deep and so narrow that it was difficult to turn or roll over. I almost had an attack of claustrophobia and it was all I could do to compose myself. Another shell landed near us and the concussion knocked Packer out for a few minutes. Olson and LeCrone were wounded by the same burst. Packer, Sturgis, and Moores pulled them into their dugout and dressed the wounds in Olson's leg and LeCrone's shoulder.

Moores, Tompkins, Scheufler, and I carried Olson, who weighed about 225 pounds, partway to the aid station before we met a jeep. LeCrone was able to walk and did not tarry on his way to the aid station; he seemed happy to have a ticket to the rear. Vic Popa had taken a piece of shrapnel through the stomach and our medic was hit in the leg.* LeCrone came back to us in February and Olson and Popa returned in May.

With Olson gone, Pete Ruffin told me to take charge of the squad.†

We heard that an artillery shell had struck our kitchen area yesterday, wounding three men and killing Busby, who had helped me on the litter detail on the 10th.‡

At 2100 we rolled up our bedrolls and quickly and quietly walked two miles beyond Mon Schumann, where we climbed onto trucks.

OTTS The men were breaking up fast. Some of them were crying, and many were telling me they couldn't stand many more barrages. I explained to them the system that Rocco, Germain, and I used to keep from going crazy—we pretended that the company area was a target as on a rifle range and that our foxhole was the center or bull's eye. We would lie in our hole and score the Heinies on their artillery rounds according to how close they came to our hole—five for a bull's eye and four, three, two, and one as they landed farther away. We gave them a "Maggie's drawers," as the red flag on a rifle range is called, for a complete miss of the target. This helped pass the time, but I could think of things I would rather do.

Bananas LaFlam would bring us hot chow in thermite cans every day, leaving some at my CP and carrying some to the other platoons. Quite a few men went several meals without eating because they didn't want to leave their holes for fear of being hit.

Each regiment had an officer and group of men called the "Graves Registration" team. They came up with a truck and loaded American and German dead alike in stacks on the trucks. I furnished them with guides to places where we knew some of our men had been killed, but we had a hard time talking the graves registration men into going anywhere forward of the road.

The dead were easy to handle as they were frozen stiff and were not decayed or smelly. I would have hated to be around Mon Schumann

---

*S/Sgt. Vernon S. Olson and Pfc. Fonrose N. LeCrone were both listed as "slightly wounded" and S/Sgt. Victor M. Popa as "seriously wounded," all near Mon Schumann on Jan. 13. All three were hospitalized.

†Egger was promoted to staff sergeant on Jan. 28 to accord with his new position as squad leader.

‡Pfc. Marvin L. Busby was listed as killed in action near Mon Schumann on Jan. 12. The wounded men were T/4 Alfred Morin, T/4 Theodore Tymkowiche, and T/5 Frank Tomsick. Morin returned to duty nine days later; the others never came back to G Company.

when the thaw came as there were numerous dead soldiers covered with snow lying all over the ground and in the bottom of foxholes.

About 2100 we left "Purple Heart Crossroad" or "88 Junction," as we called Mon Schumann, and marched back to Kaundorf, where we entrucked and rode almost to Berle. We walked on into town and after standing around for some time waiting for orders assigning us to certain buildings, we finally got tired and took over a cellar in a building occupied by some other company. I had only fifteen men left now, so there was plenty of room for all of us.

Jan. 14, 1945. G Company moves to battalion reserve near Berle.

EGGER Shortly after midnight we arrived in Berle, where the 3rd Platoon stayed in a barn at the edge of town. We left a sentry behind and moved into town about daylight. We were here for a short rest.

I found a small piece of shrapnel about one-third of the way through my Bible. The New Testament was a 1942 Christmas present from my parents and I carried it in the left breast pocket of my field jacket. I was sure the sliver of steel had struck me during yesterday's shelling. In our previous position I had noticed several holes caused by shrapnel in the frozen ground at the edge of my foxhole, and the two or three I checked extended in depth beyond the length of my bayonet blade. My narrow foxhole had been confining, but it had protected me well.

Wendell Wolfenbarger (from the 1st Squad) and I found a hayloft, spread out our bedrolls, and slept most of the afternoon. Wendell was an outgoing person with an infectious smile. He had remained cheerful through all the hardships we had endured. He was especially happy that day because he had received a letter from home in which his wife had told him about Christmas and their two children. She had sent some photographs of the family, which he proudly showed to the men in the platoon.

An enemy 88 fired an occasional round into town to harass us.

We had two hot meals today. It seemed like I never had enough food or sleep.

OTTS We spent the day in Berle enjoying hot meals. It was Sunday and I attended church and communion services held by Chaplain Grover B. Gordon, the Protestant chaplain assigned to the 3rd Battalion. Father Francis X. Bransfield was the chaplain for our battalion, and although I am a Protestant I attended many of his services. They were both very fine men.

I went on reconnaissance in the afternoon to an observation post (OP) located in a factory building on the north edge of town. The building was located right beside a road and on top of a steep hill which dropped off to the front giving an excellent view. My platoon was to occupy the building as an OP and guard the road against possible enemy patrols.

We were to stay in the building, but as soon as it was dark we dug holes on each side of the road to fight from if we were attacked. It was really hard digging since the exploding shells had melted the snow and ice in some places and it had frozen over again, fusing with the ground.

Jan. 15, 1945. G Company enjoys a day off in Berle but moves back on line that night.

EGGER Stribling rejoined the squad today after a ten-day absence.* He said he got lost and had been fighting with the 1st Battalion. Captain Goldsmith told him to quit trying to fight the war by himself and to stay with us. I thought the captain phrased his chewing out in a positive way. I did not doubt that Stribling had been with the 1st Battalion but I was sure he had been with the unit that was furthest to the rear.

The 3rd Platoon was taken about fifteen miles back for the day to the small town of Bavigne, where Battalion HQ was located. My hopes for a shower were in vain. I bought some candy bars and fruit juice. Wolfenbarger stole a bottle of champagne from H Company and offered to share, but I remembered my other experience with French wine and did not partake.

Sturgis received a backlog of ten packages of cookies, candy, and cake. The parcels had gone to the artillery unit to which he had previously been assigned and were just now catching up with him. He shared his bounty with the members of the squad and all the rich food made me sick.

In Bavigne, the house we were staying in was near a battery of 155s, which rattled the windows and shook the plaster loose every time they fired.

Two 2½-ton trucks went through town loaded with dead American GIs. They were not exactly stacked in like cordwood, since the bodies were frozen in grotesque positions and occasionally an arm or leg protruded at an awkward angle.

We returned to Berle shortly after dark and were told to be ready to move in an hour.

Captain Goldsmith, who was six-foot-five, must have been leading the column, as we set out at a fast pace carrying our bedrolls. It didn't

*The morning report of Jan. 12 listed Pfc. Oscar Stribling AWOL as of Jan. 5. He is shown as having returned to duty on the 15th.

take long to cover the three miles, but only about half of the men kept up. The rest were gasping for breath and cursing between gasps. The Captain was in a hurry because the road was subject to shelling.

FROM EGGER'S LETTER OF JANUARY 15

. . . This is a bleak and desolate looking country. I'll never forget it for more than one reason. It seems like I have been moving around in an endless nightmare.

. . . I have a squad to look after now and I don't care much for the responsiblity. . . .

A bunch of the old timers were wounded the other day. That leaves me the third to oldest man in the platoon.

I found a little piece of shrapnel in my Bible the other day. I hope we never go through another barrage like that. Pray for me, my nerves are getting a little more shaky all the time. I don't know how long I'll be able to stand it. . . .

We relieved Item Company, 3rd Battalion, in a wooded area at the edge of the road. The relief of troops on the front was usually carried out under cover of darkness and it was done quietly and efficiently with experienced men. We disliked having new troops relieve us because they didn't know how important it was to keep quiet. My counterpart from Item Company met me at the road and showed me our positions. While I assigned pairs to each dugout, his men moved out to assemble at a prearranged location. The I Company sergeant told me that the Germans were dug in about two hundred yards to our front in the woods at the edge of a clearing. The open area in our front was no man's land.

I approached Coolidge's position while he was on guard tonight and, although he was awake, he never heard me even after I deliberately made some noise. His having been in the artillery may have caused a partial loss of hearing. I thought the infantry was no place for him but it took a month to transfer him back to the artillery.* Until then I didn't let him be on sentry duty alone.

---

*Pfc. Ralph Coolidge was transferred to the 102nd Field Artillery Battalion on Feb. 10, 1945.

OTTS The night at the OP was uneventful and we moved back to Berle the next morning. I went with Captain Goldsmith to the Battalion CP for an orientation meeting to show us what had happened and to explain the plans for the next few days.

This was the first time I had seen much of Major Arthur W. Burke, who had been our battalion commander since the last week in December. He was about twenty-eight and very eager and daring about everything. Burke was an excellent officer who liked to be out in front at every chance, but he could plan some of the most daring and hazardous movements I have ever heard of. If Major Albert Friedman, his executive officer, and the company commanders hadn't held him back we would either have taken Germany single-handed or all been killed. Fortunately, he would always listen to reason and usually could be talked into changing some of his plans.

I went on reconnaissance late in the afternoon with Major Burke and Captain Goldsmith to look over some defensive positions in the woods east of Doncols. I was glad to have the chance to look over the terrain in the daylight since I was to guide the company there that night. We climbed back up the mountain to Berle, and around 2000 I led the company back down to the woods. We were relieving another unit, so the foxholes were already dug. And although it was a dark night, we made the relief with less confusion than usual.

Benny and I placed our men while the lieutenant and men we were relieving collected their gear and cleared out of the foxhole that was to be our Platoon CP. It was the best foxhole I ever stayed in. The Germans had dug it, probably with slave labor, and it was about seven-by-five-by-ten feet deep with a covering of six-inch logs, dirt, and snow. Bruno had come back from the hospital and he, Benny, Lamb, and I all stayed in the one hole. We had a little gasoline stove, a candle, and a bottle gas lamp, so we really had most of the comforts of home.

Jan. 16, 1945. G Company continues to outpost the town of Berle.

EGGER The dugouts the Germans had left were covered with logs and dirt and were located in a dense young stand of conifers. Keeping dry was no problem since the temperature was near or below freezing all day. I had noticed that any time the Germans were in a position for very long they constructed comfortable, well-protected dugouts. The Wehrmacht evidently provided the men with the tools needed for the job. The enemy needed protection from our artillery, which was highly effective and for which they had a healthy respect.

Stribling and Packer pulled guard at the Company CP and Scheufler and Tompkins were together as usual. Sturgis, Coolidge, Moores and I occupied the two adjacent positions. H Company had two heavy machine guns between us and the 2nd Squad, which was on our right.

When I had heard about the five-percent plan at Metz I had reservations about the quality of the men we would be getting. Obviously every rear echelon CO who had to give up a percentage of his men to the infantry would comb out the gold bricks an disciplinary problems and those with the least experience. Surprisingly, the majority of the five-percenters were as good soldiers as the replacements that were sent to the division.

For example, Ed Sturgis developed into a good infantryman after about a two-week period of withdrawal and adjustment. His being selected as a five-percenter may have damaged his self-esteem, but the ready acceptance of him by the squad members should have helped. Sturgis, who was twenty-five years old, was from Brooklyn but didn't fit the stereotype of being cocky and brash. Alton Moores was another five-percenter who turned into a good combat soldier, but he had a problem when he was in a rest area and had access to liquor, which I will discuss later.

OTTS I went to Battalion HQ in the town of Bavigne today to pick up the payroll for the men. To my way of thinking, there was no earthly reason for paying the men in foxholes where they had no place to spend the money and not even a pair of dice or a deck of cards to gamble with. We were paid in French francs, but even the small change was in paper currency. I had to run from foxhole to foxhole with a bagful of paper money, a fountain pen, and a payroll form for each man to sign.

The Jerries, playful as usual, dropped in an occasional mortar round while all this was going on, and it's a wonder I didn't scatter francs all over the area in my mad dash from one hole to the next. The Army is very strict about every man getting exactly what is coming to him down to the last penny, but in this case whenever we got close to the amount due I would dash off to the next hole.

Even though a few mortar shells came in each day, generally it was not enough to bother us much. Mostly we just took it easy in the woods outside Berle and sent out an occasional patrol. The nights were dark, though, and we stuck to our policy of always moving in pairs. The Germans were not so quick to try to capture or shoot two men as they were one.

Jan. 17, 1945. G Company continues outposting Berle and suffers some tragic losses.

EGGER The Germans occasionally dropped mortars or artillery on the road to Berle, but our area had been relatively free of shelling until a mortar barrage came in during the afternoon. Ray Tompkins, who was caught away from his dugout, suffered a severe arm wound. A shell fragment had almost severed his right arm at the elbow.* Sturgis dressed the wound and we carried him to the jeep, which took him to the aid station. We were not surprised to learn later that he lost his arm. The 3rd Squad needed an assistant leader and I had planned to recommend Tompkins.

I learned in the evening that Wendell Wolfenbarger had not returned from a patrol with Morgan and Montgomery. The three men had stumbled upon a German position and Wolf had provided fire cover for the other two as they withdrew. He was all right the last time they saw him, so we didn't know what had happened to him. I had heard the firing, but since it was to our right front I thought it involved another platoon. I knew nothing about a patrol being sent out. Lee Allen took another patrol out that night to look for Wolfenbarger but couldn't find him.

OTTS I went back to Bavigne to turn in the signed payroll forms and get a shave and some clean clothes. I took along a form Captain Goldsmith had filled out requesting my promotion to first lieutenant. On the way we passed a pile of dead Germans about the size of a small three-room house. They had been gathered up and brought back in 2½-ton trucks and dumped there.

Our company kitchen and supply room were in Bavigne, and we had a house there to which we were sending a few men each day to wash up, get clean clothes, and get a night's sleep in a building. There was only one catch to it, as I discovered when my turn came.

I was sitting on the bed in an upstairs room reading the mail from home and chatting with some of the company headquarters people when I heard and felt the damnedest explosion I had ever experienced. I immediately hit the floor.

The others all burst into laughter, but I didn't see anything funny until I looked out the window and saw the cause of all the noise. There was a 155mm Long Tom in our backyard with the barrel pointed directly over our roof. It was the muzzle blast from the big gun that I had heard and felt. I discovered that the gun fired all day and all night, which explains why the men who were sent back to this "rest camp" said they would rather stay in their relatively quiet foxholes.

---

*Pfc. Raymond O. Tompkins was listed as "slightly wounded" in action near Berle on Jan. 17 and hospitalized.

The gun finally had to be moved as it was literally shaking the building apart—the plaster was falling off the walls and the mortar was coming out from between the bricks.

But despite the terrible roar of the Long Tom, the day wasn't a complete loss. I was able to shave, take a sponge bath, and put on some clean clothes. I also got a GI watch from the company supply sergeant, S/Sgt. Stan Aras. I would have been issued one in the States if I had come over with the division, but I hadn't received one as a replacement.

Jan. 18, 1945.   G Company pulls back into Berle that night.

EGGER   Moores and Lundy discovered Wolfenbarger's body early this morning in some timber about fifty yards to our right front and brought it back to the road.* I don't remember whether he had died where he was shot or if he had traveled some distance after being wounded. He was facing our positions and had been shot in the back. I wished the 3rd Squad had been notified that a patrol was out so we could have been watching more closely instead of just having minimum security posted.

Another unit relieved us shortly after dark and we filed past Wolfenbarger's body on the way out. I knew it could not be helped, but it never seemed right to walk off and leave our dead. There was no formal way to pay our respects, but it seemed a shame that only strangers, to whom the dead were probably only a statistic, would be at the burial.

The wind drove snow into our faces and the Germans were shelling the road to Berle. They always seemed to know when our troops were moving. Packer, Sturgis, and I dug a shallow foxhole at our outpost outside Berle. The falling snow was so thick that we could only see about five feet.

OTTS   We were relieved tonight by Charlie Company. During the change I was able to have a quick chat with Law Lamar. The Heinies must have become wise to the switchover as they started throwing in a few shells. We made the trip down the long, flat stretch and up the mountain to Berle in record time.

OPERATIONAL BACKGROUND   The advance begun on January 9 had registered slow but steady gains that had largely eliminated the German

---

*The G Company morning report of Jan. 25 listed Sgt. Wendell W. Wolfenbarger as killed in action near Berle on Jan. 18. Wolfenbarger was posthumously awarded the Silver Star for his action in covering the withdrawal of Morgan and Montgomery.

resistance south of the Wiltz River. North of the III Corps sector elements of the First and Third Armies had linked up at Houffalize on January 16, thus sealing off the waist of the Bulge (see Map 5). It was too late, however; the tenacious German delaying tactics combined with the deliberateness of the American advance had allowed most of the enemy troops to withdraw from what might have been a sizable pocket. Now the obvious strategy was simply to force the Germans out of the Ardennes and back across the Our River, from whence they had launched their attack on December 16.

Toward that end, on January 18 XII Corps of Patton's Third Army had struck north across the Sure River to attack the enemy on the extreme eastern end of his line, close by the German frontier. This had unhinged the last remnants of the German line further to the west, thus allowing the 26th Division to draw up to the Wiltz River. After crossing that stream the Yankee Division, along with all other American units advancing north of it, would wheel eastward toward the German border.[2] [P.R.]

Jan. 19–20, 1945. G Company receives some replacements and reorganizes.

EGGER   Six inches of wet snow fell during the night and the company pulled back to houses in Berle to dry out.

Lee Allen from the 1st Squad was appointed my assistant. Frank Gormley became platoon guide, replacing Popa. Stew Rorer was transferred to the 2nd Squad and was made its leader, with Tom Montgomery as his assistant. Joe Treml, who had been wounded at Moncourt and had returned to G Company two days ago, took Wolfenbarger's place as assistant leader of the 1st Squad.

After being gone for over two months, Treml hardly knew anyone. Stribling, Treff, Rorer and I were the only men from the 3rd Platoon still with the company and he knew Ruffin, who had been in the 1st Platoon. Army policy was to return the recovered wounded or ill to the unit in which they had last served, but it didn't always work that way.

G Company received twenty-three new replacements, which did not come close to bringing it up to full strength. Of these, the 3rd Platoon was given five: Elbridge Walker and Merle Ward went to the 1st Squad; Clay Williams and Tony Clemens [pseudonym] were assigned to the 2nd Squad; and the 3rd Squad got Jesse Wiseheart. Bill DeSota had returned to the 1st Squad several days ago after being hospitalized for frostbite, and Solomon Rubin transferred from the 1st Squad to the 3rd.

My squad had lost four good men—Lee, Olson, LeCrone, and Tompkins—in the last two weeks and some of the survivors were not

ROSTER AND LOSSES OF THE 3RD PLATOON BETWEEN DECEMBER 19 AND JANUARY 18

Platoon Leader: 1st Lt. Chester Hargrove was acting CO from Dec. 21–26. 1st Lt. Charles Walter replaced him as leader of the 3rd Platoon until Walter was hospitalized on Dec. 26. Lt. Hargrove returned to the 3rd Platoon that same day, but himself took sick and was hospitalized on Jan. 2. 1st Lt. Leroy Lassiter filled in until a non-battle injury on Jan. 10 sent him to the hospital. Newly commissioned 2nd Lt. Edward Germain then took over the 3rd Platoon until Hargrove returned on Jan. 27.

Platoon Sergeant: T/Sgt. Robert Starcher asked to be relieved of the job on Dec. 21 and was later transferred to the Battalion Patrol. S/Sgt. Pete Ruffin, who had been wounded at Moncourt and had returned on Dec. 18, then took over. He was made T/Sgt. on Dec. 29.

Platoon Guide: S/Sgt. Victor Popa was wounded on Jan. 13. S/Sgt. Francis Gormley replaced him on Jan. 19.

1st Squad

S/Sgt. L. Treff, Ldr (to 1/7*)

Sgt. Nachman, Asst (to 1/7), Ldr

Sgt. Wolfenbarger, Asst, KIA 1/17

Pvt. Bob Adis, frostbite 12/25

Pfc. Lee Allen

Pfc. Bill DeSoto, sick 12/26–1/15

Pfc. Henry Huckabee

Pvt. Bob Lees, frostbite 1/11

Pfc. Tom Oakley, WIA 12/23

Pfc. M. Pearcy, frostbite 1/11

Pfc. Stewart Rorer

Pvt. Solomon Rubin

Pfc. Alex Stoddard, WIA 1/11

2nd Squad

Sgt. Dan Dafoe, Ldr, WIA 12/25

Sgt. Gormley, Asst (to 12/27), Ldr

Pfc. Albert Evans, WIA 1/5

Pfc. Junior Letterman, WIA 1/11

Pfc. W. C. Lundy

Pvt. Tony Messina

Pfc. Tom Montgomery

Pvt. Rufies Morgan

Pvt. Rene Poirier, WIA 1/7

Pvt. Frank Santarsiero, WIA 1/5

Pvt. Harold Schroaf, WIA 1/11

Unidentified Replacement

Unidentified Replacement

3rd Squad

S/Sgt. Vern Olson, Ldr, WIA 1/13

Sgt. Egger, Asst (to 1/13), Ldr

Pvt. Ralph Coolidge

Pfc. J. Fockler, frostbite 1/8

Pfc. Fonrose LeCrone, WIA 1/13

Pfc. Walt Lee, KIA 1/5

Pfc. Alton Moores

Pvt. Harley Packer

Pfc. Paul Scheufler

Pvt. G. Schmitt, frostbite 1/13

Pfc. Stribling, AWOL 1/5–1/15

Pvt. Ed Sturgis

Pfc. Ray Tompkins, WIA 1/17

*S/Sgt. Larry Treff was promoted to T/Sgt. and appointed platoon sergeant of the 1st Platoon on Jan. 7. Sgt. Stan Nachman became leader of the 1st Squad and Pfc. Wendell Wolfenbarger moved up to assistant.

always dependable. Packer was not emotionally stable and would go to pieces when he heard a German machine gun, which was understandable considering the experience he had undergone. Stribling, who made a habit of slipping away when the going got rough, was totally worthless. Coolidge, besides being hard of hearing, was a gold-bricker who could not keep up on the hikes. I did not doubt Rubin's courage and dependability, but he was a poor walker with bad feet. Moores, Allen, Scheufler, and Sturgis were the best in the squad. Wiseheart—who was thirty-two, an old man by infantry standards—was of unknown quality. John Grieco, our new medic, was first rate. He did not wait for the men to ask for help but contacted the platoon members to see if they needed him. He even offered to wash our feet in order to reduce the trench foot cases.

We traveled to Doncols by truck in the evening of the 20th and the platoon was assigned a house for the night. We had a short briefing about the next day's plans. The 2nd Battalion was to cross the Wiltz River before daylight and take the high ground beyond. This was expected to be the Germans' last big defensive stand in Luxembourg. The briefing did not tell how wide or deep the river was or if we would have assault boats. I didn't say anything to the rest of the squad, but it sounded like a tough objective to me. Of course I prayed, as I always did when the going was rough, which was every day. The responsibility of being a squad leader weighed heavily on me and I prayed for courage and wisdom and for the safety of my men and myself if it was the Lord's will. There was always the specter of another Moncourt. I was worried about the next day and consequently had a fitful sleep.

OTTS We rode on trucks to Doncols and the men grabbed a few hours sleep in a hayloft while the company officers attended a briefing at the Battalion CP. This was to be the big push, and George Company was to be one of the attacking companies, with my platoon one of the lead platoons. We studied our maps and waited for the report from a patrol that had gone across the river to check on the enemy positions. The patrol returned about 0400 and reported one machine gun nest and a few other outposts, which we marked on our maps.

Jan. 21, 1945. The 2nd Battalion advances across the Wiltz River.

EGGER In the early morning darkness we walked to the Wiltz River and crossed the five-foot-wide stream on two planks. Back home this would have been called a creek, not a river. We climbed the steep snowy banks on the opposite side, expecting to be shot at any minute. George Company took the town of Grumelschied on the high ground to the right of the crossing, but the only German troops left were an anti-tank crew who immediately surrendered. By nightfall we had walked the eight miles to Derenbach, where we set up positions in a wooded area. I was thankful for the way the day had turned out and I was happy to have a bedroll and to heat a ration over some hot coals. We were tired after the steep climb and long walk through the foot-deep snow.

To quote from the battalion history: "This was the biggest surprise in the whole campaign, because the Germans had easy ground to defend and could have made the crossing a most bloody event; apparently the German units had become weakened, however, and had withdrawn quietly just a few hours before that attack began."[3]

OTTS At 0630, just as dawn was cracking, we marched out in single file down the mountain to the Wiltz River. It turned out to be only a five-foot stream that we crossed on two planks. Bruno cracked up again on the way to the river and was missing for two days.

The ground on the other side of the stream rose almost perpendicularly. There was an open stretch for about three hundred yards and then thick woods and brush up to the top. The climb was difficult through the foot-deep snow. We were in a skirmish line, expecting every minute to be mowed down by German machine guns. I don't know why the Jerries didn't try to stop us; one enemy platoon could have held up our whole battalion for hours and inflicted many casualties.

We reached the top of the mountain and rested a few minutes before heading off to take the town on our right, Grumelschied. I took my platoon to the crossroads just beyond the town to set up positions against a possible counterattack while the rest of the company went into the town, where they captured a Kraut anti-tank crew.

Grumelschied was our objective for the day, but we hadn't expected to take it so quickly. Major Burke therefore decided we should push on. A patrol was sent out to the next mountain, and when they returned reporting no contact with the enemy we started moving again with our platoon leading the way. It was tough going blazing a trail through the knee-deep snow with overshoes and combat boots on. My feet were bothering me for the first time—I had worn a blister on my heel and the soles of both feet ached.

We were standing around in the middle of an open field when an 88 shell landed right in the middle of a group of us. No one was hurt, but we certainly did scatter quickly.

We stopped so many times along the way while someone up ahead was trying to decide which route to take that it was almost dark when we took up positions for the night in the woods to the right of Derenbach. While Benny and I were laboring away trying to dig in among the rocks and tree roots, we heard something going overhead in the darkness that sounded like an airplane with the motor gone haywire. We all decided that it must have been a German V-1 or V-2 rocket.

Jan. 22, 1945. Following a patrol led by Otts, the 2nd Battalion occupied the twin towns of Kleinhoscheid and Knaphoscheid.

EGGER In the morning we rode on tanks behind a cavalry reconnaissance group but dismounted when mines were found placed in the frozen snow over the road. We then walked cross-country to Selscheid, where about fifteen of the enemy surrendered. The 2nd Battalion went on to clear the twin towns of Kleinhoscheid and Knaphoscheid. George and Easy companies outposted the former but we were aroused during the night to dig positions at the edge of town in case of a German counterattack. After completing that job we were allowed to return to our billets. The town received regular 88 and nebelwerfer fire throughout the night.

OTTS The next morning Major Burke called me up to Battalion and said he wanted me to take out a patrol. There were three towns about six miles to our front—Selscheid, Kleinhoscheid, and Knaphoscheid. The purpose of the patrol was to find out whether there were any German troops in these towns and also to find a route for the battalion to follow us.

We were to be a motorized patrol, with three jeeps for the eight of us, but we were only a few hundred yards out of town before the jeeps got stuck in the snow and we had to abandon them. I had told Captain Goldsmith that my feet were hurting too much to walk and that if the jeeps couldn't make it I would have to let T/Sgt. Treff take the patrol on without me. But I decided I didn't want the men to think I couldn't take it so went on anyway.

About a half-mile further the flat hilltop dropped precipitously to the valley and roads below. We walked and slid down the hillside and found an intersection at the bottom where two roads met. Some of our tanks on the hill behind us couldn't get down the way we had so they turned around and left. The roads weren't on our map, so I had to radio back to Major Burke that I didn't know how the rest of the battalion could catch the road coming out of town. Besides, it was full of big German Teller mines that we weren't about to try to clear.

Despite not knowing how or when our troops would be able to follow, we continued on down the road toward Selscheid and walked boldly into town, not knowing but what there might be a whole battalion of Krauts there. As it turned out some civilians met us at the edge of town and told us there were several German soldiers there but they all wanted to surrender. With the civilians as guides, we toured the town, barging into the rooms where the Jerries were eating or sleeping or just sitting around and we ended up capturing eight of them. They all came with us peacefully.

On the way into town S/Sgt. Dave Seeney and I had agreed that if we took any prisoners he would get any watch they had and I was to get any pistol, since I had wanted a German pistol for a long time. Seeney took a P-38 from one of the prisoners and gave it to me. Another of the Krauts had a nice cigarette lighter I wanted, but when he gave me some tale about his father having given it to him and its great sentimental value I got soft and let him keep it even though I knew some MP would end up with it.

While we were searching and investigating the prisoners, George Company, which was leading the battalion, arrived. It was getting late in the afternoon, but Major Burke ordered us to push on and clear the twin towns of Kleinhoscheid and Knaphoscheid—"North Kingtown" and "South Kingtown" we called them—on top of the next hill. As it turned out, elements of the Sixth Cavalry Reconnaissance Group, who we were in support of, had already taken Knaphoscheid so we outposted Kleinhoscheid that night. We had nice buildings to stay in but spent a good part of the night out in the field to the north of town digging foxholes in case we were attacked.

Jan. 23, 1945. The 2nd Battalion lays over in Selscheid for the day.

OTTS We moved back to Selscheid and took over some very nice buildings with our Company CP in a barroom. The barkeeper spoke English, and we talked with him quite a while even though he didn't have anything left to drink. The cooks set up the kitchen and we had a hot meal. My platoon was in a big empty room over a garage. The company had to move its CP out of a nice house when a lieutenant and a sergeant from General Paul's staff took it over for the Division CP. That was as close as I came to seeing a general during my whole stay in the European Theater of Operations; we were in the same town even if I didn't see him.

Orders had come out awarding some of the men Bronze Star medals, and we had a good time joking about them. The way medals were given out really was a joke. In the first place, the Bronze Star should not have been given out for both meritorious service—in other words, simply doing a good job—and heroism in combat. There should have been two medals. A combat man does not enjoy wearing a medal that clerks in Paris were wearing because they could pound a typewriter faster than anyone else or that a cook was awarded because the general liked his apple pie.[4]

Purple Heart medals were handed out at the aid station for any scratch that drew blood. Gilluly got one when he dived into a foxhole to escape a barrage and his steel helmet scraped the bridge of his nose and a second one when a brick fell from a building and scratched his nose.

Whenever we had a breathing spell regiment would send down word to battalion that the other regiments were getting more Bronze and Silver Stars than we were, so we would sit down and think up past acts of valor to write someone up for a medal. My stories always had to be rewritten because I couldn't make them sound heroic enough. George Idelson, the leader of my 1st Squad, proved to be a master at writing up citations, though. He could make an ordinary patrol sound like it should rate the Congressional Medal of Honor.*

We weren't as bad as the Air Corps, with its Flight Medal, but we did throw a good many Bronze Stars and Oak Leaf Clusters around. Many acts that should have merited medals went unnoticed and many of the medals that were awarded were well deserved, but I thought that medals should be given only for something beyond the line of duty and not for just a routine patrol. It makes a man very proud to receive a medal, so we should take care not to cheapen the honor.

Jan. 24, 1945. The 2nd Battalion continues the advance with Otts leading the way.

EGGER We walked over roads all day following the 1st Battalion, which was pursuing the retreating Germans. We spent the night in an open field, but bedrolls were brought up and we had C rations to eat. Allen, Moores, and I dug a large foxhole and with three bedrolls we had fourteen blankets. The dry ones went on the bottom and directly over us, while the wet blankets were on top. We slept in our clothes and kept our shoes and canteens under the blankets to keep them from freezing. We stayed warm despite subfreezing temperatures.

OTTS Shortly after midnight Captain Goldsmith sent me over to the Battalion CP in Knaphoscheid. Major Burke informed me that I was to lead our battalion and a platoon of tanks to another town six miles away, where we were to contact the 1st Battalion and follow them. They told me to pick up T/Sgt. Treff back in Kleinhoschied to serve as guide; he

---

*See the end of Chapter 8, for Egger's concurring opinion on the inequity of the awarding of medals and on S/Sgt. Idelson's skill in writing citations.

was supposed to have explored the road leading out of town to the northeast, which was covered with snow and hard to distinguish, especially at night.

It turned out that Treff had not been out on the road at all. His feet were in such bad shape he could hardly walk. We stood around in Kleinhosheid for a while trying to decide what to do. I talked with Lt. Kahzo Harris of Danville, Virginia, the tank platoon commander, and he agreed that the infantry could walk through the snow easier if the tanks went first. But since we couldn't see the road, he was afraid the tanks might get stuck in a snowdrift. He was game for anything, though, so we started out—Lt. Harris and I on foot in front of the four tanks with the battalion of infantry following behind. We came to several intersections and crossroads where we had to stop and study our maps.

I ran into Harris after the war at Fort McClellan, Alabama, and he got a great kick out of telling everyone how cautious I was and how I cursed him for shining his flashlight all around. I wanted to get under a raincoat or up close to the tank before using our flashlights to examine the map, but he would just stand out in the open waving his flashlight around as if he were on a Boy Scout outing. Lt. Harris didn't seem to give much of a damn about anything. Although he was only about five-foot-six and of small build, he talked big enough to make up for his size. Having seen him in combat, I believed more of his tall tales than most people did, but there were still some even I couldn't swallow. One of his favorite stories—which also happened to be true—was about how General Patton was with him in the battle for Nothum and recommended him for promotion to first lieutenant right there while the battle was going on.

Harris and I took one fork to the left that ended up at a dead end after about a quarter-mile. We had to turn around and go back. As we passed the troops who had bunched up behind us I heard some of my men remarking jokingly, "There's Lt. Otts goofing up again!" We laughed with them and shouted back that the walk would do them good.

Just before daylight we made contact with the 1st Battalion and halted for a couple of hours outside a small town. Around mid-morning George Company climbed aboard the tanks and the other companies loaded on trucks and we set out following the 1st Battalion. After riding several miles we came to a valley, where we spent most of the day trying to keep warm over scattered campfires.

I never drank much coffee at home, but every time I had a chance overseas I would make a cup just to have something inside me. The breakfast K rations contained a packet of Nescafe and three lumps of sugar. We always carried coffee packets and sugar in our pockets and bartered them among ourselves. Some of the K rations had powdered lemonade or orange juice in the breakfast ration. Some people really liked the stuff, but I couldn't stand it.

Whenever they were available we were issued small cans of Sterno. They gave off a lot of heat with no smoke and very little flame and were excellent for use at the front, especially at night. We were also issued heat tablets, but they smoked a lot and made a big flame. The K ration boxes were covered with a thick coat of paraffin and they would burn long enough to heat a cup of coffee.

Late in the afternoon we moved on up to the edge of Eselborn and dug in—in a frozen field, which turned out to be the hardest digging I had experienced. We insulated the bottoms of our foxholes with hay from nearby stacks.

My cough and cold were worse than ever, so I went into Eselborn to the aid station. It was dark as pitch and I did a lot of stumbling through doorways and down dark stairs before I found the aid station. Captain Streepy, the medical officer, gave me some cough syrup that tasted like rum and was really good. It must have contained a good bit of alcohol. To top it off, the medical administrative officer then gave me a shot out of a bottle of rum he always carried.

Jack Hargrove and Charles Walter returned from the hospital that night. On the 29th Jack was given command of the company and Captain Goldsmith was transferred to the 3rd Battalion to replace their executive officer, who had been killed the day before. I was really glad to see Jack and Walt come back, especially since we needed officers so badly, Ed Germain and I being the only ones left at this point.

Jan. 25, 1945. G Company moves on to Clervaux.

EGGER In the morning George Company moved several miles from Eselborn to a wooded area. Later in the day we walked to the town of Clervaux, but the 101st Regiment was taking the town and didn't need our help so we went back to the woods.

Packer went back with frostbite today.*

Our winter footwear, which consisted of snow pacs with felt liners, arrived today, only two months late. Proper foot gear would have prevented many of the frostbite and trench foot casualties. The pacs were about ten inches high, with the sole and lower part of thick rubber and the uppers made of leather. A removable felt liner kept the feet warm. I

---

*Pvt. Harley Packer was listed as "slightly injured" near Eselborn on Jan. 25 and hospitalized but returned to duty on Feb. 26.

carried a spare pair of liners and alternated them every day in order to have a dry pair. Since I was just a dogface I never knew why we hadn't been given snow pacs earlier. It was probably just another miscalculation by some brass hat that the poor infantrymen had to pay for.

I received a letter from my sister, Bonnie, in which she announced that she was going to be married on January 31. I didn't know that Bonnie even had a boyfriend, so this came as a real surprise.

OTTS We marched through Eselborn and up a long hill to a fir grove beyond the town where we occupied some former German foxholes. Lt. Germain and Rocco led a patrol to investigate a monastery that was located on a cliff above Clervaux, which was being attacked by the 101st Infantry. The rest of G Company soon arrived, and we had a big time exploring around in the monastery buildings. It was truly a beautiful place, situated on the side of a steep, snow-covered mountain with a high stone wall running all around the courtyard.

One of our men was wandering through the dimly lit cellar when he came face-to-face with a German soldier. Both were scared half to death, but the German didn't have a weapon and our man recovered enough to take him prisoner. He looked half starved and told us he had been hiding there from his own troops for several days. We were looking over the buildings with the hopeful thought of staying there a few days, but some of the troops that were attacking Clervaux took over the monastery as an observation post and chased us back to our own sector.

We were to be supplied with some new boots, so we took turns going back to Eselborn to get them. Called "snow pacs," they had rubber bottoms and leather tops and were just what we had been needing all along.

Jan. 26, 1945. As G Company comes to the end of the Ardennes Campaign, Egger is given a three-day pass to Longwy.

EGGER I was the 3rd Platoon's recipient of a three-day pass to Longwy, France. There were four men from George Company and a total of twenty men from the 2nd Battalion given passes. We arrived at Longwy about noon after a cold sixty-mile ride in open trucks. I didn't know it, but this trip was to provide me with my last view of Luxembourg. I am sure it is a beautiful country if viewed under different circumstances, but if I ever go back it will be in the summer.

Giovinazzo from F Company was the only man in the group I knew.

OTTS We were still in reserve the next day when we moved down through the valley town of Clervaux and up the steep mountain beyond to the village of Reuler on the top. After we deployed along the mountain top, we dug in to await further orders. After a couple of hours I went into town to look up Jack and find out what the story was.

It turned out that this was the end of the chase. The forward units had

---

FROM EGGER'S LETTER OF JANUARY 26

. . . I was lucky enough to get a three day pass back to a division rest center.

They issued us pacs yesterday. . . . I am afraid my feet are just about gone. They are swollen and are turning dark, too much exposure and walking. I'll have to stick it out as they won't take you [to the hospital] with bad feet. . . .

I still can't get over being back in civilization again. People at home don't realize what these little things mean to us, things that are a matter of fact at home. This will be the first time I have slept in a cot or any kind of bed for months.

---

reached the German border at the Our River, where the Ardennes offensive had been launched on December 16, and our mission of wiping out the salient had been accomplished. I was told that the 26th Division would be relieved tomorrow and would be transferred back south.

Jan. 27–31, 1945. While Egger relaxes in Longwy, the 26th Division pulls out of Luxembourg and heads south.

EGGER Upon our arrival at Longwy on the 26th we were issued clean clothes and I took a shower before lunch—my first since December 19. The food, which was well prepared and plentiful, was served family style. The rooms were steam heated and for the first time since I had left England I had a cot to sleep on. We had to answer roll call in the morning but the rest of the time was ours. There was a reading room, a room with a radio, and a barber shop in the building. The Army did some things right.

Longwy had a population of 14,000. The smokestacks and railroads indicated that it was an industrial city, as did the grime and polluted air. There were no signs the city had suffered any damage from the war.

I went to town one day to look the city over and to buy a pocket knife. The remainder of the time I was content to rest, read, listen to music, write fourteen letters, and shower as often as I wanted. I remember that when I awoke the first morning it took some time for me to realize I was not at the front. I had trouble sitting still very long to read. Listening to the music was the most relaxing pastime.

FROM EGGER'S LETTER OF JANUARY 28

. . . I'll give you a rough idea of what my pockets are full of: billfold, paybook, notebook, two boxes of lead, two tooth brushes, bottle of halazone [water purification] tablets, sometimes as high as eight D-bars [chocolate], three bags of cocoa, string, Bible, matches, knife, can opener, and a number of other pieces of equipment, can't hardly call it junk.

. . . We have a lot of fun despite the hardships. One has to be able to laugh over here. It's surprising how a cheerful person can help the rest of the men. They admire someone who is cheerful. I am not as sober as you probably think I am.

. . . We are living on hopes all the time, hoping we will soon get rest, that the war will end, and etc.

The 26th Division Headquarters was located in Longwy and all the hundred or so men here were from the various units of the division. The men talked quite a bit about their war experiences or told war stories, but I preferred to put the war on a back burner. That was hard to do because it had become such a big part of our lives. The man who was bunking next to me showed me his helmet, which had a bullet hole through the metal of the helmet, helmet liner, and the toilet paper in the top of the liner. It may have even removed a few hairs from his head.

I went to 328th Regimental Headquarters and found out that my promotion to staff sergeant had come through on the 28th. As a staff sergeant I was earning $125 a month and was sending all but $20 home.

Our pass was extended for three days because the division was moving south out of Luxembourg to Germany, so trucks were not available to come after us. I did not care if they ever remembered us.

The blisters on my feet had healed long ago but my feet still itched, were discolored and swollen. Other than that I was in good shape.

Ice cream was served one day, my first since September 17. Pancakes with syrup and cereal with milk were served regularly for breakfast.

I felt fortunate to have been here so long, but I didn't look forward to going back to the front.

FROM EGGER'S LETTER OF FEBRUARY 1

. . . I have had a good rest here, but the other fellows have had to keep pushing and I know when I left I was so worn out that I didn't know if I could keep going or not.[5] I don't care what they say but the infantry gets all the dirty work and the least praise or appreciation. The Air Corps gets a rotation after so many missions, but the infantryman keeps on going as long as he can last. . . .

OTTS   The relieving unit came up on the 27th, and because we were the reserve battalion we were the first to leave. We climbed back down the mountain, walked through Clervaux, and went back up the long road to Eselborn. Everyone was in high spirits; we didn't know where we were going but didn't think it could possibly be as bad as where we had been.

We loaded on trucks and rode back to Derenbach, where we spent the night. A new officer, lst Lt. Oglesby [pseudonym], had joined us on the 26th, and today we picked up several EM replacements in Derenbach who had to be assigned to the different platoons. Some of them were T/4s and T/5s who were allowed to keep their rank until they had had a chance to try out for squad leader or assistant squad leader or a job that their rank called for.

We had a hot meal and a few hours rest before boarding trucks again and heading south in the early morning of the 28th.

AFTER ACTION SUMMARY   The Battle of the Bulge was over. On January 14 Hitler had finally acceded to the pleas of his generals and allowed the remaining German forces to withdraw from the salient, though there had still remained the problem of extracting them before the converging American attacks could cut them off completely. By means of skillful defensive tactics the German commanders had somehow managed to accomplish this difficult feat. Thus when Egger and his comrades crossed the tiny Wiltz River unopposed, it was because the enemy had already ceded the victory in the Ardennes to the Americans and was by that time concentrating on getting what remained of his forces back across the Our River and into defensive positions in the West Wall (Siegfried Line).

The final week of the campaign, from January 22–28, was mostly in the nature of a mop-up operation. By January 26, the day Bruce Egger departed for a three-day leave in Longwy, France, forward elements of the 26th Division had reached the German border at the Our River, where the Ardennes Offensive had been launched on December 16.

The only laurels gathered on either side belonged to the opposing fighting men, Americans and Germans. The entire Ardennes operation had been a hare-brained scheme on Hitler's part, and only the skill of the German officer corps and the superior fighting qualities of the individual German soldier allowed it to achieve the degree of success it did. On the other side of the line, the American troops surprised the Germans with the tenacity of their defense, particularly at various key crossroads in the early stages of the campaign; with their endurance in almost impossible weather conditions; and with their dogged, if not always enthusiastic, determination on the attack.

Few laurels were due the American commanders. The Third Army's achievement in shifting three divisions out of Lorraine and getting them to the southern flank of the Bulge in such a short time was a notable one, but in the combat operations that followed nobody, not even the famed Patton, showed to distinction. The official Army history of this phase of the campaign notes that

> To the Germans, American tactics appeared to consist of a series of quickly shifting attacks that probed for weak spots. . . . the Germans deemed [their adversary] slow in following up retrograde movements but doggedly determined. A constant nibbling away at German positions forced German commanders to weaken one spot to shore up another, only to see a new penetration develop elsewhere. What saved them in a number of instances, the Germans believed, was an American tendency to stop at a given objective rather than to exploit an advantage fully and quickly.[6]

The losses on both sides had been heavy. During the entire campaign, from December 16 through January 28, the Americans had suffered some 81,000 battle casualties, including more than 6,000 who were killed or died of their wounds and as many missing or captured. Estimates of enemy losses run from about an equal number as the Americans to somewhat over 100,000, but the Germans had managed to save most of their arms and equipment.

With the Ardennes completely cleared of the enemy, the Allies were determined to continue on the offensive, attempting to achieve a decisive penetration of the West Wall. Montgomery's 21st Army Group, bolstered by Simpson's Ninth U.S. Army, was to make a major drive to the Rhine north of the Ruhr industrial area while the First and Third American Armies were to drive through the rugged Eifel—the German extension of the Ardennes—to reach the Rhine south of the Ruhr. The 26th Division was to play no part in this operation, however. On January 25 the Yankee Division was notified that it was being transferred to XX Corps in northeastern France, where it would participate in a renewed assault into the Saar Basin. On the morning of January 28, while Bruce Egger was still on leave in Longwy, the division began its move by truck to its new assignment.[7] [P.R.]

6 The Saarlautern Interlude
January 28–March 5, 1945

OPERATIONAL BACKGROUND   At the conclusion of the Ardennes campaign the Third Army was stretched along a front of nearly a hundred miles, from the vicinity of St. Vith, Belgium, to Saarlautern, Germany (see Map 6). In the north, with hardly a pause, the trio of Third Army corps that had participated in clearing the Bulge pressed on across the Our River into the rugged Eifel region of Germany, between the borders of Belgium/Luxembourg and the Rhine River. Significant gains were registered during February in the southern half of that sector, where, operating over some of the most forbidding terrain on the Western Front, VIII and XII Corps punched through the West Wall and some twenty-five miles beyond.

On the extreme right flank of the Third Army sector, life was considerably quieter, however. The American response to the crisis in the Ardennes in late December had shifted the center of gravity of Patton's army well to the north, with XX Corps left to conduct a holding operation on the southern end of the line. This stretched along the west bank of the northeasterly-flowing Moselle River to roughly the southern border of Luxembourg. Then the line dog-legged eastward for a few miles until it reached the Saar River, which it followed south to just below the city of Saarlautern, where the Seventh U.S. Army zone began.

The Saar River itself represented an imposing obstacle, the more so since the strongest fortifications of the entire West Wall lay along its east bank. At this time the American forces' lone bridgehead over the Saar, and toehold in the West Wall, was immediately east of Saarlautern. This lodgment had been achieved at considerable cost by the 95th Division in mid-December, just before operations on that front had been suspended to respond to the German assault into the Ardennes. Saarlautern itself, which lay on the west bank of the river, had posed no difficulty. But the transpontine suburbs of Saarlouis-Roden, Fraulautern, and Ensdorf were bristling with pillboxes and fortified bunkers, 126 of which the 95th Division had managed to reduce in bloody assaults.

General Patton had been concerned to hold on to this dearly bought bridgehead after that sector of the front had gone inactive following the shift of attention northward. After a brief rest, the 95th Division had been returned to maintain an active defense of this vital toehold in the West Wall. There it remained until relieved by the 26th Division on January 29, 1945.[1] [P.R.]

Jan. 28–Feb. 4, 1945. The 26th Division is transferred to Saarlautern, where Egger joins them in the cellars of suburban Fraulautern.

OTTS We loaded on trucks before daylight on the 28th and traveled eighty miles to the village of Berviler, France, arriving late in the afternoon. Some of my platoon were already there and had our house picked out. Everyone had a wonderful glow from just being away from the continuous shelling and in a warm building.

The next afternoon, January 29, we loaded on trucks and drove into the heart of the city of Saarlautern, where we detrucked and went into buildings in order not to be seen in the streets by the German observers in the hills to the north. According to the 2nd Battalion history, *Handcar White* [p. 47], Saarlautern had been a city of 30,000 before the war but was now practically deserted. Across the Saar River, which looped around the north side of the city, were several suburbs (see Map 7). The steep hill beyond bristled with pillboxes whose guns commanded the entire area, keeping up a steady fire on any American troops spotted on the roads and bridges or in the buildings. This was one of the most formidable sections of the West Wall.

We stayed in the buildings until after dark then marched through the snowy streets and across the bridge over the Saar River. Beyond the bridge was an open area for about a quarter-mile where any movement drew small arms and mortar fire from the pillboxes in the hills. This sector always had to be crossed at night and at high speed, which was not easy for foot soldiers carrying bedrolls and equipment. Our destination was the battered suburban town of Fraulautern, where we were met by guides from the unit we were relieving.

In Fraulautern we went through three factory buildings on our way to my CP. The night was very dark and the paths through the wreckage were narrow. We had to hold on to the person in front of us and move slowly. The last building was a warehouse that was heaped with pots and pans with only a narrow path in between. This was alongside a railroad track, across which we made a quick dash after the guide told us the Germans had a machine gun that raked the area when there was any noise. Just beyond the tracks was a building that was to be my

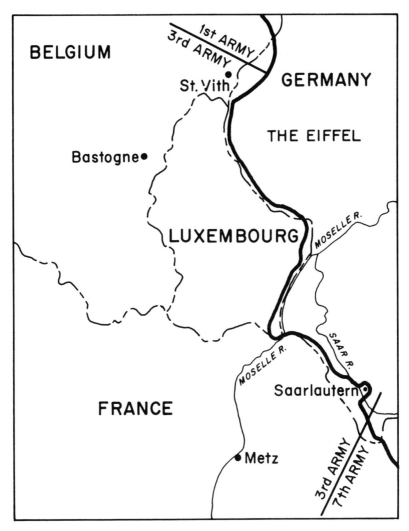

Map 6. Third Army Front on February 1, 1945

platoon CP. The two upper stories were in shambles with no roof, holes in the walls, ruined furniture, and trash and wreckage everywhere. We lived in the cellar, which was about ten by twelve feet and dark twenty-four hours a day.

I kept three men besides my headquarters group with me and sent about five men to each of the posts, which were necessarily in the upper stories of buildings with sleeping quarters in cellars, if available. The Germans were in buildings adjacent to and just across the street from

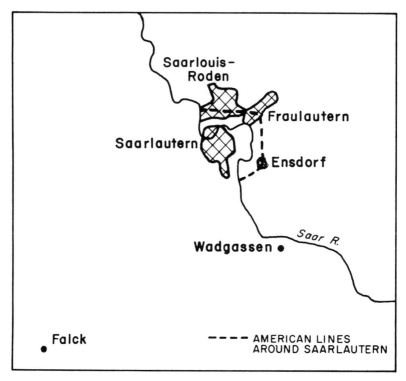

Map 7. Saarlautern and Environs

some of our positions. There were frequent exchanges of rifle fire and
hand grenades. We could leave the Platoon CP in the daylight without
too great a risk by dashing across the railroad tracks and running across
any other open space, but the men in the observation posts could come
out only at night. They couldn't even stick their heads outside in the
daytime.

We spent most of the first day cleaning up our CP. We had old mattresses across one side of the floor, a table, four chairs, and a stove.
Light was supplied by candles made from C-ration cans with wax from
a local wax factory and a tent rope for a wick and also from gasoline
bottle-lamps. They gave a fairly good light, but a lot of smoke, too. The
ceiling was black with soot.

All day and all night bursts of automatic weapons fire from the pillboxes in the hills and the enemy-held buildings in town raked the
streets and the positions we held, while we answered them tit for tat
with our .30 caliber machine guns and BARs. Mortars were used a lot
by both sides until we had to cut back to a few rounds a day because of

shell rationing. Since we couldn't expose ourselves during the day, all the water, rations, and mail had to be brought up at night. The paths to the various posts wound through narrow hallways and alleys and through windows and "mouseholes," as we called the access holes we sometimes blasted in a wall with a bazooka shell or a dynamite charge.

The phone lines were always getting blown out or cut and having to be repaired or new ones strung. Communication with the other posts was vital since we could not see them and they could be attacked without our knowing it except for the phones. We usually repaired lines at night, but sometimes it was necessary to get volunteers to string a new line in the daytime with enemy bullets splattering all around them. Gilluly and Seeney both pulled that detail.

We were eating ten-in-one rations, which were much better than the usual C or K rations. There was enough in one box for ten men for one day. But the real attraction was that they contained breakfast food, bacon, canned milk, jelly, and several other items we didn't get in the other rations. Also, our cellar was full of potatoes, and Lamb, our medic, cooked us some pretty good meals.

There was a large brewery in Saarlautern, and we kept two or three kegs of beer in the Company CP all the time—carrying it out to the platoon CPs in five-gallon water cans and then to the OPs in canteens. It was rather weak and flat but better than the water. We spent several hours each day drinking beer and playing poker.

The 3rd Platoon had a big barrel of wine in their CP, and when I paid them a visit one night I brought back a couple of bottles for my men. The wine parties ceased after Jack Hargrove, who was now the CO, visited the platoon one day and found most of the men tight. He relieved the platoon sergeant of his command and poured out the wine.

Our new lieutenant, Oglesby, accidently shot himself in the foot one night so we were back down to four officers again.*

There were no inside toilets in the buildings. Since we couldn't venture outside during the day, we just used one of the upstairs rooms for a toilet, moving to another room when the first became full or smelled too bad. The frozen foxholes had been awful, but at least they were clean. Here we were always tracking some filth into the cellars and all over our blankets and mattresses.

The candles and lamps smoked the cellars up so much that after a few days we were black all over. The soot got in our throats and lungs and

---

*Lt. Clyde Oglesby was shown on the G Company morning report for Feb. 2 as "slightly wounded" (non-battle) and hospitalized.

we were continually coughing and spitting it up. Three months after we left the area I was still spitting up black filth.

At night every noise called for a shot. Our men were trigger-happy in the dark, and many an alley cat drew our fire. Usually at dawn the Heinies would stage a real or mock attack and everyone would fire like hell. Since our OPs and the German OPs were so close together, the men would frequently pay visits to each other, leaving a hand grenade as a calling card but not stopping to chat. This kept the men from getting bored. We had our cellar fixed with baffle-plates inside the doors to stop the grenades, and surprisingly few men were wounded.

We were relieved by George Company of the 104th Regiment around 2000 on February 4. It proved to be a very exciting night. Tommy Thompson and I went back to the Company CP to lead the relieving platoon up. It was one of the darkest nights I had ever seen, and the new men kept getting separated and stumbling over machinery and junk. We finally reached the warehouse that was heaped with pots and pans. I made it through, exited through the hole in the wall, and raced across the tracks, breathing a sigh of relief to be safely on the other side, when I heard the loudest, most nerve-shattering clatter you can imagine. It turned out that the last squad had become separated from the others and were floundering around among the pots and pans. I had to rush back across the tracks and direct them out of there, but for some reason the Heinies didn't open fire. They saved that for when my men were going back after being relieved, creeping along as quiet as commandos, when the Germans began spraying the place with machine gun fire. Fortunately, no one was wounded.

The only casualty we suffered during the change-over came when a machine gun crew from the 104th Regiment fired on the men in one of our posts across the street as they were being relieved. S/Sgt. Seeney pushed everyone else down but in the process a round raked him across the lower chest and arm. Fortunately, it was only a flesh wound and he was able to walk to the Platoon CP. I had been detailed to stay for twenty-four hours to help the new company commander get oriented. The next morning we sent for a stretcher and four of us carried Seeney back to the battalion aid station.*

EGGER On February 1, thirty GIs from the 328th Regiment crowded on a 2½-ton truck for a sixty-five mile ride to Saarlautern, Germany. We didn't make it all the way in one day and the group from the 2nd Bat-

---

*S/Sgt. David Seeney returned to duty with G Company on May 16, 1945.

talion spent the night with Service Company in Buris, Germany. We were transported to our units in Saarlautern the next day.

I stayed with our kitchen until late afternoon when Junior Servoss, one of the G Company jeep drivers, took me across the bridge to the Company CP. Once over the bridge we had to race at full speed across the five-hundred yards of open area. Troops could not travel to Fox and George Company positions among the scattered buildings at the fringes of town in the daytime, so I remained at the command post until dark. The 3rd Squad was staying at the 3rd Platoon CP, which was located in the cellar of what had been a dance hall/tavern or a beer hall. All the buildings I had seen had been damaged by bombs or artillery; very little remained of the upper stories of any of them.

Seeing the familiar faces of my squad made me feel better about returning. While I was gone a number of replacements had joined the company, which was now close to full strength. G Company had been pulled off the line up north on January 27 and had been here since the 29th. There had been no casualties during my absence.

Except for the close confinement, the living conditions were good. Our lighting in the cellars was homemade candles in C-ration cans, which didn't provide much illumination. Our ten-in-one rations we were provided were supplemented by whatever canned food or vegetables we could find in the cellars. Stoddard, Pearcy, and LeCrone, our best providers, were missed. The platoon had a coal stove and fuel for cooking and heating, and we had mattresses to sleep on.

The nine replacements for the 3rd Platoon had not been assigned to squads yet and were staying at the Platoon CP with the 3rd squad. There had been ten to begin with but Lt. Clyde Oglesby, who was to have been our platoon leader, had shot himself in the foot with a carbine while outside relieving himself. Therein lies a tale.

Lee Allen told me that when the platoon arrived here there was a full barrel of wine in the cellar. Pete Ruffin, who had stayed drunk during the five days the wine lasted, was just now beginning to sober up. It was a large barrel that was already empty when I arrived, so I am sure Pete had help from the rest of the company. He had been temporarily relieved of his command until he recovered, and Gormley, the platoon guide, was acting platoon sergeant. After two days of observing Fraulautern, Pete Ruffin, and the platoon, Lt. Oglesby evidently decided he preferred not to lead this unit into battle.

I went upstairs and looked around but didn't venture into the streets or yards as there were snipers watching our position. The slight cover of snow melted today exposing the bodies of several dead enemy soldiers.

Allen and I went to the attic to get a good view of the city and surrounding area. There were a few patches of roof remaining to provide protection from snipers. We watched the German sector for an hour with our rifles ready but none of the enemy appeared. Smoke could be seen coming from the ruins of the houses in the area we were observing. I decided that it took more patience than I had to be a sniper, and besides that the flimsy roof didn't provide any protection from mortars.

A strong wind blew over the stove pipe, which exited from a cellar window. Two replacements, Em Gazda and Tony Catanese, righted it despite harassment from snipers.

Allen found some fresh potatoes in the cellar and we had them with our rations. They were a real treat after the dehydrated potatoes our kitchen served. I had not had the real thing since leaving the States.

The platoon sent a detail to the Company CP every night for rations and water. Water was in such short supply we were taking it from a nearby canal and treating it with halazone tablets.

Shortly after dark on February 4, Allen and I walked to the 1st Squad positions, which were about a block away, to pick up a .50 caliber machine gun. As we neared our quarters on the return trip a shot rang out and a bullet whistled overhead. The flash from the muzzle blast momentarily lit up the narrow street and the sound of the report reverberating from the walled streets sounded like a mortar shell had exploded on top of us. We hit the deck and shouted our identity to the sentry, a replacement named Bob Gelinas. He claimed he had challenged us and shot when there was no reply, but we sure hadn't heard anything.

The 104th Regiment relieved us at about 2000 on that night and we quickly crossed the bridge to Saarlautern. Trucks then took us twelve miles to Falck, France—a rest and training area.

Feb. 5–12, 1945. The 2nd Battalion enjoys a rest at Falck, France.

EGGER The 2nd and 3rd Platoons occupied the same house in Falck. This made it pretty crowded, so my squad moved to the basement, cleaned it, covered the sleeping area with straw, and set up a stove.

One of the first tasks was to get the replacements assigned to squads. The 3rd Squad got Eugene Holt, Ellis England, and Tony Catanese. Holt was a national guardsman who had spent time in the South Pacific. England, a logger from Kelso, Washington, had served in Alaska. Catanese was the third man in the squad from Brooklyn. Robert Gelinas, Reginald Drew, Barron Lintz, and Delbert Livermore were 1st Squad replacements. Emelion Gazda and John Marron went to the 2nd Squad. There were thirty-six men in the platoon.

While I was on leave Captain Goldsmith had transferred to Headquarters Company, 3rd Battalion, and Lt. Hargrove, who had returned from the hospital about the same time, was acting CO. Lt. Walter had also come back from the medics and was leader of the 1st Platoon. Lt. Lee Otts had the 2nd Platoon and Lt. Germain was in charge of the 4th Platoon. S/Sgt. Rocco Clemente had replaced Germain as 1st Sergeant.

The 3rd Platoon had no leader after the abrupt departure of Oglesby, but while we were in Falck 1st Lt. William Schulze, a transferee from the 87th Division, was assigned to us. The rumor was that Schulze had been a captain but had been demoted for some reason. I never did learn if this was true. I found him to be a capable officer, but none of the squad leaders were close to him. The officers received a weekly liquor ration and he occasionally shared his with the non-coms in the platoon.

This was an area that had been contested by France and Germany for centuries, so the people here spoke both languages. George Company's kitchen had set up here and was serving three hot meals daily. Crowds of little German-speaking French kids hung around the mess lines at every meal looking for handouts. Both children and adults snatched up any cigarette butts discarded by our soldiers.

Every fourth day we hiked to a mine four miles away for a shower.* An eight-mile walk was the price of cleanliness but it was worth it; besides the walk helped keep us in shape.

The training schedule included close order drill, which did not help in combat unless it conditioned us to respond to orders, and combat experiences. Some of the sergeants promoted in the field had trouble giving close order drill, but my training at Kansas State was of benefit. Being a leader in combat was more important. Pete Ruffin could perform all the duties of a garrison non-com efficiently, but he did not provide leadership by example when we were on line.

Moores and Lundy found a place in a neighboring town, five miles from Falck, where they could buy schnapps. They would take off in the evening and be back in time for roll call the next morning. There may have been other attractions besides the liquor.

There was a theater in Falck and several American films were shown during our stay.

LeCrone, who had recently returned from the hospital, looked older since he had been wounded and had become moody and morose. Rubin, who was from Brooklyn, was Jewish and about twenty-eight

---

*According to an article in the 26th Divison newspaper, YD Grapevine (Mar. 3, 1945), Lt. Ed Germain and Cpl. Bill Frost discovered the mine director's private bath. The two gained admittance by bribing the old guard with D-bars and received "an escorted tour through endless passageways, corridors, and secret panels." This led them to a lavish bath, "with sex interest attached" in the form of "a pretty well-developed mermaid." Best of all, there was no six-minute time limit.

years old. He could be comical and entertaining but he had some rough edges that rubbed some people the wrong way. This never caused any real problem in the squad; we had to put up with each other's idiosyncrasies.

Ed Sturgis and Ralph Coolidge were transferred to the artillery. I hated to see Ed leave but was glad for his good fortune—if that was what it was. He had formed a strong attachment to the squad and platoon. We corresponded until after the war ended, and he wanted me to keep him informed about how the fellows were doing.

While we were in Falck I became better acquainted with Grieco, our medic. He was compassionate and humble, by far the best medic the 3rd Platoon had had. He checked squads every day to see if the men needed attention. He was a devout Catholic who planned to study for the priesthood after the war.

Scheufler, who had been down for a while after Tompkins was wounded, was in better spirits of late. While the company was in Falck he received a letter from Tompkins, who was still in the hospital, saying that his arm had had to be amputated.

My feet had recovered from what I considered a near case of trench foot, except that they were sensitive to the cold.

The 3rd Squad missed breakfast one morning because Frenchy, the platoon runner, forgot to wake us. In the army if you were late for breakfast you did without. Allen was really upset and he and Frenchy had a heated discussion. Then he turned on me and we had a little tiff, for which he apologized later in the day. He liked to eat so well that missing breakfast ruined his day. We learned after the war that he had a stomach ulcer, so his stomach was probably giving him fits that morning.

Tonight Scheufler returned from guard duty at the kitchen with butter and frankfurters, so we had a midnight snack. For a small man, Allen could put away the food—he ate like there would be no breakfast.

OTTS I spent the day in Fraulautern and met the other officers from our battalion at Battalion Headquarters. From there we rode in a jeep to join our battalion in a rest and training area in Falck, France, some twelve miles away. Falck was a dreary coal mining town, but it was safe and quiet. The most remarkable thing about the town was its electric lights, the first I had seen since setting foot on the continent.

A new first lieutenant had been assigned to us, Lt. William Schulze from Evanston, Illinois. Bill was tall, good looking and every inch a soldier. He had apparently been busted from captain since his mail came addressed to him in that rank, but he never spoke of it and we never asked him about it. Whatever caused him to lose his rank, I am sure it was not inefficiency or cowardice. He knew his infantry tactics and weapons better than any of us and was as daring a man as I have ever seen. He talked a lot about his wife and kid, Bea and Randy.

Falck hadn't been hurt much by the war, consequently we had nice quarters. The Company CP was in one half of a duplex apartment; the other half was occupied by civilians. All the officers stayed in the CP. We had two bedrooms upstairs and a couch downstairs. Bill and I slept in one of the bedrooms, Jack and Walt in the other, and Germain on the couch downstairs. The first night there, after I had been asleep about an hour, a battalion runner woke me up and handed me an envelope. I woke up long enough to read the orders promoting me to first lieutenant and then promptly went back to sleep.

I started out with my platoon the next day looking for the showers that were in the mines. We got lost and walked about six miles but found some other showers which served just as well. They were really nice with tile floors, plenty of hot water, and no one to tell us to stay only three minutes. We certainly needed a bath after the cellars of Fraulautern. I shaved, but left my mustache on.

I was really feeling sharp with a bath, shave, clean clothes, red-top boot socks my mother had sent me, and on my collar a silver first lieutenant's bar Jack had given me. Our bags had come up from the rear and I got my camera out and took some pictures.

A Red Cross clubmobile stopped beside our kitchen with three American girls, coffee, doughnuts, and American music on the record player. Most of the girls I saw with the clubmobiles on the continent were tall and rather large. They had to be fairly strong to drive the truck and move the heavy coffee urns around.

On February 8 I was getting ready to reconnoiter the area with the other officers of the battalion when I was informed I had received a seventy-two hour pass to go to Paris. I had been scheduled to go to our division rest camp at Longwy, France, but passed it up for this trip to Paris. I was glad to get the pass but would rather have gone when we were fighting than from a quiet rest area.

I dressed up in a suit of greens, with a brass belt buckle, a new combat jacket, and even polished my combat boots. Our supply sergeant kept a supply of cigarettes on hand just for men going on pass so I loaded my musette bag with cigarettes and D-bars (chocolate). We climbed aboard a 2½-ton truck in front of Battalion Headquarters at nine a.m. and left for Paris. Lt. Myles (Mike) Gentzkow, a Fox company platoon leader; Lt. Elmer Burke, the battalion S-2; and I were the three officers from our regiment going to Paris. Rocco Clemente,

Bruno, T/Sgt. Larry Treff, T/Sgt. Pete Ruffin, the Fox Company first sergeant, and several other enlisted men were on the truck with us.

We stopped over for the night in Reims, where we were quartered in barracks used primarily for men passing through on leave from various outfits. After a delicious meal served in a dining room with tablecloths, silverware, waiters and all, Mike, Burke, and I decided to go into Reims, which was about two miles away.

We borrowed our truck from the driver and drove into town. The three of us wandered into several cafes and bars where we listened to the music and drank wine, beer, champagne, and cognac. In one of the cafes two GIs from an antiaircraft outfit came over to our table and upon noting our combat infantryman's badges started questioning us about the infantry. Several men from their outfit had been transferred to the infantry and they were undecided about requesting a transfer. They were getting tired of the spit and polish and stiff regulations of a rear echelon outfit. We told them we wouldn't take anything for being in the infantry and that we certainly had no "spit and polish" but that we would advise them to stay where they were—they really didn't know when they were well off.

In another cafe we met some French girls who joined us for a drink and danced with us.

We left about eight o'clock the next morning and arrived in Paris at noon, where we were taken to a large building in the middle of the city to register and be assigned quarters. While we were waiting beside the trucks we noticed some men, women, and children, old and young, scrambling for cigarrette butts. Some street peddlers approached us trying to sell vulgar pictures and naked rubber dolls.

We dropped the enlisted men by their hotel and went on to the Independence Club on Concorde Square, where we were to stay. It was really a beautiful hotel. We each had a private room and bath. There was only one drawback; there was no hot water or heat in the hotel. There was no heat or hot water in most of Paris, though. The room cost $2.40 for the three nights and the meals were forty cents each. The food was wonderful and the dining room had a ten-piece orchestra playing during all the meals.

We had said all during the trip that the first thing we wanted to do upon arriving was to take a tour, because if we didn't do it right away we would never make it. We made arrangements at the desk in our hotel to take a tour the following morning and left for a visit to Pigalle. It was the most talked about section of Paris and we wanted to see it first. We rode the subway, which was really efficient and simple.

We had no sooner entered a cafe in Pigalle than we were approached by women propositioning us. It was the same in every cafe we went to. We had always heard Pigalle pronounced "Pig Alley" and it was just that. There were no night clubs open in Paris at the time and, after having a few drinks of wine and cognac in two or three bars, we decided to leave Pigalle for another section of the city.

While riding on the subway Burke became engaged in conversation with two young French girls; Mike and I were standing and didn't join in as we knew no French at all and Burke knew very little. We happened to get off at the same place and Burke asked the girls where we could find a nice place to drink and dance. They told us of an MP Officers' Club in Pigalle and said they would take us there.

The club was jammed and packed with officers of all ranks and all branches of the service, also with all types of women from army nurses to French prostitutes. We secured a table for the five of us and set about consuming copious quantities of champagne at ten dollars a bottle.

We got back to the hotel in the wee hours of the morning. Naturally, we slept through the tour we were supposed to take that morning.

I heard there was a hotel somewhere in the vicinity where nurses on leave stayed, so I asked our hotel manager. He told me it was the Hotel Normandy and gave me directions to get there. It was Sunday afternoon and they were having a tea dance at the Normandy when I arrived. I met Merle Jones, an American Red Cross girl who worked there, and we danced and talked a lot. It was wonderful to be with an American girl again.

I went back to the Independence Club in time for supper and joined Mike and Burke. After we ate we all went back to the Normandy and talked to Merle. As all the army nurses were dated up and only coffee and doughnuts were served at the bar, we soon left to tour downtown Paris. We wandered up and down the Champs Elysees, stopping in every bar and cafe. We did see the Arc de Triomphe and the Tomb of the Unknown Soldier, with its perpetual fire.

We found a cute little place on a side street called the "Pam-Pam," where they served some kind of fruit juice in a bottle labled "Pam-Pam" that made an excellent mixer for cognac. We went to our hotel early that night as we were tired and wanted to get up early the next morning. I had made a date with Merle to go shopping.

Merle had to work that next afternoon so Mike and Burke and I went back to the Hotel Normandy, determined to have dates with army nurses that night. After waiting around a while we saw three pretty girls jump off the back of a 2½-ton truck and come into the hotel. They were dressed in steel helmets, combat jackets, pants and combat boots, so we really didn't know what we were getting but made dates with them for that night. We went back to our hotel and ate supper. Afterwards we picked up our dates and went to the Casino de Paris, for which the manager of the hotel had managed to get us tickets.

The scenery and costumes, when they had any on, were beautiful; for the most part the women in the show wore only a G-string or some feathers. It was just a musical stage show featuring pretty girls and much bare flesh.

After the show was over we took the nurses to the Officers Club in Pigalle and it was even more crowded than the night before. The first people we saw were the girls we had met our first night there and they rushed over and greeted us like long lost friends. We stayed at the club till about four a.m.

We left Paris the next day at noon without having taken a tour or having seen much of historical or cultural interest. I suppose our consciences should have hurt us, since we knew that in years to come we would probably regret not having seen more. Our seventy-two hours went by like seventy-two minutes. But I don't think we were unlike the majority of American soldiers on combat passes in spending most of our time in bars and cafes and our soft beds at the hotel. We had left the living hell that was war for the front-line soldier and were going back to it. Seeing the sights just did not appeal to us as much as having a bang-up good time. We felt as though we should get all we could out of each day as tomorrow we might die.

The only unpleasant thing about our trip to Paris was seeing all the soldiers in soft jobs. Almost every man there was wearing combat boots while many of our troops had spent the whole winter in muddy, frozen leggings and GI shoes because we could not get enough combat boots.

I had not wanted to be in the infantry and had always thought of it, as most other people do, as the lowest branch in the army. But I wouldn't take anything for having been a rifle platoon leader. I don't know whether other men are as proud of their branches of the service, but I thought there was nothing as great as being an infantryman.

Feb. 13–15, 1945. G Company moves into Saarlautern.

EGGER Allen and I were both sick this morning with diarrhea and nausea. We went back to Saarlautern today by truck but didn't have to go on line. The 3rd Squad was guarding the Saar River Bridge, which was relatively good duty since we could move around without fear of snipers and constant shelling. Our quarters were in a building adjacent to the bridge. We were supplied with ten-in-one rations, which was the favorite of the combat rations, but I couldn't keep food on my stomach and didn't feel like eating.

Wiseheart and Huckabee were wounded when the bridge was shelled heavily during the night of the 13th. Huck had been with us since November 11, Wiseheart just over three weeks.*

Tom Oakley returned to duty on the 13th and remarked upon the number of people who were missing from the platoon since he had been wounded seven weeks ago. Oakley wanted to be assigned to the 3rd Squad, so I went to the Platoon CP to clear it with Lt. Schulze, who agreed. While I was there I met Captain Seeley of Fox Company, who was visiting Schulze. Seeley had been praised for his bravery and leadership in a recent *Stars and Stripes* article about the action at Eschdorf on Christmas Day.

I spent the morning of the 15th looking through the demolished buildings near the bridge. There had been nice homes and apartments in this part of the city in addition to butcher shops, grocery stores, a movie house, a drug store, and a furniture store. The furniture and appliances were still in the dwellings, but personal possessions had been removed by the owners or by looters, who could have been German civilians or soldiers of either side. Moisture entering through the damaged roofs had stained the interiors of the buildings and damaged the furniture. What a job of rebuilding the inhabitants faced when they returned! And this was only one of hundreds of damaged cities in the country. Collectively I did not feel sorry for the German people, for now they knew how it had been for the countries overrun by Germany.

I took some canned fruit and dill pickles I found in a butcher shop and helped Allen move the bed springs and mattress he found in a furniture store to our quarters. We only used them one night but no doubt successive relieving forces enjoyed them after us.

Allen had recovered from his stomach disorder but it was still bothering me. Food didn't appeal to me but I craved salt, so I ate the jar of dill pickles and drank the brine. Grieco took me to the aid station, where the medic gave me some pills.

OTTS After again spending a night at Reims on the way back from Paris, on the afternoon of the 14th I rejoined the company, which had moved into Saarlautern the day before. The buildings we occupied there had suffered little damage and were quite comfortable.

Everyone was eager to hear about my trip to Paris and quite a few were glad to see that I had survived the "Battle of Pigalle," as I had borrowed money from them to make the trip. No one was surprised

---

*Neither Pfc. Jesse Wiseheart nor Pfc. Henry Huckabee ever returned to G Company.

when I told them that Bruno had missed the truck back. He showed up about a week later and we busted him to private for a week or so, then made him a staff sergeant again.

Feb. 16, 1945. G Company moves across the river into Saarlouis-Roden.

EGGER We learned that tonight we would be moving into Saarlouis-Roden, a suburb of Saarlautern, to help the 1st Battalion. According to *Handcar White* [p. 48], the plan was to attack in the morning to clear the fringes of the town so permanent defensive positions could be set up where better fields of fire were available. It was deemed necessary to hold the bridgehead here and better defenses had to be prepared against expected counterattacks in this area. The more Germans we could tie down in this diversionary attack the fewer would be used against the main XX Corps effort further northwest up the river.* I was not told all this at the time, just that we were going to attack.

Troops from the 104th Regiment relieved us in the early afternoon. A sergeant from the relieving force asked me if I was sick and told me that my face and eyeballs were yellow, which, along with the dark orange color of my urine, were indicators of yellow jaundice. He recommended that I go to the medics. The truth was, I was feeling lousy; it was an effort to keep going. But I decided to stick it out until after the attack rather than go through a hassle at the aid station, which was usually crowded whenever the troops knew that an attack was scheduled. Those suffering from such timely infirmities were naturally suspected of being malingerers. Besides, I had been vocally critical of the men who went to the medics just before an attack.

The 3rd Squad had left Falck three days ago with twelve men but now we were down to nine. Wiseheart had been wounded, Scheufler had taken sick on the 14th, and England had run the tip of a bayonet into the corner of his eye today.

The platoon assembled in a building near the bridge to wait until dark before we moved up. The 3rd Platoon was split and was to be used in reserve. My squad was assigned to the 1st Platoon under Lt. Walter. After dark we moved across the bridge, turned left past the marshlands and stopped in a building near the 2nd Battalion Hq. I noticed that one of the officers at the headquarters was drunk and hoped he had nothing to do with planning or directing tomorrow's activities.

About 2400 we moved to a building near a badly damaged church.

---

*The 10th Armored and 94th Divisions were then engaged in clearing the Saar-Moselle Triangle. This operation will be discussed in Chapter 7.

This was a hot spot; mortars and 88s were landing all around us and we could hear burp guns and machine guns. It was difficult to tell where enemy territory began, as it sounded like they had us surrounded. A shell landed outside our building, wounding two men.

OTTS   We were being sent across the river tonight to Saarlouis-Roden to help the 1st Battalion clear the fringes of the town the next morning. I went over there with the advance party to locate our positions. As we were taking over Charlie Company's positions I inquired anxiously about Law Lamar. I was told that he had been wounded a few days before. He had been sitting in a chair in the doorway to his CP (the same one I took over) when a mortar shell landed in the street and some of the fragments hit him in the forehead. I was very distressed to hear this but his men assured me that he would be all right.

The rest of the battalion came over later that night and George Company went into forward positions comprising a group of buildings clustered around a battered church on a corner. The church was occupied by the 1st Platoon, with my platoon on the right flank. Baker Company of the 1st Battalion was to our right rear. We settled in as best we could, waiting for the attack the next morning.

Feb. 17, 1945.   George and Fox Companies engage in vicious house-to-house fighting in Saarlouis-Roden.

EGGER   Just before daylight the 1st Platoon moved north to the house on the street corner across from the church (see Map 8). I was told to follow with my squad in twenty minutes. I sent Stribling with the 1st Platoon so he could come back and guide the squad. He came back all right but was so scared and flustered he couldn't find his way forward again. I should have known better than to entrust him with the simplest responsibility. We followed the communication wire and had no problem.

The 1st Platoon was to cross the street, turn right, and proceed east through the demolished buildings down the street parallel to the church. F Company was to move straight ahead (north) on both sides of the street and on the street west of Schul Strasse. Machine guns were up in the church with the 2nd Platoon. The 1st and 2nd Squads were behind the church and the 1st Battalion held positions to the right rear of George Company. My squad was to wait at the corner to be used as the 1st Platoon saw fit.

A short artillery barrage preceded the attack and our mortars lobbed shells into the houses just in front of the attacking forces. The 1st Pla-

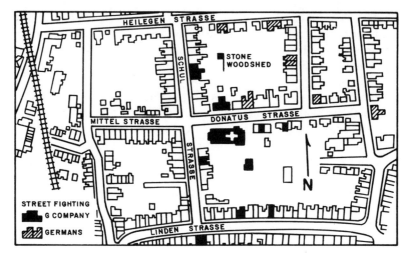

Map 8. Area of House-to-House Fighting in Saarlouis-Roden

toon and F Company were using explosives to break through the connecting walls of the houses because the big open courtyard inside the block was exposed to fire from the Germans and all the streets were raked by automatic weapons fire from the pillboxes on the hill to the north. Fox Company moved a block to the next cross street (Heilegen Strasse) before running into heavy resistance. The advance by our 1st Platoon was limited to half a block because of the Schu mines and booby traps scattered throughout the houses and the heavy fire from fortified machine gun nests.

Four men from the 1st Platoon whose feet had been injured by exploding Schu mines limped and hobbled back to our position to wait for jeep transportation to the aid station. A kid from F Company, who had been blinded by dirt from an exploding shell that killed his two companions, had been left here to wait to be evacuated. The dirt covering his face was furrowed with tears seeping from tortured eyes. I could imagine what was running through his mind.

We waited on the corner until 1600 when the 3rd Platoon was assembled to move across the street and up behind F Company to protect their right rear from Germans who could move across the block. My squad's dash across the street alerted the Germans, who began spraying the intersection with machine-gun fire. We quickly moved up through the houses until we made contact with Fox Company. My squad then moved back to the middle of the block and took positions in a stone woodshed in the courtyard (see Map 8). We took cover behind a stone wall that extended north and south on the east side of the shed. It took an hour for the rest of the platoon to cross the street, a few men at a time at irregular intervals. The 1st and 2nd Squads occupied the basement of the house southwest of the shed.

Shortly after dark a party of five or six Germans tried to slip in between F Company and our position but they were driven off with small arms fire and phosphorous grenades. The Germans screamed from the burning fragments of phosphorous, which stick to the clothing or body and burn, burn, burn.

After the attack German mortars and artillery started to drop around the woodshed, which did not provide much protection. I went to Lt. Schulze and suggested that we leave a machine gun and two riflemen behind the four-foot-high wall near the woodshed and have the rest of the squad join the platoon. He agreed, but before I could return a shell landed at the entrance of the woodshed, wounding Allen and the machine gunner in the legs. We carried them to the cellar and Grieco dressed their wounds. Neither man was badly hurt, and it was not long before Allen was asking for something to eat.*

Our jeeps didn't dare venture beyond the corner by the church, nor did the troops try to cross the street in that area except at night, so we weren't able to get Allen and the machine gunner across the intersection and to the aid station until shortly after midnight. By that time the fighting had died down and we remained holed up in the cellar of our house half-a-block north of the church.

We learned from the stretcher bearers that Captain Seeley of F Company had been killed shortly after dark when he stepped on a mine.

OTTS A brief artillery bombardment at 0930 signalled the beginning of the attack. Fox and George Companies both advanced north from the church in what turned out to be the most grinding type of house-to-house fighting. Machine gun fire swept the streets, mortars pounded the buildings, and desperate riflemen let fly with hand grenades right and left. Fox Company managed to clear both sides of the street for a block north of the church intersection, but our 1st Platoon had been stymied in its attempt to advance eastward down the street that ran by the church.

Although my platoon was in reserve and we didn't move out of our positions, we lost one man killed and five wounded. My Platoon CP was on the back side of the block and there was one squad in a building on the front side of the block on the same street as the church. The path to

*Sgt. Lee Allen was listed as slightly wounded in action on Feb. 17. He returned to duty with G Company on June 5, 1945.

this building had to be traveled fast to prevent being hit by sniper fire or a mortar shell. Beside the path was a dead American soldier; the enemy had slipped in one night, booby-trapped his body, and left a field of Schu mines all around him, making it impossible to remove the corpse.

This detached squad called over the sound-powered phone for a medic so I sent Lamb and a rifleman. They came back in a few minutes, bringing Pfc. Charles Nunley, who had been wounded by a mortar shell. The fragment had broken his arm but it wasn't too bad a wound, though he was suffering a lot from shock. Bobby Phipps had been wounded by the same shell and Nunley asked Lamb how Bobby was. Lamb replied that he would be all right, but that he was waiting for things to quiet down before he moved him. At the same time Lamb wrote a note on a piece of paper and passed it to me. I unfolded it and read, "Phipps is dead."* Bobby and Nunley were both from Tennessee and had been friends as children. I felt that I had known Bobby better than any other man I had lost and Lamb's note really hit me hard.

That afternoon we moved up and took over the 1st Platoon's positions, manning an OP in the battered church and in the one house we held on the corner across the street. The church was in shambles. The roof was gone and there were great gaping holes in the sides. There was only one opening that we could get to on the side toward the enemy as the windows were about fourteen feet above the floor. The street in front was filled with Schu mines and booby traps, but the Heinies would slip out into it and toss grenades into the church. The building was so large and so strewn with rubble that we could always hit the prone and escape being wounded.

Fox Company caught hell that day and night, fighting off a number of desperate German counter-attacks, including one with tank support. The Jerries were throwing everything they had at them to get back the block north of the church that F Company had taken in the morning. I heard later that Mike Gentzkow and some of his men had had a brick wall collapse on them when the Germans fired a panzerfaust into their building. Mike suffered head wounds and had to be evacuated. With old friends like Mike and Lamar Law both getting it in one week, I felt like I was living on borrowed time. Later that evening Captain Seeley of Fox Company was killed when he stepped on a Schu mine.

Feb. 18–19, 1945. G Company hangs onto its positions in Saarlouis-Roden.

---

*Pfc. Bobby Phipps is listed as killed in action on Feb. 17, 1945. Pfc. Charles Nunley recovered from his wound and returned to G Company on May 16, 1945.

EGGER Stribling had been missing since yesterday afternoon; evidently he never crossed the street with the platoon and just faded away during the excitement.

The Germans had left a machine gun in the open about sixty feet northwest of the wall near the woodshed. Just as I was preparing to go after it I received word that Lt. Schulze wanted to talk to me. While I was gone Drew of the 1st Squad went out to get it and was shot by a sniper. Grieco crawled to Drew, inspected the wound in his stomach, and crawled back for assistance. Grieco and DeSota, who was Drew's buddy, took off their helmets and, with the red cross the medics displayed on their arms, walked out and carried Drew back without drawing fire. Drew was suffering from the wound and he kept repeating, "I don't want to die." Despite the machine gun fire at the intersection he was immediately carried to the aid station.

Drew and DeSota richly deserved the Bronze Stars they got for their action that day. Evidently it was a normal day's work for a medic, since Grieco received no special recognition for his part in this episode other than the admiration of the platoon.

Scheufler, who had been hospitalized on the 14th because of illness, returned to the platoon after dark with the ration detail.

The 3rd Platoon was to attack eastward in the row of houses on the south side of Heilegen Strasse, so we moved up to the corner house to spend the night. In the early morning the Fox Company men who had been holding the house moved west across the street into the buildings occupied by the rest of their company. The 3rd Squad slept in the cellar on a coal pile. It was a decidedly lumpy bed.

On the 19th the 3rd Platoon waited all day at the corner house expecting an order to attack. A dead German soldier lay on the floor inside the front door, where a Fox Company man had shot him yesterday. He had run across the street and burst in, only to be greeted by a blast from an M-1. The room was small and the dead soldier occupied more than his share of the space. His lifeless eyes stared into all corners of the room and seemed to follow my every move. His upper uniform was soaked with dried blood from his chest wound. The face was lacking in expression except for the look of surprise his staring eyes seemed to convey. He was probably in his early thirties as there were deep lines in his dingy colored face, indicating that he may have spent the winter in smoky cellars and pillboxes.

In the afternoon we were told to start firing at the German positions and at the same time our mortars and artillery started shelling the houses occupied by the Germans. The Germans returned the fire with mortars and, for the first time, heavy artillery. The 150 mms. sounded like freight trains as they roared in on us. The enemy shelling was concentrated on the positions farthest from the houses occupied by the Germans. The 3rd Squad, being closest to the German positions, was little affected by the shelling; the other two squads didn't fare so well. The concussion of an exploding shell shook up Stan Nachman, the leader of the 1st Squad, and Gazda of the 2nd Squad and gave them splitting headaches for the rest of the day.

After dark some troops from F Company came back to the house we occupied. We moved back to the building in the middle of the block and could hardly recognize the place, it had been shelled so heavily. Six men from the 1st and 4th Platoons had been killed here today, five by artillery and one by a sniper.

OTTS I thoroughly enjoyed the next few days in Saarlouis-Roden. I had always loved to shoot any kind of gun and I spent those days doing just that. Bruno, Gilluly, and I formed a three-man harrassing force and spent our time worrying the enemy, when he wasn't worrying us. Whenever things became quiet and a little dull we would go out and raise a little hell. I fired several hundred rounds of M-1 carbine ammunition from the hole in the church wall and the debris outside. We would just sit there for long periods at a time firing into every window and door in the German-held houses on the next block to let the Heinies know we were still thinking about them.

We found several hundred rounds of bazooka ammunition in a building in our area, and since we had often wondered how much damage could be done with a continuous pounding of bazooka shells we decided to form a three-man house wrecking detail and find out. There was a building in the center of our block where the 1st Platoon had a squad and we carried several rounds up there. From a hole in one end of the cellar we had a good field of fire to three enemy-held buildings in the next block. We had previously noted a sniper in one of these buildings so we started working on it first. After a while we were getting direct hits every time. Following several well placed rounds the building began to crumble and fall. We fired a few white phosphorous rounds as fire for effect and moved to another building.

Tiring of that we tried rifle grenades and experimented with hand grenades fired with adapters from the end of rifles to get timed fire over the enemy's buildings. Anytime during the day if things were getting quiet and dull the three of us would go out and stir up some excitement with rifles, carbines, Tommy guns, pistols, bazookas and grenades. Whenever the Heinies tossed grenades in the windows of the church we would toss one back as soon as the first one exploded.

Gilluly wanted every weapon and explosive made to be on hand for his personal use. We started gathering things in case we were ordered to make a push into the next block and I just turned Gilluly loose to get what he could. We ended up with three bazookas, two flame-throwers, nineteen bangalor torpedoes, three one-pound and two forty-pound cone-shaped charges called "bee-hives," booby-traps, TNT, composition C, cases of grenades, and thousands of rounds of machine gun, rifle and carbine ammunition. There was only one thing that Gilluly didn't have that he wanted, a tank. Jack said he nagged him every time he saw him to get him a tank.*

We had all these explosives stored in the hallway above our cellar, but upon thinking what would happen if a shell set them all off we moved everything to a cement shed next door. The night after we moved them a shell tore the roof off the shed but none of our explosives were set off.

Each morning we had to check all the unoccupied buildings in our block to see if any enemy had infiltrated during the night. This was fun, as all we had to do was walk up to the stair leading into the cellar and shout, "Anyone down there? If there is, you had better come out in five seconds because a grenade is coming down." After the five seconds were up we would pull the pin and toss a grenade down the stairs. As soon as the smoke cleared we would creep cautiously down for a quick look around. We never did catch anyone in our buildings.

One of the battalion anti-tank guns was in position a block south of the church and fired at regular intervals down the street beside us at a pillbox on the far end. We could stand in our doorway and watch the 57mm shells go by. Also several times during the day a TD or tank would fire a few rounds from behind us and then drive up to the corner by the church, firing a couple of rounds while coming up, two more while turning around, and a couple more while leaving. They never stayed long enough for the enemy to get a shot at them. The last few days a new TD with a 90mm cannon instead of the usual 76mm fired down the street beside us. The muzzle blast would almost knock us off our feet if we were standing in the doorway.

As I said before, the days were fun but no one enjoyed the nights. The army used searchlights aimed at the sky to provide some light, and the artificial moonlight made the ruins of buildings appear ghostly. The shadows were very dark and everything was just too quiet. The men at

---

*Lt. Hargrove noted in his postwar scrapbook, concerning the period in Saarlouis-Roden: "I had two boys (Gilluly and Bruno) who claimed to be G Co. artillery in Saarlautern—they were firing AT grenades and bazookas indirect over the church."

the observation posts had to be rotated frequently, as their nerves could not stand the silent darkness too long. We had booby-trapped the door at the front end of the church, but there were many places where a patrol could slip in and wipe out a whole outpost.

Before coming to Saarlautern we had had only one 300 radio per company and the inter-company communication was by EE-8-A and sound-powered telephones. At Saarlautern we picked up a 300 for each platoon, tying us into the battalion network, and still had our EE-8-A's and our phones. Each OP had to check with the Platoon CP every fifteen minutes, we checked with the Company CP every half hour, and they checked with the battalion every hour or so. In the divisional and regimental headquarters network, our regimental name was "Handcar," with the three battalions "red," "white," and "blue," which made our battalion "Handcar White." This is where the title of our 2nd Battalion history comes from.

Feb. 20–21, 1945. G Company hangs on in the cellars of Saarlouis-Roden.

EGGER This morning we cleaned out the basement and found a tunnel connecting the cellars of the houses on this side of the block. We found out later that the area was honeycombed with tunnels, which may have accounted for the Germans' sudden appearance on several occasions.

The snipers really had our positions covered. If we kept low we could move to the woodshed and stone wall to the east of it, both of which were still standing despite the heavy shelling. Four men were killed yesterday by a single shell burst as they crouched behind the stone wall; and a sniper shot James White of the 4th Platoon just outside the back door. His body was carried into the first-floor room facing the street directly above the basement we occupied. We had to walk past it several times a day for a week.

I was feeling much better and regained my appetite. All symptoms had pointed to yellow jaundice, but my quick recovery was unusual. The incubation period for the virus is two to eight weeks and I became ill about two weeks after drinking the canal water. As of this writing, the medical profession has not yet discovered the dill pickle cure.

Stribling, who had been at the Company CP since the 17th, was sent back to the platoon on the 21st. We could use him on guard, but I was sure he would fold under pressure.

We were receiving a canteen of water (about a quart) a day, which was not enough to make coffee or bouillon to wash down the dry rations and crackers. I had noticed that the non-com who doled out the water to the platoon found enough for himself to heat and shave every day. I told him that we would be in sad shape if everyone shaved daily. I started to accompany the detail that went back to the Company CP each night for rations and water, and we usually managed to steal an extra five gallons of water and sometimes additional rations. I had noticed that the men at the CP were clean-shaven so I figured they could spare the water.

OTTS One night, one of the men reported a noise that sounded like digging under the church so I went over to investigate. I couldn't hear anything, but they were so positive that I called the Company CP and Jack called battalion. They sent up a couple of engineers with two forty-pound "beehive" charges. They wanted to put them on the floor, one on top of the other, and set them off to blow a hole down to meet whoever was digging. There was a lot of debris in the way, and as we didn't hear any more digging, I thought it best not to risk demolishing the church.

The next morning Jack and I decided to see what a ten pound "beehive" would do. We set one on the concrete floor of the cellar in an empty building and lit the fuse, running to safety across the street. We thought it would probably blow a hole through the floor about six inches in diameter and three or four deep. Instead, it collapsed the whole building down into the cellar, so we didn't have a chance to see what kind of a hole it had made. The walls were probably already weakened. I was certainly glad we hadn't tried the two forty-pound charges in the church if one ten-pounder did that much damage; it might have shaken down every building in the block.

While sitting around in our cellar one day, someone noticed that part of the cement wall looked a little newer than the rest. On tapping it with a rifle butt, it was discovered to be hollow. Someone found a sledge hammer and quickly knocked a hole in the bricks. The former civilian occupants of the house had dug a hole back of the cellar wall and stored all their valuables, along with preserves and other things, then cemented it back over. We then visited every house in the block, tapping on the cellar walls and digging for souvenirs. One man got a sword, another a large Nazi flag, but all I got was a few World War I medals. We only found one other cellar cache besides the one in our CP.

Feb. 22–24, 1945. G Company's ordeal in Saarlouis-Roden continues.

EGGER There were guards posted at the woodshed, behind the stone wall, and one man in the room facing the street. Other than that we were confined to the cellar. The inactivity and close quarters frayed a few nerves. LeCrone was extremely nervous and became upset if anyone made much noise for fear the Germans would hear them. Pete

Ruffin was jittery and nervous but we never saw him above ground. Gormley, the platoon guide, and the squad leaders were performing more and more of his duties while Pete spent almost all his time in the cellar.

The inactivity was apparently too much for Moores and Lundy, who crossed the street to our left and prowled through the buildings F Company had cleared. They came back with a nice looking radio, which was of no use to us and which they could not take with them. Some of the men were uneasy about pulling guard in the room with the dead man, the "stiff room" as Rubin called it. I told them it is the living you have to worry about, not the dead. Fortunately, the weather was still cold enough that there was no odor from the corpse, but it wouldn't be that way much longer.

Stribling scampered back into the cellar tonight while he was supposed to be on guard. He couldn't face the phosphorous shells the Germans were sending in. I made him go back on guard and went with him for a while. We couldn't leave the positions unattended and we all had to accept whatever the conditions were during our tour of guard duty.

An enemy machine gun in the pillbox at the end of the street fired down the street occasionally and sprayed the front of our house. One of our anti-tank guns near the church periodically wheeled into the street and fired at the pillbox, chipping a little concrete away each time. A burp gun in the pillbox would reply in what appeared to be a gesture of contempt.

Ellis England came back from the hospital on the 23rd. The bayonet scratch in the corner of his eye he had suffered a week before apparently hadn't been too bad.

A fellow from the Battalion HQ Company came up this evening to set out anti-personnel mines in front of the stone wall and woodshed. These would provide a warning and an additional weapon in case the Germans tried to move in on us at night. Before I went out with him I told him about the dead men in the area so he wouldn't be startled by them. It was evident that he was scared and not happy about his assignment and my attempts to downgrade the immediate danger did little to ease his mind. He kept hearing noises that had no meaning. He lost no time in getting the job done and didn't tarry at the Platoon CP but quickly returned to his unit. Feeling secure must have been relative. This man was fearful in a position where we felt reasonably safe, but he had ventured into the unknown from out of a situation in which he felt secure.

OTTS Suspicions were aroused at Battalion Headquarters by the fact that the Germans had been entirely too quiet the past few days, so orders came down that we were to capture a prisoner to try to find out what they were up to. Several patrols had been sent out to no good effect. Finally, on the night of the 23rd Jack told me that my platoon would have to furnish a patrol to try to take a prisoner. I picked Pfc. Albert Krause, who spoke German fluenty, Gilluly, Bruno, and a couple of other men, and we went back to the Company CP for briefing. Each man armed himself with a Tommy gun and several grenades.

The patrol set out at 0500 the morning of the 24th and went up to the barricaded back door of a building on the far side of the block in front of our position. There was a German soldier on guard at the door and Krause told him in German that they were a ration detail that was lost and to let them in or come out himself. He refused and told them to go around to the front door, which they couldn't do as they would have been exposed to all the enemy in the block on all sides. The patrol stood there in the dark for about ten minutes talking to the German, but they were unable to convince him. Finally they gave up, backed off a few yards and every man let go with a burst from his Tommy gun, and then all ran like hell for cover. Gilluly kept us laughing for an hour, telling how Krause had argued with the Heinie.

Feb. 25, 1945. The 3rd Platoon draws a suicide mission that is fortunately called off.

EGGER The 2nd Battalion Headquarters could not figure out what the Germans were up to, since the last few days and nights had been so quiet, so they ordered George Company to take a prisoner. Lt. Hargrove, our CO, decided that the 3rd Platoon would have the honor, and Lt. Schulze assigned the job to the 3rd Squad. The plan was for us to file to the woodshed, move out behind the wall, and dash north to the houses on the south side of Heilegen Strasse, take a prisoner and return. (These were the same row of houses we were going to attack on the 19th.) We were given the choice of returning the way we came or going to the corner house occupied by F Company. I voiced my objections to the plan, saying we didn't have a chance of success in broad daylight, that a night patrol would be more effective, and that if they insisted on a day patrol we should be taking the shortest route to the Germans, not the longest. I did not say so, but if the enemy soldier was no better informed than we were, the battalion would not learn much from a prisoner.

Lt. Hargrove came up in the afternoon to observe the operation and we prepared to leave. Catanese had an infection in his trigger finger so I left him behind. I appointed LeCrone assistant to replace Lee Allen and told him to bring up the rear. I figured that if there had ever been a suicidal mission this was it, but there was nothing I could do about it when people wouldn't listen to reason.* Many of the men had so little confidence in the plan that they left their billfolds with friends in other squads to mail home if they didn't survive.

Lt. Schulze was to accompany the squad as far as the woodshed. We crouched low and filed out singly and entered the back door of the shed. All the men followed except Stribling, who would not leave the house. He was a coward but he was not stupid. Just as I started out the front door of the woodshed the Germans opened up with machine guns. Stone chips and dust filled the air and bullets plowed the ground at the end of the stone wall. The tracers appeared to be coming from the sky, which indicated that the machine gun fire was coming from the pillboxes on the hill. I looked at the lieutenant without saying anything. He shook his head and called it off.† In a few minutes mortar shells began to fall around us, so we waited in the shed until dark. Moores and I stayed a while longer and fired rifle grenades at the house occupied by the Germans. They must have observed our movements and thought we were undertaking a full-scale attack. I was thankful they had not held their fire until the squad was in no-man's-land.

OTTS Since the patrol failed, battalion decided that we would have to pull a daylight attack to try to capture some prisoners. The 3rd Platoon was going to attack and we were to give them fire support. Baker Company, on our right flank, was to attack also. We were to have tank support to neutralize fire coming from a pillbox in the far corner of the block to our front. The tank officer came up and I showed him exactly where I wanted him to place his tank and which building to fire on. We were planning to cross the street behind the tank and follow the 3rd Platoon as they advanced through the buildings. Jack and Rocco went forward with the 3rd Platoon to direct the attack. Rocco was carrying the radio, even though he was now first sergeant and did not have to be up front.

The attack started at 1400 and everyone fired like madmen. We almost shot out of ammunition before time to move up. The tank came up but stopped short of where I had planned for it to stop, and instead of

---

*During the preparation of this work Bruce Egger wrote to the editor that "the Feb. 25 incident made me lose confidence in our higher command. I knew how a man condemned to die felt on Feb. 25 and all the men in the squad felt the same way."

†In a brief journal he kept, a copy of which he made available to Bruce Egger for this work, 1st Sgt. Rocco Clemente noted on this date, "Acted as radio operator in attack. German machine gun and mortars stopped us. Mission called off due to impossible routes of attack."

firing at the pillbox, fired several rounds into the ground floor of the corner building where a squad of my men was in the cellar. We couldn't cross the street, as the tank was firing across our path. I don't think I had ever been so mad at anyone before; I cursed, threw rocks, and bounced a few carbine rounds off the tank, but they paid no attention to me. Finally the tank withdrew and we were able to cross the street. We cursed all tankers and one in particular for weeks afterward.

The 3rd Platoon was stopped cold and the attack was called off. I heard that our machine gun had fired a bit wild and wounded several Baker company men as they were crossing the street to attack. It must have been true, as they weren't very friendly towards us after that.

Feb. 26, 1945. The 2nd Battalion moves back into the rest area at Falck.

EGGER It was a beautiful sunshiny day, which was wasted on us because we were confined to the cellar as usual.

A unit of the 101st Regiment relieved us after dark. I made sure to point out to one of their sergeants the location of the mines. I wondered how long the location would be passed along. Someday American forces would move beyond this point and the mines would probably remain a hazard to our grave registration units and to returning civilians.*

We walked to Saarlautern and trucks took us to Falck. Understandably, we were happy to leave Saarlouis-Roden for good.

OTTS We were to be relieved tonight and, as the day was unusually quiet Jack and Rocco came up to help Bruno, Gilluly, and me stir up a little excitement. We had a big day shooting everything we could get our hands on.† I had never been able to shoot as much as I wanted to in the States but really made up for lost time then. I fired an M-1 until my shoulder got sore and my lip was swollen. I also took some good authentic pictures, as the enemy was just across the street from where we were firing.

---

*In late May, almost three weeks after the war had ended, *Stars and Stripes* published an article headlined "Saarlautern Still a City of Peril, Where 10 a Day Die by Violence"—from mines and booby traps. The story went on to note that "there is no water in Saarlautern and no lighting system. As dusk comes to this metropolis of the dead, the living pause in their endless searching of the ruins and light fires and sit around them in the ravaged streets. . . . Only the undertaker has business in Saarlautern."

†In his journal Clemente noted at this time: "Went out with Lt. Otts, Gilluly, and Bruno. Fired rifle grenades, bazooka, rifle, fragmentation grenades at Heinies."

Feb. 27, 1945. G Company returns to Falck.

EGGER Gormley, our platoon guide, had come back early yesterday and found good quarters for the platoon. We walked to the mine today for showers.

Packer and Schmitt rejoined the squad today. Schmitt had been assigned to us at Metz, but had been in the hospital with pneumonia since January 11.

We heard today that Drew had died in the hospital but we were never sure about this; his name was not listed among the dead in the 328th Regimental History, which was written immediately after the war.*

OTTS The first day back in Falck we went to the showers to remove the cake of soot and filth. There was a very modern theater in town so we all went to a picture show.

Feb. 28, 1945. The men of G Company relax in Falck.

EGGER Moores and Lundy went to the neighboring town last night and didn't show up until this afternoon. They had made an unusual accommodation with a married couple there. In return for material considerations—I suppose cigarettes, soap, or food—and with the consent of the husband, they were sleeping with the wife. Some arrangement!

I could see now why they were five-percenters, but they had been dependable in combat. Neither Oakley nor LeCrone wanted to be assistant squad leader so I had suggested Moores, but this little escapade killed that proposal. Cpl. Hank Sosenko from the 4th Platoon, who had joined the company on January 25, ended up with the job.

OTTS We didn't do much of anything today, just took it easy. Our whiskey ration came in, one quart each of champagne and Scotch and one pint of gin for each officer. This was the first chance we had had to have an officers' party so that night we shut ourselves up in the living room and drank, played cards, and shot dice.

There were five of us—Jack, Walt, Bill, Germain, and I. We each opened a quart of champagne first and when it was gone started on the Scotch and gin. Benny, T/Sgt. Robert Streeter, and T/Sgt. Harry Cooley came in and had a round of drinks with us. About midnight

---

*For the circumstances of Drew's being wounded see Egger's entry of Feb. 18–19. Pfc. Reginald H. Drew's name later appeared on the 328th Regiment's casualty list in *The History of the 26th Yankee Division,* p. 258.

Walt went up to bed and Jack went to sleep on the couch in the living room. Bill and Germain got very playful and started throwing each other around jujitsu fashion. Every now and then they would grab me and toss me across the room. After this happened a few times, I decided it was time to go to bed so I left them and went upstairs.

Mar. 1–3, 1945. G Company continues its rest in Falck.

EGGER A training schedule similar to the one used during our previous stay in Falck was soon established. One day was spent sighting in our rifles and practicing marching fire.

I learned from a fellow in Fox Company that Giovinazzo and ten other men had been taken prisoner in Saarlouis-Roden on February 19.

Joseph Bergeron, who was wounded at Moncourt and had a brother killed there, returned from the hospital and was assigned to the 1st Squad. W. S. Thompson, who had been hospitalized with a non-battle injury in October, also rejoined the company and went to the 2nd Squad. Holt was transferred to the I&R [Intelligence and Reconnaissance] Platoon with the 2nd Battalion and Catanese was sent to the hospital because of the infection in his finger.

Pete Ruffin tried to have Stribling court-martialed for deserting in the face of the enemy at Saarlouis-Roden. Stribling didn't cross the street near the church with the platoon and he refused to go out with the squad the day we were to try to take a prisoner. None of the men, including me, would testify against Stribling, even though we had often complained of his unreliability. I think the fact that Ruffin's performance had been so poor caused the men to bow their necks when he asked them to give evidence against Stribling. Getting rid of him would make my job easier, but I didn't want to see him spend time in prison so I was glad to hear that he had been transferred to the artillery.*

Schmitt, Rubin, England, Holt, and I went with Moores and Lundy to the neighboring town where they had the arrangement with the married couple. Rubin and Schmitt must really have been bored to join us on this expedition, since they were poor walkers and usually had trouble keeping up on a march. Our two guides dropped off at the married couples' house and we went to the town bistro. Holt had developed a

---

*Although this was apparently the rumor going around G Company, there is nothing in the morning reports to substantiate it. On the contrary, on Mar. 2 Pfc. Oscar Stribling was shown as having been remanded to the 114th Medical Battalion because of sickness (non-battle). On Mar. 7 he was reported to have been sent on to the 106th Evacuation Hospital. Presumably the problem was "battle fatigue," which was the Army's all-purpose term for any nonphysical condition that made soldiers unfit for combat.

3rd PLATOON PERSONNEL BETWEEN JANUARY 20 AND MARCH 5

Platoon Leader: 2nd Lt. Germain was leader of the 3rd Platoon until 1st Lt. Hargrove returned from the hospital to duty on Jan. 27. Two days later Captain Goldsmith was transferred to 3rd Battalion HQ and Lt. Hargrove took command of G Company. Newly arrived Lt. Clyde Oglesby took over the platoon on Jan. 26 until he shot himself in the foot at Fraulautern on Feb. 2. 1st Lt. William Schulze, a transferee from the 87th Division, was given command of the platoon on Feb. 5.

Platoon Sergeant: T/Sgt. Pete Ruffin was the 3rd Platoon's sergeant during this whole period.

Platoon Guide: S/Sgt. Francis Gormley, leader of the 2nd Squad, became Platoon Guide on Jan. 20.

1st Squad	*2nd Squad*	*3rd Squad*
S/Sgt. Stan Nachman, Ldr	*Sgt. Stewart Rorer, Ldr	S/Sgt. Bruce Egger, Ldr
Sgt. Joe Treml, Asst	Pfc. Tom Montgomery, Asst	*Sgt. Lee Allen, Asst (WIA 2/17)
Pfc. Bill DeSoto	Pfc. W. C. Lundy	**Pvt. Ralph Coolidge
Pfc. Henry Huckabee (WIA 2/13)	Pfc. Tony Messina	Pfc. Alton Moores
	Pvt. Rufies Morgan	*Pfc. Solomon Rubin
		Pfc. Paul Scheufler
		Pfc. Oscar Stribling (hosp 3/2)
		**Pfc. Ed Sturgis

Replacements who joined the Platoon January 20

Pvt. Elbridge Walker   Pvt. Tony Clemens, hosp 1/26–3/3   Pvt. Jesse Wiseheart (WIA 2/13)

Pvt. Merle Ward   Pvt. Clay Williams

Replacements assigned to squads on February 5

Pvt. Reginald Drew (WIA 2/18)   Pvt. Emelion Gazda   Cpl. Tony Catanese (hosp 2/25)

Pvt. Robert Gelinas   Pvt. John Marron   Pvt. Ellis England

Pvt. Barron Lintz   †T/5 Eugene Holt

Pvt. Delbert Livermore

Men returned from hospital

Pvt. Joe Bergeron (2/28)   Pfc. Albert Evans (1/23)   Pfc. Fonrose LeCrone (2/10)

Pvt. Rene Poirier (2/14)   Pfc. Tom Oakley (2/13)

Pvt. W. S. Thompson (3/1)   Pvt. Harley Packer (2/26)

Pvt. George Schmitt (2/22)

‡Cpl. Henry Sosenko, asst 2/27

*Transferred from the 1st Squad   **Transferred to 102nd Field Artillery Battalion, 2/10

†Transferred to I&R Platoon, 2nd Bn, 2/25   ‡ Transferred from 4th Platoon, 2/27

considerable thirst during the long walk and the schnapps was strong, so he was unable to walk back to Falck. Rubin, who was our interpreter, left instructions for the bartender to wake him up so he could return to the company in time for roll call and we went back without him.

OTTS That evening we saw the World Premier of "My Reputation" with Barbara Stanwick and George Brent. There were newspaper men and photographers interviewing the men and taking pictures of the audience. There was also a USO show, the only one I had seen in the European Theater of Operations.

There were two girls living across the street from our kitchen who were always standing around watching us and hoping someone would offer them food. They were cute looking and, although rather small, said they were eighteen. That night T/Sgt. Cooley and I were talking to them and they, with Cooley's help, invited us into their parlor. Cooley, being from the Bronx, knew how to strike up acquaintances better than I did, so I just followed along. The girl I was with was named Margo, and she had already picked up a good bit of English.

We sat around for two or three hours talking to the girls and their family and drinking schnapps. Cooley had bought a bottle from one of the civilians for 500 francs ($10.00). When we first liberated a town everything was free, but it did not take many days for the French people to commercialize and start cashing in on the GIs. Ten dollars a bottle for the "white lightening" was outrageous, but we paid it.

One of the cooks had found an old motorcycle and we rode it around until it broke and wouldn't start again. I wanted to ride some more, so I tied it behind a jeep and we took off. The jeep stopped suddenly and I couldn't find the brake pedal on the motorcycle, so I ran into the back of the jeep and was thrown over the handlebars. I wasn't hurt and didn't have sense enough to quit, so we started over again. We had gone several blocks when the jeep whipped around the corner by our kitchen, popping the motorcycle around like the end of a whip. The motorcycle turned over and I was dragged several yards by the jeep with me under it. I got out with a few scratches and bruises, but decided not to try any more.

Our last night in Falck, Cooley, and I took Margo and her sister to the picture show and then stopped by their house for a while.

Mar. 4, 1945. G Company moves to a quiet sector near Saarlautern.

EGGER We hiked to the mine for a shower today. A light warm rain had fallen for the last two days and it felt like spring.

This evening we traveled nine miles to relieve L Company, 3rd Battalion, at Wadgassen, a suburb south of Saarlautern. I took Messina and Gazda from the 2nd Squad and Moores, Oakley, and Rubin while Hank Sosenko took the rest of the 3rd Squad to another outpost. Our outpost was in a house at the edge of town near the west bank of the Saar River. The Germans occupied pillboxes on the other side of the river, so we couldn't move around during the day.

OTTS   This evening our battalion went back to the Saarlautern area, but this time our positions were at Wadgassen, on the south side of town where there wasn't much activity. We moved up at night and the trucks stopped about a mile from the town. It had been raining and we had difficulty climbing the steep muddy hill to get to the town.

Wadgassen had been only slightly damaged by the war, and as there were no civilians in the town we had our choice of buildings. My platoon occupied four houses and almost every one of us had a bed. The houses and cellars were filled with jars and cans of all kinds of preserved food. There was one cellar that covered a whole block and had several small rooms with shelves full of jars and bottles.

There was no shelling or shooting and we really enjoyed ourselves eating and resting. One of the men shot a cow—he swore there was a Kraut hiding behind it—and we had a wonderful dinner in my Platoon CP of steak; soup made from carrots, peas, meat, rice, beans, potatoes, and onions; sausage patties, mashed potatoes, pineapple, peas, apples, apple butter, bread, coffee, tea, and chocolate milk. I ate so much I could hardly move for hours afterwards.

The left flank of the Seventh Army was about 200 yards to our right and we heard an occasional rifle shot from that direction.

Mar. 5, 1945.   That night the 26th Division departs from Saarlautern.

EGGER   During the day we had men on guard at the upstairs window facing the river. At night there were three men on the second floor—one on guard and two asleep. A field telephone provided communications.

This morning while Oakley was on guard and Rubin and I were sleeping, the Germans fired three rifle rounds through the upstairs window. The bullets struck the wall above our heads and knocked some plaster down on us. After that we kept out of line with the windows.

Tony Messina, whom I had borrowed from the 2nd Squad for this detail, was an interesting person. He had been born in Sicily and had migrated to New York City, where he became a dress designer. He didn't speak English very well, and when he was excited, which was most of the time, we could hardly understand him. In those days it was difficult for us to realize that a dress designer could be masculine enough to be in the infantry, but he was a good soldier. Messina, who was about five-foot-two, and Gazda (also from the 2nd Squad), who was six-one, were good buddies and made a Mutt-and-Jeff combination.

The 65th Division relieved us this evening. We knew that this was too good a setup to last. This was the first time on line for the 65th. In the usual manner of green troops, they were noisy during the relief and were loaded down with barracks bags and packs. We walked into town and waited in the street at the Platoon CP for trucks. No one seemed to know when the trucks would arrive so I told my squad to move into the house next to the CP where they would be more comfortable. I joined them after informing Gormley of our location.

I woke up at 0400 to discover that there was no one at the Platoon CP. I roused the squad members and we hurried to the area where we had de-trucked two days earlier. We arrived just as the last of the company was loading on trucks. Would they ever have missed us? I wondered sometimes how we could be winning the war.

OTTS We had a bicycle on which I had lots of fun riding around the town. Tonight I dressed up in a collapsible opera hat, red necktie and walking cane, hopped on my bicycle and rode over to the Company CP to a meeting Lt. Jack Hargrove had called. I thought it was only a G Company meeting so I made a grand entrance wearing all my accessories, smoking a cigar, and twirling the cane. I was certainly embarrassed when I found the 2nd Battalion S-2 and S-3 and the relieving battalion commanding officer there. They all looked at me as if they thought I was crazy. Jack smiled and made motions to show that I wasn't exactly right in the head.

We all agreed that Wadgassen was too good a deal to last, and sure enough we were told at the meeting that the new 65th Division was moving into this "inactive" front. We had been in and around Saarlautern for a month and gladly told the new men they could have it. We liked the south side of the river but did not want another turn at the north side.

The relieving unit came up loaded with duffle bags and bedrolls; they looked as though they were going on a bivouac in the States, except that they had enough clothing and equipment to last a year. They were a trigger-happy group too; one of them almost shot a man in our 1st Platoon as he was coming in from an outhouse behind his quarters.

I was with the last squad to leave the town and when we reached the other side of the hill we found everyone gone and no trucks left for us.

After waiting on the road for a while, we decided to start walking—
anywhere back was better than just standing there. Someone had remembered us though, and we met a truck coming for us. We rode back
about ten miles to the regimental assembly point in the town of Merten,
Germany, where we joined the rest of our company and our kitchen
served us hot coffee.

Some members of the 3rd Squad, 3rd Platoon, in Linz, Austria, September 1945. Front row, left to right: Pfc. Ray Peck, S/Sgt. Bruce Egger, Sgt. Hank Sosenko; back row, left to right: Pfc. Harry Gibbs, Pfc. Albert Evans, Pfc. Paul Scheufler, and Pfc. Wilbur Munns. (Egger personal collection)

Lt. Lee Otts near Falck, France, February 1945. (Otts personal collection)

Captain Jack Hargrove, CO of G Company. In the jeep are (left) Cpl. Bill Frost, forward clerk, and Pfc. Leonard "Bananas" LaFlam, company driver.
(Courtesy of Mrs. Marlene Hargrove)

Non-coms of Lt. Otts' 2nd Platoon at Falck, France, February 1945. Front row, left to right: S/Sgt. George Idelson, S/Sgt. Alfred Bruno. Back row, left to right: Sgt. Dave Smith, T/Sgt. Benny Bergeron, Sgt. Donald Thompson, S/Sgt. Vernon Hedgpath.
(Otts personal collection)

Two G Company battle casualties at Halloran General Hospital, Staten Island, July 1945. Left, Lt. Ernie Greup, who was wounded in both hands and the left arm on Dieuze Plateau, November 14, 1944; right, T/Sgt. Larry Treff, who took a dozen machine gun bullets in the right leg and thigh on Hoecker Hill, March 13, 1945. (Courtesy of Ernie Greup)

Some G Company veterans. Front row, left to right: Pfc. Alton Moores, S/Sgt. Ed "Stumpy" Uttian, Pfc. Roy Epley. Back row, left to right: T/Sgt. Francis Gormley and unidentified soldier. Taken at Dupenweiler, Germany, on March 19, 1945. (Courtesy of Rocco Clemente)

The two leaders of the 1st Squad, 2nd Platoon: S/Sgt. George Idelson (left) and Sgt. Donald Thompson. (Courtesy of Mrs. Donald Thompson)

Lt. William Schulze, who was killed in action at Deggendorf, Germany, April 27, 1945. (Courtesy of Mrs. Marlene Hargrove)

Two G Company wheelhorses: S/Sgt. Stan Nachman, leader of the 1st Squad, 3rd Platoon (left), and 1st Sgt. Rocco Clemente. Taken at Linz, Austria, in September 1945. (Courtesy of Rocco Clemente)

Lt. Lee Otts at Saarlouis-Roden, February 1945. (Otts personal collection)

Captain Jack Hargrove. (Courtesy of Mrs. Marlene Hargrove)

Several members of the 2nd Platoon. (Courtesy of Mrs. Donald Thompson)

7 The Drive to the Rhine
March 6–25, 1945

OPERATIONAL BACKGROUND While the men of G Company were spending an uneasy interlude in the cellars of suburban Saarlautern, events had been transpiring slightly to the north that were to lead to a sweeping Allied breakthrough to the Rhine. In mid-January the front covered by the Third Army's XX Corps stretched southwesterly along the west bank of the Moselle River from the point of its confluence with the Saar River to approximately the southern border of Luxembourg, then eastward to the Saar, which it followed southward to just below Saarlautern. The area from where the Saar River emptied into the Moselle in the north to where the XX Corps line cut eastward between the two rivers was known to the Allies as the Saar-Moselle Triangle. The base of this one-hundred-square-mile triangle was a westerly reaching extension of the West Wall called the Orscholz Switch (see Map 9).

In mid-January, while the Battle of the Bulge was winding down in the north, the XX Corps commander, General Walker, had ordered the green 94th Division to undertake a series of probes against the western end of the Orscholz Switch. Though these were limited in scope and the advance was slowed by the weather, by mid-February it had become clear that the opportunity to clear the entire Saar-Moselle Triangle lay at hand. Walker and Patton readily agreed that the 94th should give it a try and Patton, after much hassle, managed to procure the 10th Armored Division from SHAEF reserve to exploit a breakthrough should it occur.

The 94th Division launched its big attack on February 19, breaching the German defenses so decisively that the next morning the 10th Armored rolled into action. Sweeping northward in three fast-striking columns, the tankers met so little organized resistance that they reached the apex of the triangle on February 22. The next day elements of the 94th Division secured bridgeheads across the Saar River at Serrig and Taben, in the strongest sectors of the West Wall. The 10th Armored crossed the river on the 26th, quickly ripped through the German fortifications, and struck north toward Trier on the upper Moselle River, securing that ancient city in the early morning hours of March 2. The Third Army had torn a gaping hole in the West Wall.

General Patton, the most aggressive and daring of the Allied generals, was now formulating a bold plan that was destined to destroy the bulk of the German armies west of the Rhine and south of the Moselle. It was toward that end that on March 6 the 26th Division was moved north to the Serrig bridgehead on the east bank of the Saar River.[1] [P.R.]

Mar. 6–7, 1945. The men of Company G, sleepless and exhausted, relieve elements of the 94th Division outside Serrig.

EGGER We rode in a northerly direction until late afternoon, through parts of the Siegfried Line* and past numerous pillboxes and dragons teeth (concrete tank barriers) that had been demolished with explosives. There had obviously been some heavy fighting in this area. We unloaded at Kastel, which was on a high hill on the west side of the Saar River not far from Trier, and waited until dark.

Lt. Schulze was on pass so Pete Ruffin briefed the platoon. We were to relieve the 94th Division on a heavily wooded hill where the German positions were just fifty yards away. All the men with coughs, which included Moores and Scheufler, were to stay with the Company CP. This is one time a smoker's cough paid off.

We started out in the rain shortly after dark. The road was muddy and full of puddles and our feet were soon wet. We crossed the river on a pontoon bridge marked at the water's edge with white engineering tape and passed through the town of Serrig in a column of platoons. Some of the houses were lit up and we could hear men laughing and singing. I sure wished we could join them. We walked until 2000 before stopping at a barn to wait to be led into position. The pace quickened after the guides joined us, and a number of men fell behind. I knew the guides were in a hurry to carry out the relief before daylight. I just hoped that the Germans would never attack us shortly after our arrival from one of these forced marches while we were short-handed.

By midnight the going was getting noticeably tougher as the grade steepened and we began to gain elevation. It was still raining and we were wet and tired. I fell asleep the few times we stopped to rest. About 0400 we turned off the road onto a narrow trail that led to the top of

---

*The 26th Division was probably passing through the eastern end of the Orsholz Switch, at the base of the Saar-Moselle Triangle, which had been cleared by the 94th Division two weeks before.

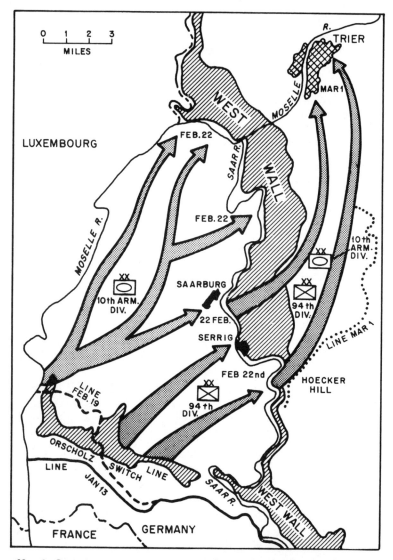

Map 9. Operations in the Saar-Moselle Triangle, February 19–March 1, 1945

Hoecker Hill. It was a dark night, the path was steep and slick with mud, and at times we had to pull ourselves up by grabbing at shrubs along the edge of the trail. We finally reached the top of the hill about 0600 and relieved a unit of the 94th Division.

The five of us in the squad who had been able to keep up occupied two adjacent muddy foxholes. I told the others I would pull the first shift of guard duty. We had been up since 0400 on the 6th and had walked for ten hours, so I had a difficult time keeping my eyes open and had to move around to stay awake. The hill was covered with scrub oak on which there were still many brown leaves from the previous fall. As I fought off sleep and tried to keep my eyes focused on the German positions, they started playing tricks on me—the oak trees and leaves turned to brick walls and houses similar to those in Saarlautern. I would have given anything if I only could have grabbed a quick nap. After an hour of battling to stay awake I awoke Sosenko and asked him to take over, but it was so wet and cold I only slept fitfully. Fortunately, the Germans, who had outposts just 150 yards away, did not attack.

About 1000 the men began to stir around. Oakley, LeCrone, and I ate some rations and tried to improve our foxhole, which proved to be an impossible task. We enlarged it but it was still a muddy mess and became more so as the rain continued.

I walked out the line to our left, which was occupied by our 2nd Squad and heavy machine guns from H Company. Two German soldiers walked up to the machine guns and surrendered this morning.

In the afternoon our platoon took up new positions to our left covering about two hundred yards along a trail. Oakley and I set about building a home. The soil in our new position was sandy and well drained, so we soon had a hole about three feet deep dug into the bank along the trail. We found a heavy door about four by eight feet that we put over our hole and covered with a foot of dirt and rock. I have never been able to figure out why that door was way out in the boondocks, so far from any town or buildings. Sosenko and England were together while LeCrone shared a foxhole with Tony Clemens of the 2nd Squad.

The stragglers, Rubin and Packer, arrived about noon. Schmitt had been sent to the hospital with a collapsed lung. The men with coughs, including Moores and Scheufler, were brought up on line when we discovered that the main body of the Germans were a quarter-mile from us, far enough away that a smoker's hack was not going to reveal our positions.

During the night mines and booby traps were set in the brush and trees along the company front. A telephone was strung from each squad CP to the Platoon CP, which was in a timber-covered dugout. We called every hour during the night. One man was to be on watch at all times.

OTTS It was almost daylight when we left Merten. We rode forty-five miles to the town of Kastel, which was on a hill overlooking the Saar River. We had been on the move without any sleep all night, but we had been in Kastel only a couple of hours when all the company commanders and platoon leaders were called to the Battalion CP. We were to go on a reconnaissance to view the positions occupied by the units of the 94th Division, which we were to relieve.

After a brief orientation we climbed aboard jeeps, crossed the river on a pontoon bridge, and passed through Serrig. With a guide directing us, we followed a narrow, winding road up a steep mountain called Hoecker Hill, which was the highest point in the vicinity. The ground to the left of the road rose almost straight up to the top of the hill and to the right dropped precipitously to the Saar River below.

We left our jeep on the road and spent forty-five minutes climbing up the steep cliff. We used our hands as much as our feet to negotiate the narrow path and were forced to stop and rest several times. I remarked on reaching the top that we would either have to push ahead or I would have to be carried off that hill on a stretcher, I would be damned if I would climb back down.

Right at the top of the hill was a concrete bunker which was to be our Company CP. The CO of the company that we were to relieve explained the setup to us and had guides take each platoon leader over his area. About the middle of the afternoon Jack left to go back and lead the company up. He left his platoon leaders up there, as there was no need for us to make the climb again.

I later learned that the company left Kastel about dark and started the long march down to Serrig and then up Hoecker Hill. Somewhere along the way Jack took a wrong turn and became lost. They wandered around in the rain and dark all night, finally straggling in about 0600. We had spent the night waiting, expecting them to show up any time.

The men had had no sleep for two days and nights and after walking all night were exhausted. I led them to our area and placed them in their foxholes, relieving the other unit. I pointed out the direction of the enemy to each man and tried to impress on everyone the great necessity of staying awake until daylight because the enemy was very near and was in the habit of sending out patrols at night.

Mar. 8–12, 1945. There follows a period of quiet days and uneasy nights for the men of G Company atop Hoecker Hill.

OTTS The next few days were some of the most nerve-wracking we had experienced. The holes we took over were about fifty yards back from the crest of the hill running in a line along a path. The hill was covered with scrub oaks and bushes about six feet high and so thick that we couldn't see more than fifteen or twenty yards in any direction. The Germans were dug in just under the crest of the hill to our front, not over fifty yards away, and were really closer to us than our foxholes were to each other. We could hear them talking all during the day and night.

Krause and Idelson took down several of their names and snatches of their conversations. They were so close we could hear the clink of the metal and the gurgle of the water as they filled their canteens. Being in that close proximity to the enemy and with the nights so dark you couldn't see the edge of your foxhole was enough to make one nervous.

Ordinarily we placed two men to a hole, with one standing guard while the other slept, but here with our foxholes so far apart and the Germans so close we found it best to have three men in a hole so two men could be awake at the same time all night.

A machine gun platoon from Howe Company was assigned to our company, so I had four heavy and two light machine guns in my platoon area. We had our front pretty well covered with crossing and overlapping fields of fire from the machine guns and BARs and weren't too worried about a daylight attack, but at night were kept jittery by the intense darkness and the gaps in our lines.

Searchlights across the river were used again as artificial moonlight but I don't know who they helped the most, the Heinies or us. Since the lights were behind us, we were silhouetted against the sky whenever we got out of our foxholes. The glow was reflected back at us from the bushes to our front and we were not able to see more than ten yards in that direction. Still, it made us feel better to have a little light around us.

Everything was so quiet at night that we didn't talk over the phones more than was absolutely necessary. We worked out a system of tapping on the mouthpiece of the phone with a pencil or our fingernails just to let each other know that everything was all right.

Every day or so battalion would order us to send out a patrol to contact the enemy and engage them in a fire fight. I don't know what the reason was other than to determine if anybody was there. I would send Gilluly and a couple of other men out to see if the Heinies were still there, telling them to take a look and come right back without drawing any fire. I believed in letting well enough alone. We could have gone over, tossed a few grenades and fired a few shots into their holes, but they would only have come back and done the same thing to us, with nothing gained by either side. I liked everything as it was, nice and peaceful, and couldn't see the sense in stirring up a hive full of sleeping bees. A hand grenade can do a nasty job in the confines of a foxhole. The battalion CO might have known best but he was several thousand yards from the enemy while we were only fifty.

Three engineers came up and brought us some booby traps. I followed them around, directing where I wanted them placed and watching how it was done. After the engineers left we got some more and placed them so as to cover our entire front. They were of English make of the "Bouncing Betty" type. We dug holes, placed booby traps in them, and then camouflaged them with brush and leaves. A very fine trip wire was strung from the device to a bush or tree about twenty or thirty yards away. If anybody touched the trip wire the booby trap would explode, throwing small steel balls and pieces of scrap iron in every direction. They were very effective and we felt much better with them between us and the enemy. We learned from a prisoner that the Germans also had about three rows of booby traps in front of their positions.

One morning just before daylight we were awakened by an explosion and a German's screams. We could tell from the sounds that the screaming man was running through their positions parallel to our front. At first I thought that the explosion had been a mortar shell, but as I went down the path in that direction someone told me that it had been one of our booby traps. As soon as it was light enough to see, we walked cautiously out to our front and discovered that the booby trap we had placed beside the path leading towards the enemy's position had been set off. There was a large pool of blood in the path, which led me to believe that there was more than one man wounded. I don't think a man who had lost that much blood could have been doing all the running and screaming. I put another "Bouncing Betty" in the same hole and strung another trip wire across the path.

The next morning, about the same time, we heard another explosion we recognized as a booby trap, so we jumped out of our holes and went running down the path towards the sound of the noise. It was the same place as the one that had exploded the morning before, only this time there was a German staff sergeant lying in the path. He was not yet dead, so we dragged him down the path back toward our positions.

The German was wounded in the chest and stomach, and it was obvious that he was dying. I sent for Lamb and a stretcher team but he died before they arrived. As he was dying he murmured over and over in German, "Oh God, I meant no harm, I meant no harm." Then there was a rattling in his chest and he was dead. As he was unarmed and wore no helmet, he could have been coming in with the intention of surrendering, but it was a favorite ruse of the Germans to go on patrols unarmed so if they were captured they could use the excuse that they were coming in to give up. We took his wallet, papers, and dog tags then dragged him off to one side of the path and left him there.

I took the things I had found on him back to the Company CP, where Jack and I examined them to see if we could find anything of interest. We found out that his name was Rudolph Mueller and that he was from Hamburg. He had several pictures that were obviously of his wife and of some other girl, probably another girlfriend. He had his platoon roster on him but nothing else of value to us. It was a good sign for a platoon sergeant to want to surrender, as it showed the Germans were not too happy with their setup. I imagine quite a few more would have surrendered but it was impossible in the daytime, as their own men would shoot them, and at night they were afraid to try to run our gauntlet of booby traps and machine guns.

My mother had written that Dr. Brooks May from my hometown was a medical officer (a captain) with the 26th Division, but I was still surprised when I was called down to the Company CP one day and found Brooks sitting there looking very tuckered out. We had a good time talking about everyone at home, but he swore that if he had known what a hard climb it was to get up here he would have waited until I came to him. I soon did.

All our food and ammunition had to be carried up the steep hill on packboards strapped to the men's backs so their hands were free to aid in climbing. We sent details from each platoon to carry our own rations, but for three days the Battalion A&P and anti-tank platoons carried rations and ammunition to a supply dump on the top of the hill to prepare us for the coming attack.

The weather continued wet and dreary and the men were beginning to crack under the strain of the dark, foreboding nights and the nearness of the enemy. Bruno, the tough taxi driver, the courageous, even foolhardy leader of patrols, the man who wanted to be up front in every attack and scorned wearing a steel helmet, came to me crying—not like a baby, I can stand a baby's cries, it is usual for them—but like a man. Have you ever seen a man crying? Not from some sorrow, or because he is afraid, but because he has just had all he can take. Bruno said to me, "Please, Lieutenant, let me go on a patrol, attack, or something; I can't stand this quiet and dark any longer." This was the third time Bruno had cracked under the strain so I sent him back to the aid station and also sent a note to the medical officer telling him to see that he had plenty of rest and then was transferred to some rear echelon outfit. He had already had more than his share of combat and I was afraid that any more might cause his mind to snap completely.

We were relieved on the night of March twelfth and moved to the back side of our hill to get ready to attack the following morning.

EGGER I had noticed on the long hike up Hoecker Hill that my elbows itched excessively; if I had scratched every time I felt like it they would have been raw. The problem was particularly bad after I had warmed up and was sweating from exertion. I went to the medics in April and found out that I had scabies, or the seven-year itch, which I had contracted either in the dirt of the foxholes or in the cellars of

Saarlautern. It took until December of 1945 for the prescribed ointment to clear up the condition. The members of my squad were lousy again—we must have picked up the critters in the house at Wadgassen.

The Germans shelled our positions frequently, and Rorer was wounded on the 8th during a barrage that landed near the Company CP. Tom Montgomery became leader of the 2nd Squad and Bob Gelinas of the 1st Squad became his assistant.

Tony Clemens of the 2nd Squad shot himself in the foot that same day. Clemens was a big man and it was three miles by trail to the aid station. I heard that the two medics who went with him made him walk all the way—there was no free ride for those with self-inflicted wounds. LeCrone, who had been sharing a foxhole with him, told me later that Clemens had talked about shooting himself and he finally told him to go ahead. LeCrone was ill and said he felt so depressed he just wanted the guy to shut up, but he never thought Clemens would actually do it.

A misty rain had been falling continually since our arrival and the nights were so dark our army focused two large spotlights on the sky above our positions to improve the visibility.

We were restricted to a canteen of water a day and there were no extra rations, since all supplies, including ammunition, had to be back-packed three miles up the trail on the backside of Hoecker Hill.

Moores and I were caught in an artillery barrage while we were re-turning from the Platoon CP to our foxholes. The shells threw dirt over us and Moores was nicked on the nose by a small piece of shrapnel or rock. The skin was broken and he lost several drops of blood but it was enough to make him eligible for the Purple Heart and I put him in for it.

Moores, a transfer from an ordnance outfit, was one of the five-per-centers who had joined us at Metz. He was from Bangor, Maine, and had a pronounced downeast accent. Alton was in his early thirties and single. He was a National Guardsman who had been in the Army for 4½ years and had been busted from sergeant three or four times. He pos-sessed a dry wit, didn't display his emotions, and was calm in a crisis. He had asthma and several other ailments. We kidded him that he was unfit for the infantry and should ask for a transfer, but he said he was just waiting for things to get tough before he cleared out. Moores was a good combat soldier but didn't like to walk or dig and was frequently in minor trouble when we were in a rest area. It was during this period that he and Lundy found a German motorcycle that was in working order. They rode it down the hill to the kitchen and left it with one of the jeep drivers.

Another steady and dependable member of the squad was Tom Oakley, from Waverly, Tennessee. He was a carpenter by trade but had been a cook with the CCC [Civilian Conservation Corps] for a while before the war.

LeCrone had been sick for several days. The medic thought it might be his appendix so I sent him to the aid station. We had a different medic, since John Grieco had gone to the hospital with yellow jaundice.

The time we spent on Hoecker Hill allowed me to get to know Sosenko and England better. Hank Sosenko, who was about twenty-six years old and married, was from Binghamton, New York. Like Stan Nachman, he was Polish. Hank got along well with the men and was frequently the butt of good-natured kidding.

Ellis England, from Kelso, Washington, was another one of the older fellows, twenty-six or -seven, and single. He had worked in the woods as a logger from the time he was sixteen. Ellis was a good-natured guy who smiled and laughed a lot but he was tough as buckskin. No one pushed him around.

Lt. Schulze was still on pass and Lt. Walter was transferred to F Company, so we were short two platoon leaders for the time being.

This afternoon we heard that we would be attacking the German positions tomorrow morning. Each attack was becoming more difficult for me to face. I was beginning to wonder how many more I could survive. I had been in combat longer than any man in the platoon and only five or six men in the company had seen more action.

The 1st Battalion relieved us after dark and we moved to a wooded area where we spent the night. I wondered what tomorrow would bring.

OPERATIONAL BACKGROUND The attack Bruce Egger and his comrades of the 26th Division were scheduled to launch on March 13 was only the latest of a series of Allied blows designed to smash the German forces west of the Rhine River. On the far northwestern anchor of the Allied line, in the southern reaches of the Netherlands, Field Marshall Montgomery had on February 8 launched the Canadian First Army southeastward in a forty-mile drive through mud, flood, and cold to close to the Rhine.[2] Complementary with that offensive, General William Simpson's Ninth U.S. Army (which was still attached to Montgomery's 21st Army Group) had on February 23 forced a massive crossing of the swollen Roer River and driven northeastward to link up on March 9 with the Canadians at the city of Wesel. Though the bulk of the battered German forces in the area had been able to pull back across the Rhine, the Allies had nevertheless cleared the west bank of that formidable river barrier from Dusseldorf to Nijmegen on the Dutch-German border.[3]

In the meantime, General Courtney Hodges' First Army, a part of Bradley's 12th Army Group, had got into the act with spectacular results. It too had crossed the Roer, with General Joe Collins' VII Corps leading the way on February 23 to protect the Ninth Army's right flank, and III Corps following two days later. Collins reached the Rhine and then turned south to take Cologne, Germany's fifth largest city, on March 5. By this time the German opposition was in such disarray that III Corps, on Collins' right flank, was racing toward the Rhine practically unimpeded. On March 7 its 9th Armored Division created banner headlines at home when it seized an undestroyed bridge across the river at Remagen and established the first Allied bridgehead on the east side of the Rhine.[4]

In comparison with this exploit, the Third Army's just-completed operations in the Saar-Moselle Triangle, which included the capture of the ancient city of Trier, seemed small potatoes, but General Patton was hatching a scheme that would reclaim some of the glory for his command. This contemplated no less than the conquest of the entire Saar Basin and the Palatinate (the southern Rhineland). In conjunction with General Alexander Patch's Seventh U.S. Army to the south, the Third Army would clear the west bank of the Rhine from the Moselle to the Swiss border.

While the Allied armies to the north of Patton's sector had been smashing their way to the Rhine, the Third Army's VIII and XII Corps had been clearing the southern portion of the rugged Eifel region just to the north of the lower Moselle. Patton's plan was to turn these forces south across the Moselle in the vicinity of Koblenz and let them sweep down the west bank of the Rhine behind the German defenders. At the same time XX Corps would drive eastward and southward from its lodgements across the Saar, rolling up the West Wall from behind (see Map 10). This would greatly simplify the task of the Seventh Army, which faced the difficult job of cracking the German fortifications in the south by means of a head-on assault. Generals Bradley and Eisenhower both endorsed the plan.

The date for the thrust across the Moselle was set for March 14. In the meantime, XX Corps' attack was to get underway in the early morning of March 13 with the 94th and the 80th Divisions striking eastward from the Saar while on the right the 26th Division attacked almost due south to roll up the West Wall laterally.[5] [P.R.]

Mar. 13, 1945. The 2nd Battalion suffers heavy casualties on top of Hoecker Hill.

EGGER The battalion's objective that morning was some wooded knolls a half-mile to the east. Whether our higher command thought that the Germans were there I don't know, but they were 150 yards further on, well concealed in an area that dominated the knolls we were

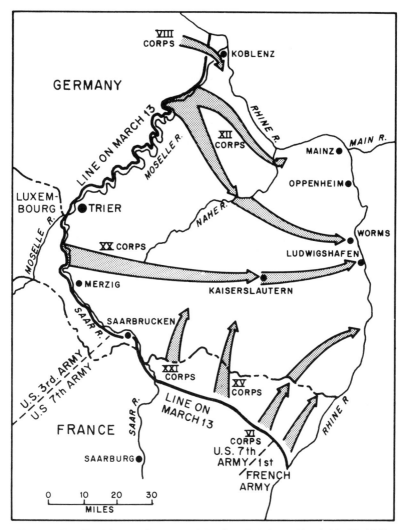

Map 10. The Third Army's Conquest of the Saar-Palatinate, March 13–25, 1945

to take. They seem to have had all their weapons zeroed in on our objective and enjoyed perfect fields of fire, but this wasn't known to us until it was too late.

Rifle and automatic weapons fire to our front indicated that Easy and Fox Companies had already begun the attack in an attempt to reach the battalion objectives under cover of darkness. We were in support and took off at daylight. As we started forward we met wounded men from the forward companies coming back. A seriously wounded sergeant was lying alongside the trail, probably carried there by the two men who sat beside him, one of whom was weeping.

A tank or artillery piece on the high ground to our right front was firing at the trail junction. The shells seemed to travel at an incredible speed as they bore down on us. Packer broke down and became hysterical so I told him to stay behind. As we traveled up the trail through scattered scrub oak trees we passed a number of dead GIs lying face down facing the enemy. The ground was torn up, probably by our artillery, even though there were no German positions in this area.

After reaching the top of the gentle slope we stopped at the edge of a grove of conifer trees. Before we could dig in we were hit by a barrage of German mortars that killed Lundy instantly and wounded Clay Williams, Walker, Treml, DeSoto, Poirier, Al Evans, and the medic who was Grieco's replacement.* This was the second time Treml, Evans, and Poirier had been wounded in action. Some of the wounded were able to walk, others had to be carried four miles down the steep trail.

It didn't take us long to dig deep foxholes. The machine gun fire from the wooded area and the shelling kept up all day. A mortar shell landed and exploded two feet from Sosenko's and my foxhole, scrambling our brains for a few minutes. I never heard it approaching, which supports the saying that you don't hear the shell that hits you.

According to *Handcar White* [p. 55], the orginal plan had been for all units to move to the attack at 0600, but there had been a change of orders to hold off until noon. Somehow the 2nd Battalion never got the word and had attacked without any support from the rest of the regiment. Perhaps a full-scale, coordinated attack would have reduced the losses the battalion suffered on Hoecker Hill that morning.

Lt. Otts of the 2nd Platoon and his platoon sergeant, T/Sgt. Benoit Bergeron, were wounded. Lt. Hargrove, who had been shaken up by the artillery barrage and wounded in the foot, had gone to the aid station.† We didn't know what had happened to Pete Ruffin, our platoon sergeant. The platoon guide, Francis Gormley, had taken charge of the 3rd Platoon. Gormley, who was in his late twenties or early thirties, was more mature than most of us. We generally got along well with him.

---

*The replacement medic was apparently Pfc. Niles W. Keenlance, who was listed on the 328th Infantry Medical Battalion morning report of Mar. 13 as "slightly wounded."

†Although Lt. Hargrove was listed in the morning report as "slightly wounded," he did not go to the aid station. Instead he had been sent back to Regimental HQ by the Battalion CO to plead for relief and ended up spending the night in Serrig. In a letter to Otts dated June 4, 1945, which gave a full account of the action at Hoecker Hill, Hargrove said that a bullet had pierced his shoe and scraped his toes.

About 1600 we received orders to renew the attack, but just as we were forming a skirmish line word came down to sit tight, which suited me fine.

With the Germans so near, we stayed awake all night. Besides that it was cold without our overcoats (which had been collected two weeks ago by the supply sergeant) or blankets.

OTTS During the previous few days the battalion patrol group and patrols from our company had been investigating the hill to our right front that was to be our battalion's initial objective in this morning's attack. It was no higher than our hill but there was a small wooded draw in between. Each patrol had returned without contacting the enemy, so we decided it must be unoccupied. Several times each day the Germans would throw a few mortar and 88 rounds into that vicinity. They must have had a pretty good idea as to what was up and were getting their mortars and artillery zeroed in on the hill, waiting for us. I thought at the time the way we were showing our hand was rather foolish but didn't have anything to say about the matter.

OTTS ON HOECKER HILL

(as described in George Idelson's letter of June 30, 1988, to Lee Otts)

My last memory of you—and it is a vivid one—is of you standing in a fierce mortar and artillery barrage, totally without protection, calling in enemy coordinates. I know what guts it took to do that. I can still hear those damn things exploding in the trees. . . . I lost one foxhole buddy to shrapnel in that barrage, and then his replacement. I don't know who was looking after me.

In the early hours of the morning Easy and Fox Companies labored up the steep backside of Hoecker Hill and quietly moved onto the objective just as day was breaking. Then all hell broke loose—German machine guns chattered away and soon mortar shells were raining down on the area. The attacking companies were getting pounded.

G Company was in reserve that day and we were moving forward to tie onto the right flank of Fox Company when we got caught in the enemy barrage. It seemed also that some of our artillery rounds were falling in the area and adding to the punishment we were taking.

Jack and his radio operator were in the lead and I followed right behind him with Thompson and the rest of the platoon. All along the way we passed Fox and Easy Company men running away from the front, yelling, "Every man for himself—it's too hot up there!" They claimed that the order had been given to retreat, but as we had not been informed of it by radio we told them to follow us and kept moving forward. At one point we were forced to hit the ground when the shelling became too intense, but after a couple of minutes we moved out again.

When we were within about fifty yards of our objective, Jack called a halt and told me to take my platoon up and tie onto the right flank of Fox Company. I started back along the line to tell the men where we were going when I discovered we had only twelve men with us. The rest of the company had not seen us get up and go on after we hit the ground that time. I didn't know how far back they were, so I started walking back looking for them without telling Jack where I was going. I finally found them almost back where we had started. Someone in the front had told them to turn around and I imagine the other officers thought the order had been given to retreat. I was furious about it and cursed and raved from the front to the back of the line, with a few extra words for the Easy and Fox Company men who had left their companies. I think I made it very clear that they were to get on their feet and follow me back to the front.

We got back to where Jack was waiting and I explained to him what had happened. Then I started off with my platoon to join Fox Company. I sent a couple of scouts out but as they were not familiar with the terrain and didn't exactly understand where I wanted to go, I took the lead myself. We found Fox Company and, after placing my men, I reported to Major Burke and told him that George Company was in position. He and the other battalion officers were busy digging holes for protection from the shells and small arms fire.

Mortar shells were falling everywhere. I was watching a couple of my men digging in when a 50mm round hit about five yards from us. Fragments whistled by my ears but none of us was hit. I went back to the position we had selected for our Platoon CP and had just removed my equipment and both field jackets to help Benny dig us a hole when all hell broke loose. Mortar shells started falling almost as thick as rain drops and we all hit the ground fast. Instead of covering my head, I, like a fool, propped up on my right elbow with my chin resting on my hand, looking around to see what was going on. All of a sudden something hit me on the left side of my jaw that felt like a blow from Jack Dempsey's right.

It has always been a subject of controversy whether you can see the shell that hits you or not. I think I did. A 50mm mortar shell hit about fifteen yards to my left and I believe it was a fragment from that one which hit me. It didn't hurt when it hit, just felt sort of numb. I stuck my hand up to feel the wound and it felt as though half my face was missing. Lamb was lying about six feet away and I crawled over to him to get a bandage put on my face. As he was tying the bandage in place he said, "Oh God, Lieutenant, this is all for me too." I later heard that he cracked up that night and had to be evacuated.

The shelling slacked up a bit and I put one of my jackets back on, stuck my pistol in my hip pocket, and told Tommy to come with me. I wanted him along in case I became weak from loss of blood and needed help getting to the aid station. Just as we were about to leave Jack came limping up. He had been hit in the foot and was looking for me to tell me to take over the company. When he saw the big bandage on my face, he said, "My God, no, not you too," turned and walked back to his foxhole.

Tommy and I started out following the wire that had been strung up to the battalion phone, but the shells had torn large gaps in the wire and as there were no paths we became more or less lost. All the scrub brush looked alike to me.

I was walking along holding the bandage tight against my face trying to stop the bleeding with my left hand and pushing the bushes aside with my right hand, when something hit me in the shoulder and knocked me flat. At first I didn't know what had hit me, but as I did not hear any nearby explosion and no one else was hit I guessed it was a rifle or machine gun bullet. I don't know whether it was just a stray bullet or a deliberate shot by a sniper. I remember getting up from the ground and letting go with the longest string of cuss words I had ever used. I already had my free trip to the hospital with the wound in my jaw and that was adding insult to injury.

I decided that we must be going in the wrong direction so we veered to the left and after a while recognized some familiar landmarks. We followed the path on down to the forward aid station. In all we had probably walked about two or three miles. I didn't know how bad my shoulder was hurt but had noticed I couldn't raise my arm to knock the bushes out of my face after I was hit.

One of the medics at the aid station put a new bandage on my face, since the one on it was coming off. He then took my jacket off and bandaged up the holes in my shoulder. There were a couple of neat little holes; a small one in the front where the bullet had gone in and a larger one in the rear where it had come out.

There were no jeeps at that aid station so I had more walking to do. I gave Tommy my pistol, telling him to keep it for me, that I would probably be back in a few weeks. Then I started walking down the path to look for a jeep to ride back to Serrig. After walking about a mile I came upon a bunker that was the 3rd Battalion CP. There were a couple of jeeps outside and I went in and asked some major if I could get one of his drivers to take me into town. My tongue was very swollen by then and I had a hard time talking. I think he could see that I needed help so he told one of the drivers to take me to the aid station.

Neither of my wounds had hurt very much until that six-mile jeep ride down the rough, rocky road into Serrig. The bouncing up and down hurt my shoulder as it was not in a sling or any sort of splint. Upon reaching the 3rd Battalion Aid Station I sat in a chair while they gave me several shots; morphine and penicillin I guess. There was a vacant stretcher on the floor in front of me that looked very inviting. I told the medics to wait a minute and staggered over to the stretcher; I had just about had it. The medics changed my bandages and Chaplain Gordon presented me with a New Testament.

From the aid station I was taken by ambulance to a collecting station where I was carried in and placed on the floor beside several other litter cases. I saw Brooks May and tried to attract his attention but my tongue was so swollen I could barely mumble. He finally noticed me and came over, but he still didn't recognize me at first as my head was covered with bandages. He removed the bandage from my face and told me I had a broken jaw. Then he put a tighter bandage all around my head. I asked him to write my mother and he said he would. He had to move on to other patients and I was carried out to another ambulance. The next stop was the Division Clearing Station, where I was carried inside another building and all my clothing removed. They had no pajamas to give me, so I was naked except for the blanket over me and all the bandages.

[This ends Lt. Lee Otts' account of his combat experiences in World War II. The story of his hospital stay in England and return to the United States is summarized in the epilogue. The remaining narrative is Egger's alone. P.R.]

EGGER *Mar. 14, 1945.* This morning the ground and vegetation were white with a thick coating of frost. We heard that Larry Treff, platoon sergeant of the 1st Platoon, had not returned from patrol yesterday afternoon.* Fortunately, the men with him had been able to crawl back

---

*In a letter to Bruce Egger dated December 13, 1988, Larry Treff gave the following account of what happened to him on March 13: "Before taking that patrol out I was told we would meet a patrol from another 2nd Battalion company at the top of the hill. As we approached the top of the hill, I spotted a group of soldiers and thought they were the other patrol. Within a split second or two, we knew that they were the enemy. They

under fire. We also heard that Lt. Dean, CO of E Company, had been killed yesterday. He had been wounded at Moncourt while serving with G Company and then had rejoined the 2nd Battalion in the latter part of February.

The loss of Treff left G Company without any officers or platoon sergeants on line; staff sergeants were in command in all four platoons. With Lt. Walter's transfer to Fox Company and Treff missing in action, the 1st Platoon had been left without any leaders; Lt. Otts and T/Sgt. Bergeron of the 2nd Platoon had both been wounded; Lt. Schulze of the 3rd Platoon was on leave and Pete Ruffin, our platoon sergeant, had disappeared. We learned later that he and the two leaders of the 4th Platoon, had run out on us and gone to the kitchen, which was at the foot of the hill, near Serrig. I don't mean to condemn the latter two. Every man has his breaking point, and there is ample evidence that they were good soldiers who had proved themselves in combat; I could not say the same for Ruffin.

About 0900 Marron of the 2nd Squad, who was on my left, started firing to our front and hollering that the Germans were coming. Almost at the same time a unit of the 101st Regiment moved through our positions using marching fire and met the counterattack head-on. We continued to be shelled all day as the sounds of small arms fire faded into the distance.

George Company's casualties from the shelling were not as heavy as yesterday, but Major Burke, our battalion commander, was killed and Captain Arma Andon of Howe Company was wounded. A single shell had killed four men from the 101st as they were passing through our positions. The ground was churned up from the hours of shelling by mortars, 88s, and nebelwerfers.

Shortly before dark we pulled back to the positions we had left yesterday morning. There were more dead scattered along the trail than there were yesterday. I laid down and went to sleep without taking time to dig a hole.

Mar. 15, 1945. It was a beautiful day, the sun was shining, and it was warm enough to be comfortable in shirt sleeves. I rested most of the day, washed and shaved. Our platoon strength was now twenty-seven men, down from thirty-five when we left Falck on March 5. Besides

turned machine guns and other small arms on us. I was hit immediately in my right thigh. I was immobilized and ordered the rest of the patrol back and covered their withdrawal with my carbine. I was hit again in the lower leg and this last hit put me out of action. Soon after, the German medics came for me." American medical personnel later estimated that he had been hit by from twelve to fourteen machine gun bullets.

THE ACTION AT HOECKER HILL

(as described in Lt. Hargrove's letter of June 4 to Lt. Otts)

You know the story [of Hoecker Hill] up to the time you were hit—at the time my entire company headquarters was evacuated, except Parcell and myself. We dug in and continued to get 50mm mortar barrages all day at about half-hour intervals, plus one 88 every three minutes in the afternoon.

. . . We prepared to attack at 1800 and were all lined up in the woods ready to go when regiment called it off. As we were moving back to our holes we got a mortar barrage. One round hit a 60mm ammunition bay which exploded, wounding about eleven mortarmen.

All day men were cracking mentally and I kept dashing around to them but it didn't help. I had to send approximately fifteen back to Serrig, crying. When the attack was called off I was ordered to send out a daylight patrol for which Treff volunteered. . . . the patrol got back, except Treff, who they said was cut in two by a machine gun. (He later wrote us from New York—he had been wounded in the leg and taken prisoner, then released eleven days later by the 4th Division.)

At this time . . . [the two leaders of the 4th Platoon] cracked—the former badly. . . . [All we had left leading the platoons were staff sergeants. Major Burke] had Lt. Walter come back from F Company to keep G Company together and sent me to see Col. Mott. . . . When I got to Regiment they sent me with Maj. Carrier to see Gen. Paul. I went to sleep waiting to see him, and stumbled in. Apparently he was satisfied with my story for the battalion was to be relieved the following morning. It was then about midnight so I stayed in Serrig.

They tell me the following morning was more of the same story. The other battalion attacked through ours just as the Jerries counterattacked and moved right through them. That morning Maj. Burke was killed and Captain Andon seriously wounded in the stomach. . . .

Total at Hoecker Hill was four killed: Schoenknecht (1st), Krause (2nd), Lundy (3rd), and Robinson (4th); 24 wounded, but this figure included those slightly wounded like myself—pieces of shrapnel scraped my toes after going through my shoes and scratched my cheek.

Lundy there had been three others from George Company killed on the 13th. Albert Krause, the German-speaking member of the patrol at Saarlouis-Roden, was one of them.

Lt. Schulze came back from his pass today. Carl Cullison, who had come into G Company as a replacement at the same time I had and had been wounded at Moncourt, and Dan Dafoe, who had been wounded in Luxembourg, both returned from the hospital and were assigned to the 1st Platoon. Tony Catanese, who had recovered from an infection in his finger, returned from the hospital and went to the 2nd Squad.

Ruffin and Packer, who had been back at the company kitchen for two days, were also back with the platoon. Packer was transferred to the 1st Squad, which only had five men. He told me that Ruffin had given him a bad time for breaking down and going back on the 13th. No one seemed to know when Pete himself had taken to his heels. I could forgive his cowardice; what was hard to take was his hypocrisy and intolerance of the same weakness in others.

I was getting worn down psychologically. I had never felt so nervous and frightened. It made me appreciate the mental agony Stribling, Packer, Ruffin, and those who had shot themselves had gone through. I wondered if I too was reaching the breaking point. I did not have the nerve to shoot myself, which would have been too obvious anyway. I even thought about dropping a case of rations on my foot, but I did not want to live the rest of my life with that on my mind. I decided to stick it out and trust in the Lord.

March 16, 1945. We took off early in the morning on foot. There was a welcome quiet in the heavily wooded area. We walked past our positions of the 13th and followed the route the 101st had taken. We saw some dead Germans along the way but no dead Americans. The 1st Platoon took some prisoners from a by-passed pillbox.

We heard that all our armies were advancing rapidly against the Germans. We walked about ten miles and stopped on a hill beyond the village of Saarholzbach near the Saar River.

OPERATIONAL BACKGROUND It turned out that the 26th Division, which was attacking southward down through the pillbox belt of the West Wall, had drawn the toughest assignment of the offensive. Within a few days, however, German resistance had all but collapsed, and on March 17 the lst and 2nd Battalions of the 328th Infantry were able to occupy the deserted city of Merzig without opposition. From there the Yankee Division turned eastward to join in the advance toward the Rhine.[6]

3rd PLATOON PERSONNEL BETWEEN MARCH 5 AND MARCH 15

Platoon Leader: 1st Lt. Bill Schulze

Platoon Sergeant: T/Sgt. Pete Ruffin

Platoon Guide: S/Sgt. Francis Gormley

Platoon Runner: Pfc. "Frenchy" Dumais

1st Squad

S/Sgt. Stan Nachman, Ldr

Sgt. Joe Treml, Asst (WIA 3/13)

Pfc. Joe Bergeron

Pfc. Bill DeSoto (WIA 3/13)

Pfc. Bob Gelinas (to 2nd Sq 3/9)

Pfc. Barron Lintz

Pfc. Delbert Livermore

Pfc. Elbridge Walker (WIA 3/13)

Pfc. Merle Ward

2nd Squad

S/Sgt. Stew Rorer, Ldr, (WIA 3/8)

Sgt. Tom Montgomery, Asst, Ldr 3/8

Pvt. Tony Clemens (SIW 3/8)

Pfc. Albert Evans (WIA 3/13)

Pfc. Emelion Gazda

Pfc. W. C. Lundy (KIA 3/13)

Pfc. John Marron

Pfc. Tony Messina

Pfc. Rufies Morgan

3rd Squad

S/Sgt. Bruce Egger, Ldr

Cpl. Hank Sosenko, Asst

Pfc. Ellis England

Pfc. F. LeCrone (to hosp 3/11)

Pfc. Alton Moores

Pfc. Tom Oakley

Pvt. H. Packer (to 1st Sq 3/15)

Pfc. Solomon Rubin

Pfc. Paul Scheufler

Pfc. Rene Poirier (WIA 3/13)

Pfc. W. S. Thompson

Pfc. Clay Williams (WIA 3/13)

Pfc. George Schmitt (to hosp 3/7; ret to duty 3/10)

Changes as of March 15

Sgt. Frank Micik, Asst 3/15
(from 4th Platoon)

Pfc. Harley Packer
(from 3rd Squad)

Pfc. Bob Gelinas, Asst 3/9
(from 1st Squad)

Cpl. Tony Catanese (ret from hosp 3/14 and assigned to 2nd Sq)

Squad strength,

as of March 5:	9	12	10	Platoon = 35
as of March 15:	7	8	8	Platoon = 27

In the meantime, other units of the Third Army were racing through the Saar-Palatinate region in a squiggle of columns that resembled a child's doodlings on an operational map. Beginning on March 14 XII and VIII Corps had sent five infantry and two armored divisions southward across the Moselle River just below Koblenz to go rampaging down the west side of the Rhine. Two days later General Walker, commander of XX Corps, committed the 10th and 12th Armored Divisions to join the 94th, 80th, and 26th Infantry Divisions in their eastward dash from the Saar River. All these elements of the Third Army were making spectacular progress in the face of collapsing German resistance.

Farther south, General Patch's Seventh U.S. Army on March 15 had launched an assault against the West Wall along a seventy-mile front. Here the going was considerably tougher, but with the German positions being compromised by the presence of elements of XX Corps in their rear, on the 20th two of Patch's divisions made a penetration of the West Wall in the vicinity of Zweibrucken and headed eastward for the Rhine.[7] [P.R.]

EGGER *March 17, 1945.* We started out early in the morning but progressed slowly while another battalion was taking Metlach. The next town down the Saar was a little place called Besseringen that was empty. We passed increasing numbers of pillboxes, trenches, and emplacements in the Siegfried Line that had been cleared and then entered Merzig, a town of about 15,000 that was now deserted. The men spent the rest of the day looking through the buildings. Canned fruit was my only find of value.

Moores reclaimed his motorcycle and had a big time riding it around town. We had a good house to stay in and the guard duty was light.

March 18, 1945. We took off walking this morning—all except Moores, who rode his motorcycle. Some of the men were carrying loot, which they soon discarded as the day warmed up and we started uphill. We walked about ten miles to Marbach, which was not far from Saarlautern, then, after eating a hot meal, continued on trucks for about an hour that evening. The platoon set up an outpost for the night outside the town of Duppenweiler. It was a clear beautiful night, a little cool but much warmer than we had been accustomed to.

The platoon got several replacements today. Ralph Newcity, who was about twenty-four years old and from the state of New York, and Ray Peck were assigned to the 3rd Squad. Peck was a good-natured nineteen-year-old kid from Seekonk, Massachusetts, who had only been in the Army about five months. I heard Scheufler tell them I was a good squad leader who wasn't afraid of anything. That made me feel good because Paul was an old-timer in the squad, but I didn't agree that I wasn't afraid.

March 19, 1945. We moved into Duppenweiler and found the 26th Division HQ located there. Since it was unheard of for the top brass to be out in front of the troops, it indicates how far the infantry companies had fallen behind the armor during the last five days. We stayed in town all day and outposted a bridge that night. The small villages we passed through after Merzig were inhabited and undamaged by the war.

March 20, 1945. The 3rd Squad got two more new replacements today, Russell Greasor and Harry Gibbs. Both were about nineteen years old and from Logansport, Indiana. G Company had received a total of fifty-four replacements on March 18 and 20. With the returning wounded and trench foot cases, this had brought the company close to full strength.

Besides Peck, Newcity, Greasor, and Gibbs in the 3rd Squad, the platoon had received seven other new men, with five of them going to the 1st Squad. The ones I can remember are Vassie Nelson, Charles Patti, William Prior, Ralph Goodwin, and N. S. Wingo. 2nd Lt. Kennedy Schmertz joined the company as leader of the 2nd Platoon. Sgt. Frank "Lucky" Micik had been moved over from the 4th Platoon to be assistant leader of the 1st Squad after Treml was wounded.

These last replacements were never destined to experience any of the tough fighting or severe weather conditions so many of us had endured over the past few months. After March 14 G Company lost one man killed and seven wounded.

We were told that the Germans were falling back in all areas and that we would continue to pressure them so they couldn't establish a line of defense; trucks would pick us up in the afternoon, we would move ahead as rapidly as possible, and we might outrun our supply line and have to live off the land.*

The weather had been clear and our fighter planes had strafed columns of retreating Germans, leaving numerous dead horses and burned-out vehicles along the roads. We passed through St. Wendel, but the 80th Division had been there before us. There were hundreds of German prisoners standing in a field outside of town.

We spent the night at Buprich-Huttersdorf.

---

*The 2nd Battalion had in fact been assigned to a variegated task force with orders to press on to Ludwigshaven on the Rhine by nightfall. But as Egger notes, it got so tangled up in military traffic at Kaiserlautern that it was unable to fulfill that assignment.[8]

March 21, 1945. We rode all day on trucks. Our route of travel took us through Kaiserlautern, a city of about 80,000. Parts of the city had been destroyed by bombing raids.

It seemed that all the units in the European Theater were on the move in the same area, as the roads were congested with traffic and our progress was slow. Our Air Corps had created havoc with the retreating Germans—judging by the large number of destroyed vehicles we saw along the way. There were numerous burned out vehicles along the roads and many German prisoners walked unattended while slave labor refugees were walking west, away from Germany. It was beginning to look like the end was near.

The company spent the night at Esthal.

March 22, 1945. Today we rode in trucks to a hill overlooking the Rhine. The gentle rolling hills along the river were covered with vineyards.

Troops of the 5th Division were billeted in some of the small towns we drove through. One man ran out and gave our truck two bottles of wine. There were signs painted on buildings and walls which said "See Germany and Die," "Onward Slaves of Moscow," and "Death Will Give You Peace."

We walked on to Guntersblum, which was occupied by a unit of the 4th Armored Division, so we set up an outpost in a field near the town.

The tankers never pulled guard when the infantry was with them, but we made them pay by stealing some of their ten-in-one rations. Since they were mechanized, they usually carried a several-day supply of rations.

OPERATIONAL BACKGROUND   By March 22 no less than eight divisions of XII and XX Corps were poised on the Rhine at Mainz, Worms, and Ludwigshaven, though the First Army bridgehead at Remagen was still the only American lodgement on the east side of the river. General Patton was determined to remedy that situation by immediately hurling one of his columns across the Rhine on the run. Patton was not unmindful of the headlines this feat would engender, but above all he wanted to preempt Field Marshal Montgomery, who was thoroughly detested by all the American commanders and who was due to unleash his massive set-piece attack across the Rhine in the north on the night of March 23.

With Patton's orders ringing in his ears, General Eddy of XII Corps accordingly sent the 5th Division across the river in boats on the night of March 22. The spot chosen was Oppenheim, about ten miles south of Mainz, where the Germans would least expect it; the crossing was all but unopposed. The 90th

Division started across the next day, followed by the 4th Armored on the 24th. It wasn't until the evening of the 23rd, shortly before Montgomery was scheduled to launch his massive attack in the north, that General Bradley announced the Third Army's successful crossing the day before, emphasizing that it had been carried off without so much as a preliminary artillery bombardment—this obviously in contrast to Monty's massive preparations. Bradley added that American forces were capable of crossing the Rhine wherever they chose.

So it seemed, as Patton pushed two more divisions across south of Koblenz on March 25 and 26 while General Hodges, whose forces by now were mopping up east of the West Wall, ordered two of his Seventh Army divisions across in the vicinity of Worms on the 26th.[9] [P.R.]

EGGER *March 23, 1945.* The 4th Armored moved out of Guntersblum and we moved in to spend the day waiting for trucks to take us down the river to Mainz, where we were to cross the Rhine. George Company rested and waited near a large wine warehouse in the center of the town. The owner gave the men several bottles of wine. The trucks did not show, the day was warm, and the men were bored and thirsty so they helped themselves to more wine, despite the protests of the owner. The trucks never arrived and some of us slept on the sidewalks. The heavy drinkers slept in the gutters of Guntersblum.

Our fighter planes had strafed and bombed down-river from us throughout the day.

March 24, 1945. The trucks took us to Mainz, a city of 110,000, this morning. The 5th Division had crossed the river in boats south of here the night of the 22nd, followed by the 90th Division and the 4th Armored. The city had only been slightly damaged by bombs.

I saw a Negro civilian today, which I thought was unusual in a country with so much racial discrimination. Perhaps a Negro's lot was not any more difficult in Germany than in the United States.

The men found a guitar and accordion for England and Sosenko to play and we drank wine and sang until midnight.

March 25, 1945. In the afternoon we traveled by truck to Nierstein on the Rhine [a mile north of Oppenheim], where we waited until 2300 to cross the pontoon bridge our engineers had constructed. The Germans had destroyed the main bridge behind them. Enemy aircraft tried to bomb the bridge but our antiaircraft kept them away and the bombs were dropped in the town. After crossing the river we walked for five miles and slept in a field.

AFTER ACTION SUMMARY The Third Army's Saar-Palatinate campaign had been one of the most brilliant of the war, even given the fact that it had been waged against a badly battered foe who was reaching the end of his resources in both men and material. As one of Patton's colleagues put it in a telegram on March 22: "Congratulations on surrounding three armies, one of them American" (the latter remark being a reference to the fact that Third Army units, driving southward, had penetrated deeply into the rear of the Seventh Army zone).[10]

This was stretching a point, but there can be no doubt that the enemy losses had been enormous. The American estimate was that the two German armies involved in the Saar-Palatinate campaign, the First and the Seventh, had lost seventy-five to eighty percent of their infantry. Patton's Third Army alone had taken more than 68,000 prisoners and inflicted another estimated 45,000 casualties on the enemy at a cost of only 5,200 losses itself, including 681 killed.

For all that, the enemy commanders had fought a skillful delaying action in the face of overwhelming American strength, thereby avoiding wholesale encirclement despite Hitler's refusal to allow timely withdrawals. How many German troops managed to escape across the Rhine in the face of these difficulties is impossible to determine. Whatever the number, it is clear that only fragments of an organized opposition remained to defend the heartland of the German nation against the mighty Allied host that was pouring across the entire length of the Rhine.[11]

The increasingly upbeat tone of Egger's journal entries therefore reflected the reality of the military situation; even though hostilities would stretch out another seven weeks, for all practical purposes the war was over. And, as General Patton had predicted the previous summer, it had been won west of the Rhine.[12] The remainder of the war would take on the nature of an unimpeded race across Germany. [P.R.]

8 The Race across Germany
March 26–May 9, 1945

OPERATIONAL BACKGROUND   By the last week of March the entire line of the Rhine—and with it the final German defensive barrier—had been breached by the Allied forces. On the extreme flanks, the First Canadian Army in the Netherlands and General Patch's Seventh Army in the far south of Germany continued to meet strong resistance. Elsewhere it was clear that the Wehrmacht was finished. Once across the Rhine, the other four Allied armies—from north to south the Second British and the Ninth, First, and Third U.S.—raced through the German heartland. Here and there they encountered pockets of resistance, but for the most part the battle for Germany was in the nature of a road march. Hitler's continuing insistence upon a policy of no retreat had resulted in the bulk of his forces being destroyed west of the Rhine, leaving only battered fragments to contest the invading Allied host in central Germany.[1]

On the Third Army front the crossing of the Rhine just south of Mainz had caught the German high command by surprise, since it meant that any northward thrust by the Americans would necessitate another major crossing—that of the westerly flowing Main River. This proved to be no great concern for Patton, who sent his old reliable 4th Armored Division looping northeastward, with the 26th Division in support, for a link-up with the First Army. The immediate objective was the small city of Hanau, on the Main River just east of Frankfurt, where the tankers were fortunate enough to seize an incompletely demolished bridge. Here the Yankee Division was to meet the last organized resistance it would encounter.[2] [P.R.]

EGGER   *March 26, 1945.*   The entire regiment was assembling in the area five miles east of the Rhine where we had stopped in the early hours of the morning. Rubin, who had dropped out last night, came in with the 3rd Battalion. The 2nd Battalion was loaded into trucks at daylight and we rode through Darmstadt, which had been devastated by bombs, to Grossauheim, a suburb of Hanau on the Main River. We

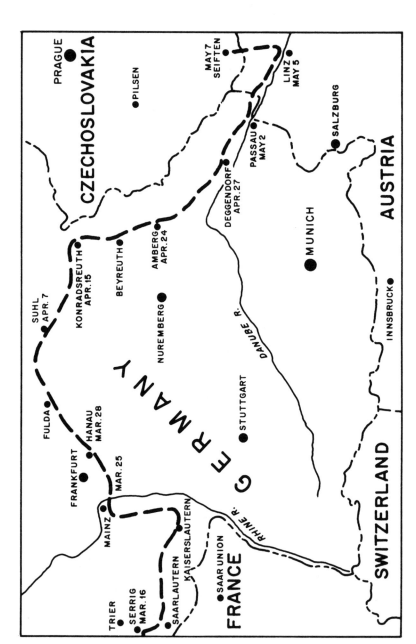

Map 11. G Company's Route Through Germany

kept encountering units of the 4th Armored with large numbers of prisoners in tow.

We unloaded about noon in a wooded area near a battery of the 4th Armored. The infantry of the 4th had crossed the bridge over the river [about a mile upstream from Hanau] and were encountering resistance. We moved to the edge of town and waited at some buildings near the bridge. There were a number of civilians in the area observing the proceedings.

At 1600 we hurried across the bridge while the Germans were firing air bursts above it and relieved the 4th. The sounds of the burp guns and sniper fire reminded me of Saarlautern. I noticed two dead GIs on the far side of the bridge. Our platoon took over a house near the river for the night. The occupants of the house, an elderly couple, moved to the basement for the night.

March 27, 1945. G Company moved through the town [Krotzenheim] before dawn. Within a block of our quarters I counted four dead American soldiers who had probably been killed by snipers yesterday. The Germans had withdrawn, so we moved back across the bridge—which was still receiving air bursts—to attack Hanau.

We began to draw sniper fire as soon as we entered the outskirts of the city. The 3rd Platoon cleared a row of houses that paralleled the railroad tracks. The civilians had left this area, which had been shelled by our artillery, and we found no soldiers in the buildings. Lt. Schulze told me to assemble my squad and move across the tracks to occupy the railroad depot. Rubin was missing so I went into the last house I had seen him enter and found him looting the place. I blew my stack and told him that there was still a war being fought and that the squad just might need his help, that his dallying here could cost lives.

The squad crossed the street and railroad and entered the depot without suffering any casualties from the scattered sniper fire. I posted guards at the four doors of the depot and the rest of us exchanged fire with some Germans behind an embankment about a hundred yards away. I emptied my rifle at two pairs of legs running behind a box car, but the legs never faltered so I must have missed.

A milk cow wandered through no man's land, perhaps looking for someone to milk her.

The rest of the platoon joined us at dark. We crossed the tracks and with a column on each side of the street started to move into Hanau. When we were within fifty yards of the embankment a German soldier hollered, a grenade exploded in front of us, and a machine gun fired over our heads. Everyone hit the pavement. The firing soon ceased. I could see a man against the skyline run for a short distance on top of the embankment and disappear on the backside. Lt. Schulze told me to take half of my squad and go after the machine gun, but before we could get started Lt. Hargrove had the company pull back to the nearest houses, where we spent the night.

March 28, 1945. That morning we moved through Hanau and found that the Germans had left during the night. The 2nd Battalion history, *Handcar White,* [p. 61] described the scene as follows: "At 0900 the battalion filed through its sector of Hanau without firing a shot. The destruction and devastation there was terrific. In the center of the city there was nothing standing and the men found it necessary to pick their way carefully through the rubble-strewn streets. The only signs of life were occasional wisps of smoke curling from stove pipes jutting out of the wreckage. Hanau had been bombed out of existence."

G and F Companies moved to the eastern outskirts of Hanau, where we set up an outpost. Four enemy soldiers hiding in a nearby house surrendered to us.

In the afternoon G Company walked four miles across town to outposts in a wooded area near a German garrison. We found German army blankets in a warehouse so we slept warm.

March 29, 1945. This morning the company moved into some barracks that had been a German Officer Cadet School. We collected all the weapons from the buildings and stacked and burned them. The 3rd Platoon found a German army liquor store. Soon men were coming from all directions, but the platoon took a fair sample of the stock. There was such a wide variety that the fellows could choose between bourbon or Scotch, cognac, gin, calvados, champagne, wine, brandy, and many kinds of schnapps.

Soon orders came down for us to move out to support the 1st Battalion and clear the woods east of the city. We walked through the woods all afternoon in the rain and waded a waist-deep stream but found no Germans. As we were returning a lieutenant and three men from F Company stepped on a mine and were killed.

March 30, 1945. I felt good considering the long, wet hike and how late it was when we finally got back to the barracks last night. We left Hanau by truck in the afternoon but did not cover much distance because of traffic congestion. Most of the men carried a bottle or two, but I opted for a two-pound brick of cheese I had found in the warehouse.

We unloaded at dark and walked to a small town. Moores and Sosenko had been drinking most of the day so I left them in a house and took the rest of the squad to a barn at the edge of town and set up an outpost.

Now that liquor was available, Pete Ruffin was drinking heavily, which only made him more surly than ever. I couldn't understand why Lt. Schulze didn't bite the bullet and get rid of the man.

March 31, 1945. We rode trucks all day. The burgermeister (mayor) of one of the towns we came to refused to surrender, so the battalion radioed for air support. Two P-47s soon appeared and fired a salvo of rockets into the town. We then proceeded through town without incident.

The 11th Armored [which the Yankee Division was now supporting] had by-passed this area. The infantry divisions could not keep up with the mechanized divisions, which had tanks and half-tracks to carry their infantry. The armored units used the main highways and we took the secondary roads, so they were usually ahead of us.

We stopped in a village and set up an outpost while the trucks went back for the rest of the battalion. The trucks were back at 2000, but it took us until 2400 to reach Hainzell, where we spent the night in a house.

April 1, 1945. The people in the house turned the kitchen over to us this morning so we could prepare breakfast. They even provided fresh eggs, which were a real treat. We had not moved in on these people unannounced, since Gormley had gone on ahead in the company jeep and made arrangements with the civilians to provide quarters for the platoon. There were times, of course, when we were taking new territory that we moved in without notice. I failed to note in my diary the age of these people, whether they had children, or their attitude toward us.

The people here were getting dressed up and ready for church on this Easter Sunday as if nothing had happened. We left on foot about 1000 while the church bells were ringing. It was a bright, clear day but the light wind had a chill to it.

Occasionally we could see where the tanks had left the road and machine gun cartridges indicated that the armor had momentarily caught up with the fleeing Germans. We stopped frequently to rest; for once the battalion was not in a hurry. After walking about eight miles we stopped at Urnshausen, where Gormley had picked out a house for the platoon. The company kitchen was set up and we had a hot meal at 1600. I wrote a few letters and shaved. We were given rations and told to be ready to move at any time as trucks would be arriving during the night.

After being Company CO for two months Lt. Hargrove was finally promoted to captain yesterday.

April 2, 1945. We loaded onto the trucks at 0200 this morning. The sky had clouded over during the night and it was threatening to rain. The trucks traveled slowly and stopped occasionally; I thought the convoy leader may have had trouble following the map. We passed two trains consisting of a long string of boxcars that had been shot up by the air force or our tankers. The event had been fairly recent, since some of the cars were still burning.

It started raining as we unloaded from the trucks in Michelsrombach at 0800. Housing was found for each platoon, but the 2nd Platoon was sent out of town for a twenty-four hour outpost. The 3rd Platoon, fortified by a squad from the 1st Platoon, was sent on patrol and to clear the woods outside town. It took us two hours to find that there were no enemy soldiers hiding in the forest. By the time we had returned we were wet to the skin from the rain. As we started to leave on patrol a German observation plane had flown over the town and escaped despite machine gun fire from the trucks and tank destroyers.

The 3rd Platoon was billeted in a large, rich house. The owner was a big burly man in his fifties who spoke English. The photographs of his five sons in the service were prominently on display. He said that three of his sons had been killed in Africa, Italy, and Russia. There were no women in the residence. I don't know the man's occupation but he seemed to be a person of substance and authority. Perhaps he was a large landowner. He was always present, undoubtedly (and with good reason) in an attempt to protect his possessions. Several of us went to a tavern in town and had a glass of dark beer, which I did not care for.

I spent the afternoon resting and went to bed early. The guard duty was light and we rolled dice to see which two pulled the duty.

April 3, 1945. It had rained all night and was still raining when the 3rd Platoon went out this morning to relieve the 2nd Platoon, which had been out for twenty-four hours. The positions were on a small hill near a patch of woods. The foxholes were full of water and we decided to use them only if it became necessary. England, Gibbs, and I went to the woods to look for pitch so we could build a fire but were called back to town, where we loaded onto trucks. The battalion had to leapfrog the companies as they did not have enough vehicles to transport the entire battalion at one time.

We were still following the 11th Armored Division. A few destroyed German vehicles along the road marked its passage. After a two-hour ride we unloaded in a small town and the trucks went back for F Company.

The 3rd Platoon spent four hours in a tavern waiting for the trucks to return. The proprietor served us beer, which did not last very long, so Nachmann and Moores snooped around the establishment and found a supply of pink champagne (but no caviar). Sosenko played the piano and the men sang, drank champagne, and were in good spirits when the trucks arrived at 1400. We rode for about two hours, unloaded, and walked two miles to the village of Geisa. There were a few German soldiers in town, but they immediately surrendered. They did not appear to be with an organized unit but were probably stragglers or deserters trying to return to their homes.

Rubin, who could speak German fluently, found a roomy house for the 3rd Squad to stay in. An old couple lived in the house, and since they seemed amiable we kept the house clean.

April 4–6, 1945. The squad had duty guarding two bridges from 0300 to 0700. The weather had cleared but there was a heavy frost. Later in the day we rode to Wernshausen, where we spent the night. On the 5th we walked to Asbach. The next day we walked five miles to the next town, which we found occupied by elements of the 90th Division, so we returned to Asbach. Naturally there was considerable complaining among the men about an unnecessary hike of ten miles. Our kitchen could not keep up with us, so we were on K rations and whatever we could forage.

Looting was forbidden by the Army but enforcement was nonexistent in our unit. Most of the looting had occurred in unoccupied houses such as we found in the Siegfried Line, Hanau, and other contested cities. Some thievery undoubtedly took place in the inhabited cities and villages, but I only saw one case of forceful theft. Perhaps the looting was kept down because we were walking up to twenty miles a day and could not transport much more than our basic needs. Rubin had the most finesse in looting; he knew what had value and he concentrated on light, small items such as stamps, jewelry, coins, and precious metal objects.

The men who looted rationalized that the Germans had done the same thing in the countries they had occupied. I maintained that we should not come down to the level of the Germans, but after I heard about the slave labor and concentration camps I realized that we had a long way to go to reach their level of degradation.

My convictions against looting did not keep me from taking a pair of field glasses, which I thought I needed worse than the civilian who had been watching us approach. The Army did not provide the squad leaders with field glasses and I felt I could put the glasses to good use during the remainder of the war.

The Army was strict about rape and the punishment was severe. About this time there was a rape reported in a town in which G Company had spent the night. The company lined up and opened ranks but the woman didn't identify anyone. The Army prohibited fraternizing with the Germans, let alone raping their women.

━━━━━━━━━━━━━━━━━━━━━━━━━━━

OPERATIONAL BACKGROUND   The reason for the leisurely pace of the advance that Egger had noted on April 1 was that the Third Army was waiting for the First and Ninth Armies, large elements of which had been engaged in eliminating a major pocket of trapped German forces in the Ruhr. Once the three American armies were lined up, they were to drive eastward, cutting a wide swath across the center of Germany, beginning on April 10. In the meantime Patton was escheloning XII Corps, to which the 26th Division was now attached, southeastward to position it on the southern foothills of the Thuringer Wald, a southeasterly stretching range of forested hills that presented less hospitable terrain than the other armies had to traverse.[3] [P.R.]

━━━━━━━━━━━━━━━━━━━━━━━━━━━

EGGER   *April 7, 1945.*   Asbach was the most northerly point on our route of travel. From there we turned south by trucks to Suhl. The 11th Armored was still out in front of us.

Ruffin was drunk again today, as he was most of the time. The cooks must have transported his liquor.

We outposted Suhl that night and Ruffin told us that German paratroopers had dropped in the area, a story that I did not believe.

April 8–9, 1945.   We walked over mountains and through patches of snow for eight miles to Schmiedefeld, where we stayed until the morning of the 10th. On the 9th LeCrone came back to us from his appendectomy. I was glad his trouble had been diagnosed and corrected, as some of the men thought he was feigning illness. Our pay for March was nine days late because we were moving so fast.

April 10, 1945.   We walked twenty-five miles today and it all seemed to be uphill. We have been in the mountains and forests of Thuringia, a state of Germany, since the 8th. We spent the night in Masserberg.

April 11, 1945.   Our hike of fifteen miles to Steinheid was slowed somewhat by trees felled, sometimes for a distance of a hundred yards, across the road. The road blocks delayed the movement of our vehicles since the road had to be checked for mines and the trees removed, but the infantry could walk around them.

I could not understand why Germany did not give up. We were in central Germany, moving toward Czechoslovakia, and the Russians were closing in from the east. Where would the Germans make their last stand?

April 12, 1945. We walked ten miles through the rain to Haselbach, where the battalion was held up by roadblocks.

There were two priorities when we entered a town, comfortable quarters and food to supplement our rations. We were eating fresh eggs twice a day, but they may not have been as fresh as we thought since the Germans stored them in crocks of salt brine.

April 13, 1945. Today was another day for walking up and down hills for fifteen miles. The men were tired and began to grumble and complain, which was not unusual. The company stopped at the wrong town so we had to load up again and walk two more miles to the next village, Teuschnitz.

The 3rd Squad had chicken and turkey for our evening meal. We were not supposed to take food belonging to the civilians, but our officers did not enforce the rule. Besides, it was difficult to do so much walking on three K-rations a day. The civilians did not like us helping ourselves, which I could understand because most of them were not wealthy people. Maybe they would realize what the German army had been doing to the rest of Europe. Newcity and Oakley were cooks and LeCrone was a farmer/butcher so we turned the details over to them. In repayment other members of the squad took some of their guard duty.

The people where we were billeted seemed friendly so I thought perhaps the turkey and chicken had belonged to their neighbor. We did wash the dishes and clean up the kitchen.

April 14, 1945. We walked for ten miles, then trucks took us to the outskirts of Naila. The tanks ahead of us had been fired on by antiaircraft guns from a wooded area, so we unloaded and captured the gunners, who offered no resistance. The company spent the night at Naila, where my squad had beer and chicken for supper.

April 15, 1945. We joined the rest of the battalion at a small village near Naila and walked to Konradsreuth, where F Company had encountered small arms fire. The tanks moved up and blasted away at the town; then

Fox Company moved through the town with little difficulty. G Company continued through town to Martinsreuth, which was about twenty miles from the border of Czechoslovakia.

Rubin and Ruffin left us today on furlough to the states.* Furloughs were given to those men who had spent a long time overseas or in combat and for emergencies at home. It wasn't clear that Rubin fit any of these categories, so we couldn't figure out why he was one of the favored. Being Rubin, he wasn't saying.

It had been obvious for quite a while that something had to be done about Ruffin. Whoever made the decision to grant him furlough had certainly shown him considerable compassion—more than he had ever shown Packer or Stribling. We were all glad to see Ruffin leave regardless of the means and to have Gormley replace him as platoon leader. We knew Gormley would be more reasonable in his demands upon us and easier to get along with. Dafoe, who had returned from the hospital on March 14, became the platoon guide.

Rubin and Ruffin were the only men from our platoon to receive furloughs during the war, and most of us congratulated them on their good fortune. One of the fellows said it helped to be Jewish, but that was hogwash since none of the other Jews in the company received furloughs. I knew I would miss Rubin because it was good to have someone in the squad who could speak German and because he was cheerful and good natured. He always informed the German civilians that he was Jewish and needled them at every opportunity. On several occasions he told the people where we were stopping for the night that he was Jewish and then requested that they prepare him a meal, which they did, probably not because of remorse for their treatment of the Jews, but because he was a member of the conquering army.

Several of the men gave Rubin items of loot to take to the States with him and mail to their homes. But when Hank Sosenko requested the same of Rubin, he told Hank he did not have room to carry any more with him. So Hank asked the squad, "Who wants this watch? I'm tired of carrying it." Rubin said, "I'll take it." Sosenko gave it to him.

April 16, 1945. The battalion was to stay in this area to rest for several days; maybe the complaining had helped. The 3rd Squad was quartered in a farmhouse at the edge of the village. A small stream flowed through the farm and it provided us with trout for breakfast. Captain Hargrove

---

*Pfc. Solomon Rubin departed for Fort Dix, New Jersey, on Apr. 16 for forty-five days "temporary duty"; T/Sgt. Pete Ruffin left for Fort Meade, Maryland, that same day and under the same arrangements.

didn't approve of our fishing with hand grenades, or "Dupont Lures," as we called them. Perhaps he was a dyed-in-the-wool fly fisherman. I suppose he wanted us to save our grenades for their intended use.

During our travels I had noticed numerous deer, so Peck, LeCrone and I went hunting in the evening and Peck shot a buck. The deer here were much smaller than the mule deer of the States but larger than our jackrabbits.

OPERATIONAL BACKGROUND   The reason for the halt on April 16 was not, as Egger had speculated, out of concern for the troops. On April 12 General Eisenhower had imposed a limit on the eastward advance of the Ninth, First and Third Armies at the Elbe-Mulde River line, where it was anticipated that the American forces would soon be making contact with the Russians. By the 15th the most forward elements of the Third Army had reached the prescribed limits of advance—the 26th Division was only ten miles from the Czechoslovakian border—and were forced to pause for further orders from higher in the chain of command.

The new plan, passed along by General Bradley on April 16, directed the First and Ninth Armies to hold along the Elbe and Mulde Rivers while Patton drove southward in a line roughly paralleling the Czechoslovakian border to prevent the Germans from retreating into a mythical Bavarian "redoubt" and to assist the Seventh Army in sweeping southern Germany.[4] [P.R.]

April 17, 1945.   The 3rd Squad had venison steak for breakfast. The men in my squad were good providers and we ate better than most.

I cleaned up, wrote letters, and rested today.

The people in whose house we were staying were poor and without modern farm equipment. A horse and cow were hitched together to pull their wagon. The old man and his daughter worked in the fields, but there were other people staying at the farm who did not look like farmers. Perhaps they were relatives from the city. If Rubin had been with us we would have known all the details. The farmer and his family were taciturn and sullen. They emphatically refused the venison we offered them. In view of their barely concealed hostility we ignored them after that.

The country we had been traveling through the last two weeks was very scenic with little war damage to the smaller cities and villages. The cultivated fields, green pastures mixed in a quilt-like pattern with the different shades of green of the conifer and hardwood forests, and the sun shining on the red tile roofs of the buildings in the villages were especially attractive when viewed from a high point. At the same time the view could be discouraging when we realized that we had to walk to that cluster of buildings in the distance.

Moores and England shot another buck today so we could dispense with the rations for a while longer.

April 18, 1945. George Company rode tanks to Oberkotzau in the morning and occupied the town without any difficulty. We helped ourselves to cans of berries from the local cannery. (This is the town where I got my field glasses.)

We were informed today of President Roosevelt's death on April 12. The German civilians may have known about it before we did. I don't understand why it took six days for the news to reach the troops.

We were relieved by the 90th Division and trucks took us back to Konsradsreuth, a town we had passed through on the 15th.

We had been traveling east toward Czechoslovakia but now the trucks turned south and we rode for twenty-five miles. Several men from E Company were wounded by rifle fire as we loaded on the trucks, but the battalion didn't stop to hunt down the snipers.

The battalion bivouacked in a wooded area at our destination near Wasserknoden. Members of the 3rd Squad had carried enough venison with us for the evening meal and had given the remainder to the 2nd and 1st Squads. That evening we had venison and fried potatoes with canned berries for dessert.

April 19, 1945. Our twenty-five-mile hike over secondary roads took us four miles southeast of Bayreuth and through Berneck. We met no opposition. The weather was clear but windy and cool. We spent the night in a small village called Lunz.

April 20, 1945. We walked another twenty-five miles today. Training in the States, where a twenty-five-mile hike had only been a monthly occurrence, had not been this tough. Naturally the men were complaining, but I always preferred walking to fighting. Some days we had to do both. Our route took us through Metzhol and east of Eschenbach. In the late afternoon we came upon a deserted village called Poppenberg, which had been used for training by the Wehrmacht. We bivouacked there for the night.

The purple ointment medication the medics had given me had helped relieve the itching caused by the scabies.

Moores and I fired at a deer in the evening while hunting but missed, and five German soldiers came out of the woods with their hands up. I bet they thought we had excellent vision.

April 21, 1945. We cleared the training area in the morning and found it deserted. We only walked seven miles today, hardly enough to work up a sweat. LeCrone seemed more like his old self after coming back from the hospital, but then everyone was in better spirits. Some of the tension had eased, since it appeared that the war would soon be over and the South Pacific seemed far away.

We stopped at Gressenwohr for the night and tried to dry out as it had been raining most of the day. When we moved into our quarters, about 1700, LeCrone lay down to take a nap. At dusk, which was near 1830, I woke him and said that he had slept through the night and that it was time to eat breakfast and get ready to leave. He never questioned me and began to collect his gear until he noticed that Oakley could not keep a straight face. LeCrone took it in good humor. We would not have considered pulling such a stunt in February, before he went to the hospital and was nervous and jumpy.

April 22, 1945. We moved by truck through Vilseck and Hahnbach to Gebenbach, which is almost due east of Nuremberg. We walked five miles to Godlricht to spend the night. A light rain had fallen most of the day.

April 23, 1945. We marched from Godlricht to Fromberg, a distance of about ten miles, which had become like a short stroll for us these days.

April 24, 1945. We were truck-borne for about four hours today. The convoy traveled through Amberg, and then we walked five miles to Zell to spend the night. Four hundred enemy troops peacefully surrendered to the 2nd Platoon today.

Ever since our troops had been encountering a civilian population in the towns and villages we had noticed a large number of younger men who were amputees. Most of them had probably suffered severe wounds from shrapnel, and those missing feet most likely lost them to frostbite in the bitter cold of Russian winters. This was only one of the prices the citizens of Germany had paid in a losing cause.

April 25, 1945. Besides walking twenty miles today the company took a hundred prisoners, more or less. We received some small arms fire in Munster but G Company suffered no casualties. The company spent the night in Munster while the 3rd Platoon outposted the town. We saw the Danube River today for the first time, but it was a muddy brown color, not blue.

After dark the 3rd Squad was sitting around a campfire visiting with several English and French soldiers who had been prisoners of the Germans and had been released by our troops that day. They were happy men and were extremely grateful toward us. One of our sentries, hearing a noise in the field next to our position, called out a challenge. When there was no response we started firing our rifles. There was no return fire or sound, so England and I walked into the field and found a dead, unarmed German soldier who had been shot in the chest. I suspected that his home was in Munster and under cover of darkness he was trying to return to his family, whose photograph he carried in his billfold. He had come so close to making it, and to die so near home and within two weeks of the end of the war only added to the tragedy. He probably didn't answer the challenge for fear of having to spend four to six months in a prisoner-of-war camp. The incident has haunted me periodically ever since.

April 26, 1945. We rode trucks all day and unloaded three miles from Deggendorf. The battalion was now moving southeast, parallel to the Danube River toward Austria.

E and G Companies captured a hill beyond Metten and took a hundred prisoners while losing four men to wounds. The resistance we had been encountering lately was token in comparison to what we had experienced from November through March. We dug in on the hill and spent the night there. Some Germans entrenched on the next ridge popped off a few rounds of small arms fire in our direction but nobody was hit.

April 27, 1945. The Germans were still dug in on the ridge on the outskirts of Deggendorf, a city of about 15,000. I don't know if this story is true or not but we heard that our battalion commander had contacted the burgermeister of Deggendorf and suggested that he surrender the city and spare the needless loss of property and life. The offer was declined with a smart remark.

Easy and George Companies attacked across the valley and up the hill while the artillery pounded the trenches and the town beyond. I believe the town was mostly defended by a home guard of older men and boys, not by an organized army unit, as we received no mortars or artillery. But anyone who could see and squeeze a trigger posed a threat.

The bullets sounded like angry bees overhead. As I write this I marvel at how much discipline it took to keep advancing into small arms fire, especially when we could not see the enemy. The two companies kept firing as we moved ahead and drove the Germans out of the trenches without losing any men, which does not say much for the defenders' marksmanship. I think many of the home guard were drunk, which undoubtedly accounted for the erratic rifle fire.

As the company was clearing some small buildings on the ridgetop, a man from the 2nd Platoon, who was two steps ahead of me, threw open the door of a shed revealing a middle-aged man in a German uniform lying on the floor. In the brief glimpse I got of the scene the man appeared to be unarmed and unconscious. The soldier from the 2nd Platoon blasted him with a burst from his M-1 and we moved on. I have often wondered what my reaction would have been if I had reached the building first. In all fairness, the GI had reacted as we had been taught to do in house-to-house combat. Those who shot first and asked questions later had a better chance of surviving.

We continued into town with G Company attacking from the west, Easy Company from the east, and Fox Company from the south. In our sector the resistance was strong and we were held up for several hours at a bridge over a canal running east and west through the city. The 3rd Platoon was strung out west of the bridge along a street paralleling the canal. The houses there protected us from snipers in the two-story buildings across the waterway.

As the non-coms of the 3rd Platoon were gathered together for a briefing by Lt. Schulze, an elderly German started to walk past us. This was the first civilian we had observed in Deggendorf, since most had left town or had gone into hiding in the cellars. Sgt. Frank "Lucky" Micik, who spoke some German, addressed the old man, first in a questioning tone and then angrily after the civilian replied. Micik raised his arm as if to strike the cowering old man, but his descending hand plucked the pocket watch and chain from the German's vest pocket. The old man hurried away without protesting, undoubtedly thankful that he had only lost a watch.

Lucky Micik had been promoted from the weapons platoon to assistant squad leader of the 1st Squad after Treml was wounded in March. I never cared much for him, but he was a good soldier, the only one I knew who seemed to enjoy combat. One time he told me, "I'm just like you, I like to be where there is action." I didn't tell him that I was scared to death most of the time and was only where the action was because I had to be. Lucky was awarded the Silver Star for bravery at Deggendorf, where he tried to retrieve Lt. Schulze's body in the action described below.

Shortly after the incident with the civilian, German hand grenades began to explode on our side of the canal, but fortunately we had no troops in that particular area. I sent Greasor and Gibbs to the second story of one of the houses adjacent to the canal while Oakley and I went into another one nearby to see if we could pick off the grenade throwers.

I scanned the south side of the waterway with my field glasses and picked up the movement of a military cap about forty yards away. When the head became visible above the embankment I took a shot at it, but its owner quickly ducked out of sight. Over the next few minutes two more caps appeared above the embankment in the same vicinity. I fired at both and the caps vanished. My last target was a bald head, which I soon drove to cover. The grenade throwing ceased, but a volley of rifle fire came through the windows, barely missing Oakley and me. Greasor and Gibbs also experienced near misses from small arms fire directed at their house. Evidently troops in the buildings across the canal had spotted us. After that we were more careful about exposing ourselves.

S/Sgts. Sullivan and Byrne, both recent hospital returnees,* had been hanging around with our platoon that morning. They and Lt. Schulze had spent much of the time chatting while we waited for E and F Companies to come in behind the German defenders of the bridge.

Perhaps the orders were changed or maybe the lieutenant got tired of waiting. Whatever the case, he told the squad leaders that the platoon was going to cross the bridge. I got that familiar sinking feeling in my gut which always appeared before an attack. I wondered why we weren't waiting for Easy and Fox Companies; it didn't sound like they were meeting much resistance so they should arrive any time now. The narrow bridge was surely covered by machine guns, and we hadn't even called for mortar or artillery support.

Lt. Schulze, together with Sullivan and Byrne, led the way. The 1st and 2nd Squads were on the west and east sidewalks of the bridge and 3rd Squad was in reserve at the rear. Halfway across the arched bridge the platoon met with machine gun and rifle fire, which killed Lt. Schulze and slightly wounded both sergeants and Marron of the 2nd Squad.† The two squads and the wounded men quickly retreated back to safety.

Fifteen minutes later the Germans surrendered to E Company and we walked across the bridge past Lt. Schulze, who lay in a large pool of blood. I had an overwhelming feeling of sadness as we passed by his body.

There were a number of German prisoners lining the street and I

---

*S/Sgt. Wallace L. Sullivan had been seriously wounded at Moncourt on Nov. 8 and had returned to duty Mar. 14. S/Sgt. Joseph A. Byrne had been hospitalized because of illness—probably trench foot—on Nov. 12 and had rejoined the company on Mar. 12.

†S/Sgt. Sullivan and Pvt. John A. Marron were shown as "slightly wounded" in action near Deggendorf on Apr. 27 and hospitalized. S/Sgt. Byrne was also listed as "slightly wounded" in that same action but was not hospitalized. 1st. Lt. William H. Schulze had just received a Silver Star for action at Saarlautern.

In his letter of June 4, 1945, to the hospitalized Lt. Otts, Captain Hargrove described the incident as follows: "Our friend and superior platoon leader, Bill Schulze, was killed noticed a tall baldheaded man with a bandaged head among them. The battalion had lost one man killed and three wounded, all from G Company, and had taken prisoner fifteen hundred German troops.

We proceeded through the center of town. To vent their anger and frustration over the death of the lieutenant, the men of the 3rd Platoon smashed the plate glass windows of the business establishments as we filed by. I heard that the burgermeister's house was torched and when the fire trucks arrived the hoses were punctured with bayonets.

After the surrender of the troops the civilians began to appear. Deggendorf seemed to be well off, as the stores were stocked with clothing and food. The 3rd Squad selected some course-grained meat from a butcher shop for our main course that evening. I suspect it was horse meat.

That evening I talked to Nachman about the events of the day. We couldn't figure out what the big hurry was to attack across the bridge. Why take unnecessary risks when the end of war was so near?

Later that night Nachman said to me, "Wouldn't it be a hell of a note to go through all this and then check out so close to the end? The thought of being killed by some fanatical thirteen-year-old or an over-age home guard scares the hell out of me." I told him that the war couldn't possibly last more than a few more days. "That's what I'm so scared about, Bruce. After coming this far I don't want to die now. Do you know what I mean?" I certainly did know what he meant. How could I forget the conclusion of *All Quiet on the Western Front?**

April 28, 1945. The battalion was moving down the north bank of the Danube. The day was uneventful and we encountered no resistance as we walked fourteen miles to Winzer.

April 29, 1945. The battalion traveled by foot today. As we were walking I noticed a fresh mound of dirt about eighteen inches high at the

---

at Deggendorf, Germany, April 27th. It was a terrible blow to all us who knew him. . . . We had been troubled with snipers all through Deggendorf and had taken about two hundred PW's so were pretty cocky. . . . Bill was ahead of his platoon with two men on a bridge. I was with the rest of his platoon. When fired on he killed one Heinie with his Tommy gun, then drew more fire and told the two men to go back; he was shot through the head before he could get back. We flanked this group with the 1st and 2nd platoons and had no more trouble."

---

*The reference is to Erich Maria Remarque's classic novel of World War I. The main character, Paul Baumer, was the lone survivor of seven German schoolboys who had enlisted in 1914. He was killed in October 1918, on a day the army report described as "All Quiet on the Westen Front." In the 1930 movie version starring Lew Ayres, Paul is killed while exposing himself above the trench parapet to reach for a flower.

edge of the road, and upon inspecting it discovered bare feet protruding from one end of a hastily prepared grave. We passed three more mounds and later in the day found three slave laborers in a barn. The heads of the men were clean shaven and tattered clothing hung on their emaciated bodies. The German soldiers had killed those who could not keep up and finally left the others as we gained ground on them. None of the slave laborers could speak English, so they expressed their appreciation for being liberated by throwing their arms around us. They stank so badly I almost gagged.

Although we didn't have time to help them, these poor souls were not left to fend for themselves. They were rounded up by rear-echelon staff officers and put in camps with thousands of other laborers and displaced persons. I have no idea what nationality they were but I suppose most of them were Russians or other Eastern Europeans.

The road was blocked about two miles outside of Otterskirchen and we received some sniper fire and antiaircraft bursts from across the river as we cleared the town.

The battalion had walked twenty miles today. The 3rd Squad stayed in a farmhouse at the edge of town.

April 30, 1945. George Company was in battalion reserve today. E and F Companies moved through Patriching, a crossroads village near Passau, after encountering fire from enemy tanks and snipers. Our artillery bombarded the German positions and the two companies moved a mile beyond the village. In the late afternoon we moved by truck to Patriching, where we spent the night. The village overlooked the Danube, and we could see considerable enemy troop movement on the south side of the river. We were subjected to air bursts from their antiaircraft guns most of the night.

May 1, 1945. The 1st and 3rd Battalions of the 328th Regiment moved through us yesterday afternoon. We were assigned to the 101st Regiment to help establish a bridgehead across the Danube at Hacklberg if the bridge was still standing.

E and F Companies moved down to the river and discovered that the bridge had been demolished, so our artillery pounded away at targets of opportunity across the river. G Company spent most of the day in Patriching and in the late afternoon we moved toward the river and spent the night in a farmhouse.

May 2, 1945. The 3rd Platoon left about 1100 and traveled on the main road to Passau to look for an 88 that had been harrassing the battalion. When we located it the men manning the gun surrendered after blowing it up with a grenade. We spent the rest of the day and night in a nearby house.

May 3, 1945. The house we stayed in must have been a temporary field hospital for the Germans, since medical supplies had been left and the severed arm of a man was in the refuse pile in the backyard.

A light snow fell during the night, reminding me of home and the springs of the Northwest. The battalion moved out on trucks and tanks to catch up with the other elements of the regiment.

After a ride of nearly thirty miles we reached the town of Ob-Kappel astride the German-Austrian border where we spent the night. As George Company was unloading, a man from the 1st Platoon jumped from the truck bed to the cobblestone street. When he landed the butt of his rifle struck the street; the impact jarred the trigger and sent a bullet through his brain.*

As one of the soldier's buddies covered the body with a blanket I heard him say, "We never could get him to keep a shell out of the chamber and the safety on when we were traveling."

May 4, 1945. I noticed a dozen or so Russian soldiers who had been prisoners of the Germans sitting around small fires heating coffee near where we had spent the night. I was struck by how sad and sober they looked, in contrast to the happiness shown by the released prisoners of other nations. Many years later I learned that the Russian soldiers who had been captured by the Germans were sentenced to five to ten years in the forced labor camps when they got back. Some "workers' paradise"!

We left in the afternoon and rode about ten miles. The traffic was so heavy with vehicles from the 11th Armored Division, which was moving to Linz, that the battalion had to wait half a day at Starz for the roads to clear. From here we could see the snow-covered Alps to the south, on our right. We traveled until nightfall and stayed at the small village of Koth.

May 5, 1945. The battalion objective today was to take posession of the high ground overlooking Linz, Austria, (pop. 180,000) while the armored units entered from the west. We walked twenty miles in a light rain and climbed the high hill on which the village of Kranabithedt was

---

*Pfc. J. W. Whited was listed on the morning report of May 8 as "deceased in Germany near Deitzing 3 May 45 (non-battle)." The "Record of Events" on that same morning report noted: "Soldier killed by accidental discharge of own weapon while jumping off of truck."

located. Then, as the armor had no difficulty in Linz, we climbed down the steep slope onto the highway and moved on into Urfahr, a northern suburb of Linz, while the tankers were still moving through.

Shortly after we reached the highway a German soldier raced by with an American GI in close pursuit whacking him in the rear with a belt. The German was a heavy young man wearing knee-high leather boots. He was breathing hard and his eyes rolled in his head. He probably wondered what fate awaited him. I never learned what had brought on this remarkable scene nor its outcome.

In Urfahr that night we had a nice apartment with electric lights, modern plumbing, a radio, and good food.

May 6, 1945. The 11th Armored had made contact with the Russians downriver from Linz, so the 328th turned due north into Czechoslovakia, the only remaining place for the Germans to retreat. Trucks took us for about thirteen miles and then we walked another five miles to Studanky, Czechoslovakia, to spend the night.

May 7, 1945. We heard rumors this morning that the war would end soon—hopefully by my birthday, which would be the 9th. We walked to a village called Seiften and waited for the word.

May 8, 1945 [V-E Day]. Today's attack was called off for lack of a war. We basked in the warm sun and rested and I wrote a letter to my parents. Our kitchen had caught up with us and we had three hot meals.

May 9, 1945. What a present for my 22nd birthday! The company moved down the hill and camped near the main road this morning.

There was a stream of German soldiers coming in all day to surrender and turn in their weapons. While my squad was on guard at the bridge, a German lieutenant drove up in a German jeep. We halted the jeep and made him and his driver get out. The lieutenant spoke perfect English and was as blond, sharp, and arrogant as a Hollywood version of a Nazi officer. He gave us a lecture about why the Americans should not have waged war on Germany; we should have joined them fighting the true enemy, which was Russia, and that it was not too late. We laughed at him, took his sidearms and jeep, and marched him and his driver off to join the other prisoners. As the Cold War developed, I often thought of his words.

POSTSCRIPT AND REFLECTIONS   After the war I went to the F Company clerk and confirmed that Dixon and Erickson had been killed on November 8. The people I inquired about were only a dim memory in Fox Company. The clerk seemed surprised that I had survived so long without injury.

I have often wondered why it turned out that I made it through the whole war without a scratch while so many others were less fortunate. Goodness and character certainly had nothing to do with it. Neither was it a result of superior military skills and knowledge, although these could increase the odds in your favor. But ultimately survival in battle was more a matter of luck than anything. Only chance dictated where lethal artillery and mortar rounds would land, and nobody knew where the deadly sniper was concealed.

There was a soldier in the 97th Division who was sent over with me as a replacement. He appeared to be very close to being mentally retarded. He was a poor marksman, uncoordinated, and a slow learner. He had been a flunky in the kitchen with the 97th. "Sad Sack" Jackson [pseudonym] was assigned to the 104th Regiment at Nancy, France. A few days before the war ended, as we were resting at the edge of the road, a column of troops from the 104th filed by us. I was pleasantly surprised to see Jackson shuffling along in his customary stooped, eyes-cast-down posture. I called to him, but there was no hint of recognition. How had he survived when so many abler soldiers had fallen? In contrast, Lt. Peterson, a platoon leader with my company in the 97th Division who was a good leader, intelligent, and a skilled infantryman, was killed in April of 1945 on his first day of combat.

Out of the group of five men from the 97th Division that I went overseas with, one (Dixon) was killed and three were wounded. During my tenure with the 1st and 3rd Squads of G Company five men were killed, sixteen wounded, eleven went back with frostbite or trench foot, three with battle fatigue, and the fate of one is unknown to me. A total of thirty-six of my squadmates had been lost while I was in the 1st and 3rd Squads.

I was one of a mere handful of frontline veterans whose service with G Company dated back to before the slaughter at Moncourt Woods and who were lucky enough to make it through the whole war without suffering so much as a scratch as a result of enemy action. But, as somebody once observed, "There are no unwounded combat soldiers."

I do not consider myself a hero, and I received no medals for action beyond the call of duty, although I am sure men in other branches of the service were decorated for what the infantryman did every day. I volunteered occasionally and was fortunate that my missions did not turn out to be dangerous.

I was like Joe and Willie, as described in Bill Mauldin's *Up Front:* "Joe and Willie . . . came from the other infantry—the great numbers of men who stay and sweat in the foxholes that give their more courageous brethren claustrophobia. They go on patrols when patrols are called for, and they don't shirk hazards, because they don't want to let their buddies down. The Army couldn't get along without them, either. Although it needs men to do daring deeds, it also needs men who have the quiet courage to stick in their foxholes and fight and kill even though they hate killing and are scared to death while doing it."[5]

Every infantryman who saw much combat knows that, as in all things in life, there was an inequity in the distribution of medals. Some of those who received awards were more deserving than others; many who deserved them were passed over. First the deed had to be recognized by someone in authority. Then a write-up of the action had to be submitted up the chain of command for review. The better the write-up, the better the chance of the individual's receiving a medal; consequently the description of the action was often embellished. I could not recognize the events described in some of the write-ups.

Our 2nd Platoon received more awards than any unit in the company; most of their non-coms had one or more medals. I doubt that it was a coincidence that they also had George Idelson, a squad leader with superior writing skills.

Lt. Schulze won a Silver Star at Saarlautern but later lost his life for taking an ill-considered chance. Wolfenbarger deservedly received a Silver Star for staying behind to cover the withdrawal of the rest of his patrol, but Larry Treff did the same thing and nobody was even aware of it. Captain Seeley of F Company and Captain Swift, Easy Company, among others, were real heroes. Some recipients of medals for action early in the campaign broke during later actions. This does not diminish their courage but only shows that every man has his breaking point.

Gormley should have received recognition for taking over our platoon on Hoecker Hill when Pete Ruffin ran out on us. Giovinazzo's truly courageous action in knocking out a German tank at Eschdorf is documented in the 2nd Battalion history, but that was the only recognition given him.

More than four decades have passed since those terrible months when we endured the mud of Lorraine, the bitter cold of the Ardennes, the dank cellars of Saarlautern, and the twenty-five-mile road marches though Germany, but sometimes these events are as clear in my mind as if they had occurred yesterday. We were miserable and cold and exhausted most of the time, and we were all scared to death that the next action would be our last one. But we were young and strong then, possessed of the marvelous resilience of youth, and for all the misery and fear and the hating every moment of it the war was a great, if always terrifying, adventure. Not a man among us would want to go through it again, but we are all proud of having been so severely tested and found adequate. The only regret is for those of our friends who never returned.

These men—Dixon and Wolfenbarger and so many others—remain imprinted in my memory, forever young, just the way they were then. I remember their personalities distinctly, though their faces are now a blur. But they are more than dim figures out of the past; they remain treasured friends over whose memory I wept as I recorded their stories. To them and to all the men of G Company who shared the great adventure of our times these pages are dedicated.

BRUCE EGGER
Prineville, Oregon

Epilogue

While the men of G Company relaxed in Czechoslovakia, quietly celebrating the end of the war against Germany, Lt. Lee Otts was more actively celebrating the occasion in Circencester, England, and preparing to leave for the States the next day. In contrast to many who went unwounded but who nevertheless bear the unseen scars of war, the sunny-dispositioned Otts was almost completely recovered from the all-too-visible wounds he had suffered on Hoecker Hill on March 13.

After being wounded Otts had been taken by ambulance from the 26th Division Clearing Station near Serrig, Germany, to the 12th Evacuation Hospital in Luxembourg City, where he was left largely unattended for some twelve to fourteen hours while more serious casualties were being looked after. Finally, sometime after midnight on March 15, an Army surgeon deadened his right shoulder with novocaine, cleaned out the bullet wound, and placed a drain in it. Since the collarbone had been shattered, Otts had to wear a cast from his waist to his chin, with only the left arm and right hand left free.

Next a team of two surgeons went to work on his broken jaw, forcing wires around the teeth and through the gums, both top and bottom. Lee vividly recalls that this procedure, which was done without anesthetic, was extremely painful. Strong rubber bands were then hooked over the wire loops to render the jaws immobile. For the next month Otts did all his eating through a straw. There was nothing to be done about the silver-dollar-sized hole in his face where the mortar fragment had hit; it would be allowed to heal naturally before plastic surgery was attempted.

The next day, March 16, Lt. Otts was evacuated by air to England. After a temporary stay of a week at one medical facility, where he received no treatment at all because the hospital did not handle broken jaws, he was transferred to the 192nd General Hospital outside the little town of Circencester. The first day there the bandages were removed from his face, and Otts became nauseated after seeing for the first time the ragged hole along his left jaw that was so deep the bone was visible. "I hadn't shaved in about six weeks," he recalled in his memoirs, "and the matted, blood-caked beard, plus the hole in my face was too much to take."

Those first days at the 192nd were not pleasant for Otts. Although he was ambulatory and was able to wander around the hospital, visiting other patients, the nights were bad. The combination of the uncomfortable cast and the pain of his wounds made sleep difficult. On top of that the drainage from the shoulder wound seeped inside the cast and enveloped him with a foul odor. And since he could not brush his teeth, his mouth tasted almost as bad as his shoulder smelled. The good news was that extensive dental X-rays showed no damage to his teeth.

Early in April Otts talked his orthopedic surgeon into removing the cast, and by the middle of the month the wires and rubber bands were removed from his mouth. Although he had to continue carrying his arm in a sling and remain on a diet of soft food for a while, Otts' sense of fun and adventure were soon in the ascendancy. And of course his keen eye for the ladies—at first the hospital nurses, but soon to be expanded to broader horizons—had not been diminished.

By this time Lee was sufficiently recovered that, with a small patch concealing the wound on his jaw, he was able to go into Circencester every evening. A friend fixed him up with a blind date with a Red Cross worker named Mary Frances Byrd, from Wilmington, North Carolina. Otts was greatly attracted to the petite, dark-haired girl, and soon they were dating steadily. There was also Angelia, the sister of one of his friends in the ward. She was stationed in England in the WAACs and came to see her brother on weekends. "As she was quite pretty, I was always on hand to give out with the fancy talk," Otts noted in his memoirs.

He and Mary Frances Byrd were together almost every evening during that last three weeks Lee was in England. They would stop at a favorite pub called the "Black Horse," where Lee would have a beer while the abstemious Mary Frances toyed with a glass of wine. Later they would go to the Red Cross Club to dance and then afterwards spend an hour or so in the parlor of the old English couple with whom Mary Frances was living. One night when she was not available Lee took Angelia to the Black Horse, but it was Mary Frances who occupied first place on his list. They celebrated V-E Day together, well into the early hours of the next morning, and two years later Otts confided to his memoirs, "If I had not wanted to see my family so bad I think I would have been content to spend the rest of my life with Mary Frances in Circencester."

Early the next morning, May 9, 1945, he was among the 165 American officers and men who left by train for Southampton to board the U.S. Army transport *Excelsior* for the voyage back to the States. They arrived in New York on the evening of May 22.

After a thirty-day leave at home, Otts was sent to Northington General Hospital in Tuscaloosa, Alabama, for plastic surgery on his jaw. For Lee this assignment in the environs of the University of Alabama could hardly have been better, and he soon became a full participant in the social life at the university, particularly in his fraternity, Phi Gamma Delta. In February, the plastic surgery successfully completed, Lee was transferred to Fort McClellan in Anniston, Alabama. Shortly thereafter he went on extended leave and in June enrolled in law school at the University of Alabama. He was released from active duty on July 10, 1946, after having been promoted to captain the previous month.

In the meantime, Lee had kept up a sporadic correspondence with Mary Frances Byrd, who, following her stint in England, had worked a year in Germany with the Red Cross and, later, in private industry in California before returning to her home in Wilmington, North Carolina. In April 1948, "after much persuasion," she accepted an invitation from Otts to attend a Phi Gamma Delta outing in Florida. The relationship they had established in England three years earlier was soon rekindled, and on September 4, 1948, Lee MacMillan Otts and Mary Frances Byrd were married in Wilmington.

After Lee's graduation from law school the following December, the young couple settled in Brewton, Alabama, where he went into private practice. They have lived there ever since, raising four daughters—now all married—and becoming leaders in the community, which he has served with the same dedication and ability he exhibited as a platoon leader in G Company. For Lee Otts the war is now but a distant memory.

Bruce Egger's life followed a considerably different pattern. The men of G Company remained in occupation in the Sudetenland area of Czechoslovakia for two months following V-E Day and were soon undergoing combat training in preparation for a possible transfer to the Pacific Theater. Later, when the war with Japan ended, Egger noted that it "was a great relief for all of us, since it meant we would not be redeployed to the Pacific."

A number of the recovered wounded, including Vernon Olson, Vic Popa, Junior Letterman, Lee Allen, Wilbur Munns, and Albert Evans, returned to the company during this period. Egger continued as leader of the 3rd Squad, which had expanded to fifteen men with all the returnees. It was also at this time that Bruce fleshed out the sparse notes from his diary into a full journal of his combat experiences.

On July 14 Egger received a week's pass to Paris. In his journal he writes of seeing the Eiffel Tower, Notre Dame Cathedral, and the Arc de Triomphe; there is no mention of his having sampled the renowned nightlife of that city. While he was gone the 26th Division was transferred to Hammelburg, Germany, where he rejoined them in time to participate in another relocation on August 8, this time to Utzeneich, Austria. Here the training schedule was confined to three hours in the morning, with afternoons left open for athletics and recreation. Bruce later remembered those two weeks as his most enjoyable time in Europe.

On August 23 the 328th Infantry moved to Linz, Austria, where Egger's platoon took over guard duties at a displaced persons' camp. One night Bruce was assigned to accompany a humorless new lieutenant on a jeep patrol of Linz looking for curfew violators. The officer told him to drive, but as the Egger family had not had a car since he was a child, Bruce had never learned how. He ended up being chauffeured around Linz by a grim shavetail who suspected he was being conned by a wise-guy combat veteran.

Soon a few of the G Company veterans were being rotated home to be discharged under the Army's infamous point system.* LeCrone left in late September on an emergency furlough because his father was seriously ill, and Alton Moores returned to the States on points in early October. Then on November 4 the bulk of the veterans in the 26th Division pulled out for shipment home.

Through one of those quirks of fate for which the Army is infamous, S/Sgt. Bruce Egger was one point short of the sixty needed for discharge at that time and had to content himself with seeing his old friends off at the railroad station. Forty years later Bruce recalled, "Parting with these old friends with whom I had gone through so much over the past year, and most of whom I would never see again, was one of the most painful experiences of my life. I have never felt so lonely and blue."

In the meantime, Egger had been transferred to the 756th Tank Battalion, which had served in Africa, Sicily, Italy, France, and Germany, and was made acting platoon sergeant. This veteran outfit was guarding

*Each month in the service was worth a point, double that for every month overseas. Any campaign decoration, including the Purple Heart, was five points, as was each battle star. Each dependent child was worth twelve points. Originally a man had to have eighty-five points to qualify for discharge. That number was reduced to eighty in September, to sixty in October, and then to fifty at the end of December.[1]

German POWs, who were assigned to rebuilding war-damaged public works and cleaning up the rubble of war in the vicinity of Linz. In early December the 756th was transferred to Ettelingen, Germany. In the shuffle Egger was reassigned to D Company of the 334th Infantry. Then shortly after Christmas his new outfit was loaded into boxcars and sent to La Havre, France, where on January 2, 1946, they boarded a Liberty ship for passage to the United States.

A little over a week later the returning veterans were thrilled to see the lights of the Statue of Liberty welcoming them. After two days at Camp Kilmer, New Jersey, Egger boarded a C-47, bound for Fort Douglas, Utah, where he was quickly processed for discharge after politely declining the chance to reenlist. Bruce caught a bus for Boise, where his parents and other members of the family met him at the bus station. An uncle drove them home to McCall. "I never thought I would be so glad to see so much snow," Egger recalled.

That spring, when the lumber mill in McCall reopened after its usual winter shut-down, Bruce returned to work there, but his long-range plans were for a career in forestry. Thus it was that in June he landed a seasonal job as a smoke jumper with the U.S. Forest Service and remained on as a temporary employee until almost Christmas. In January, 1947, Egger enrolled in college on the GI bill, graduating from the University of Idaho in 1951 with a degree in forestry. He continued working summers with the Forest Service, including two more stints as a smoke jumper in 1947 and 1948, and caught on permanently with that agency in 1952. Over the next twenty-seven years Bruce worked in the national forests in Oregon and Washington, rising eventually to District Ranger before he retired in July of 1979 at the age of fifty-six.

In 1955 he married an attractive young lady named Leora Houston of Prineville, Oregon. They have four married children—three daughters and a son—and five grandchildren, all of whom live in the Pacific Northwest. Except for an occasional bout with a creaky back and a touch of rheumatism, which he attributes to too much sleeping in the cold and wet during the war, Bruce himself is remarkably fit, tipping the scales at the same trim 155 pounds he weighed during the war.

After his retirement Bruce and Leora built a home in Prineville, where Leora is a second-grade teacher. This setting in the sparse but bracing high plateau country of central Oregon, outposted on the west by a line of majestic snowcaps, somehow seems appropriate to Bruce's gentle, austere character with its hidden reservoirs of strength that sustained him during the long ordeal of G Company's war. [P.R.]

Appendix I: The Reckoning

G Company arrived on Utah Beach on September 8, 1944, with a full complement of 187 enlisted men and six officers. By V-E Day, eight months later, 625 men had served in its ranks. Accounting for what happened to those young Americans on the battlefields of Europe provides an indication of the human costs of G Company's war. Following is a breakdown of the losses:

KIA. Fifty-one members of G Company were killed on the battlefields of France, the Ardennes, and Germany; six more died of wounds (DOW) suffered on those battlefields, for a total of 57 combat deaths.

WIA. A total of 183 G Company men suffered battle wounds serious enough to require hospitalization. Of these, 51 were able to return to duty before May 8, 10 of whom were wounded a second time.

Total Lost to Enemy Action. Adding in two men who were taken prisoner and not liberated until the end of the war brings the total to 201 G Company personnel who were permanently lost because of enemy action.

Trench Foot and Frostbite. Since trench foot was identified in the morning reports as an "illness" and frostbite as an "injury," one cannot be certain how many cases of each there were. Based on the season and the length of hospitalization, however, one can identify 116 cases of probable trench foot and 51 of frostbite. Only 24 of these men ever returned to G Company, making a total permanent loss of 143 men.

SIW. At first the morning reports identified self-inflicted wounds as such, but around mid-November started reporting them under more benign designations. As a result, it is impossible to calculate the number of SIWs. From the early morning reports and specific mention of such incidents in the two journals, we can identify eight such cases. There were probably twice that many. Only one of the eight ever returned.

Miscellaneous. The weather that helped cause trench foot and frost-

Table 1. G Company's Losses by Replacement Draft

Replacement Group	No. of Men	KIA	WIA	WIA Twice	Net Lost to Enemy Action	Trench Foot	Frost-bite	SIW	Misc	Transfer	Total Men Lost	Left On Rolls 8 May 45
Original Co	193	30	70 (25)*	5	82†	45 (5)*	1	3 (1)*	7	21	153	40
Oct (2 grps)	11	2	6 (1)	—	7	—	—	—	—	—	7	4
Nov 10	82	6	20 (1)	—	25	47 (5)	2	—	1	4	74	8
Nov 19	117	6	39 (10)	4	39	22 (1)	21 (3)	3	2	9	92	25
Dec 19	82	7	25 (9)	1	24	1 (1)	24 (8)	—	6	14	60	22
Jan (4 grps)	78	6	21 (5)	—	22	1	3 (1)	2	11	4	42	36
Mar (3 grps)	55	—	2	—	2	—	—	—	3	—	5	50
Apr & May	7	—	—	—	—	—	—	—	—	—	0	7
Totals	625	57	183 (51)	10	201	116 (12)	51 (12)	8 (1)	30	52	433	192

*The numbers in parentheses indicate the number of men who eventually returned to duty after being wounded in action or hospitalized with trench foot or frostbite. One SIW also returned to duty.

†This number includes two men taken prisoner by the Germans on 7 Nov 44.

bite also undoubtedly contributed to the permanent loss of 17 men from illness as well as to innumerable temporary hospitalizations. There were also a number of losses from injury and accident, including three cases of accidental shooting, one of which was fatal. Thirty men were permanently lost to G Company from these miscellaneous causes.

Transfers. Surprisingly, G Company lost 52 men from transfers to other units, including eight who were furloughed home in April 1945, and assigned to stateside outfits. Most of the other 44 went to rear echelon units. A number of these men appear to have been disciplinary problems.

Table 1 shows the losses broken down by original personnel and each subsequent replacement draft. Note the excessive losses the November 10 group of replacements suffered, with only eight of the original 82 still on the company rolls at the end of the war. The particularly high incidence of trench foot is an indication not only of the terrible weather conditions they were immediately thrown into but perhaps also the low state of morale, if we are to accept the opinion of the British poet and World War I memoirist Robert Graves that poor morale was at the root of the trench foot problem (see note 2, Chapter 2).

Table 2 shows G Company's losses by period. After November, as the weather turned from wet to cold, the rate of attrition gradually lessened and each successive group of replacements fared a bit better than the previous one. The January replacements all joined G Company as the Battle of the Bulge was winding down and suffered far fewer losses than previous groups. The March replacements arrived immediately after the slaughter on Hoecker Hill, which was the last serious resistance G Company encountered; consequently their losses were minimal.

G Company arrived in Europe a fully trained, cohesive combat unit. It did not long remain so. The paper trail that day-by-day documents the losses among the original personnel, as shown in Table 3, illustrates the toll that extended combat exacts upon an infantry company.

Despite the addition in October of eleven replacements, by November 7, on the eve of the G Company's first real test in battle, its ranks had been thinned to 178 officers and men. The next day came the bloody action at Moncourt, where the company suffered 60 casualties, 22 of them killed. The rate of attrition through the remainder of November was horrendous, as evidenced by the fact that replacement drafts of 82 and 117 poured into (and through) the company on November 10 and 19. The 199 new men exceeded G Company's original complement by six.

Table 2. G Company's Losses by Period

Period	KIA	WIA	Trench Foot	Frost-bite	SIW	Misc	Trans-ferred	Total Lost
Before Nov 8	2	5	6	—	2	4*	7	26
On Nov 8	22	38	—	—	—	—	—	60
Nov 9–18	7	26	72	—	1	4	2	112
Nov 19–Dec 18	4	24	38	3	1	4	3	77
Dec 19–Jan 26	9	44	—	45	2	6	8	114
Jan 27–Mar 1	8	27	—	3	1	4	12	55
Mar 2–13	4	23	—	—	1	5	1	34
Mar 14–May 8	1	6	—	—	—	5	19	31
Totals	57	193	116	51	8	32*	52	509†

*Includes two men taken prisoner by the Germans on 7 Nov 44.

†By 8 May 45, seventy-six of these men had returned from the hospital, leaving a net loss of 433.

Table 3. Losses of Original G Company Personnel, by Period

Period	KIA	WIA	Trench Foot & Frostbite	SIW	Misc	Trans-ferred	Total Lost	On Rolls at End of Period†
Before Nov 8	2	5	6	2	4*	7	26	167
On Nov 8	20	34	—	—	—	—	54	113
Nov 9–18	3	13	31	1	1	2	51	63
Nov 19–Dec 18	2	4	8	—	—	1	15	53
Dec 19–Jan 26	1	8	1	—	1	2	13	43
Jan 27–Mar 1	2	6	—	—	—	1	9	39
Mar 2–13	—	4	—	—	2	—	6	40
Mar 14–May 8	—	1	—	—	1	8	10	40
Totals	30	75	46	3	9	21	184	

*Includes two men taken prisoner by the Germans on 7 Nov 44.

†After Nov. 8 the figures in this column include men who had returned to duty. There were a total of 31 returnees—25 WIAs, five trench foot cases, and one SIW—who rejoined G Company before May 8. Five of the WIAs were wounded a second time; they count twice in the total of 75 wounded.

On V-E Day G Company had on its rolls only 40 of its original 193 men, but even that figure is misleading; of that 40, 17 had returned from being hospitalized for wounds and four from trench foot. In addition, of the 21 men who were rotated home or transferred to other units, six had returned from being wounded. Only nine of the originals still with G Company on May 8 had made it through the war without missing any duty. All were headquarters personnel.

Nor did the early replacements fare much better. Of the 292 men who flowed into G Company's ranks prior to the Battle of the Bulge, only 58 were still around on May 8, 16 of whom had been wounded in action while 18 had returned from being hospitalized with trench foot or frostbite (see Table 1). Thus only 24 of those replacements made it through the war without suffering serious physical damage at the hands of the enemy or the elements. And of these, only 17 managed to avoid at least a short stay with the medics.

These figures suggest that few of the men of G Company, the raggedy-ass riflemen who slogged through the mud and snow and spilled their blood on the battlefields of Lorraine, Luxembourg, and Germany, ever developed the passion for war that their army commander, General Patton, professed. [P.R.]

Appendix II: Roll Call

From the start of this project we believed that there should be an appendix containing short biographical sketches of the G Company veterans mentioned most prominently in the two journals. The gap between conception and execution is a wide one, however, when it comes to tracking down men whose last known address was of 1945 vintage.

Through the network of G Company men who had kept track of old war buddies and with the help of the 328th Combat Team Veterans' Association, we were initially able to come up with the addresses of some three dozen individuals. At that point we would have been stymied without a battered, chaotic old 1945 roster provided by former 1st Sgt. Rocco Clemente which listed the home addresses of most of the men who appeared on G Company's overseas rolls. Using each individual's 1945 address, Joan Roley, who is an inspired and tenacious researcher, badgered information operators all over the AT&T system for phone numbers of persons in relevant area codes who had the same surnames as the G Company veterans for whom we were looking.

She got leads in some fifty percent of the cases, with about half of these proving fruitful. Thus it was that we found ourselves talking with a bewildered niece in Hadley, Massachusetts, who told us that her Uncle Frank had moved to Colorado way back in the late 1940s and died out there; or a son in Akron, Ohio, who was eager to share with us information about the nature of his dad's war wounds and his postwar career.

What surprised us was to discover how deeply rooted these workaday Americans were; a surprisingly high percentage of the G Company veterans who had not pursued professional careers had settled down and spent their lives in their old hometowns. Most were delighted to learn that their World War II experiences were going to be recorded in a book.

Fewer names have been included in this appendix than we would have liked, but in a number of cases we simply did not have enough

Your AAA Travel Package

Travel service is the most widely used of all the many personal services available to AAA members. Whether your plans call for a one-day jaunt or a lengthy cross-country vacation, your travel package is intended to add to the enjoyment of your trip and help you reach your destination with ease.

The components of your travel package represent the combined efforts of such professionals as AAA field inspectors and road reporters, who gather the important information you need, and the editors and cartographers who compile these findings for various publications. Each item, designed for a specific purpose, is updated and revised in keeping with the changing needs of AAA members. The entire package is tailored to the special requirements of your own particular trip.

THE STRIP MAPS

Your AAA TripTik,® an exclusive Triple-A travel service, is the backbone of your travel package. The detailed, informative strip maps meet the needs of motorists traveling today's highways.

Review the legend on this pull-out page to obtain a full understanding of strip map symbols. Both the use of color and easily identified symbols key communities on the strip maps to the appropriate AAA book publication. Town names appearing in red offer Triple A-approved overnight accommodations or dining facilities. A ◯ refers you to the Points of Interest section of a TourBook,® while a ▲ indicates a CampBook.® The ⒶⒶⒶ identifies a Triple-A club. The ▉ designates a city containing a hospital with 24-hr emergency room service in the US; in Canada, check locally for hours. The symbol also spots the location of a hospital. Hospital Data Source * 2000, Healthcare InfoSource, Inc.

Strip maps also solve one of the major problems of traveling controlled-access highways: Where is the next gas station, restaurant or motel? Symbols inform you at a glance of the availability of gas or AAA-approved lodging ▉ at or near interchanges, as well as the location of rest areas ◉ along the primary route. A ▉ indicates a AAA-recommended restaurant near the interchange. A ▉ means that, although there are no TourBook listings, at least one "family type" restaurant is there.

Printed in U.S.A.   Copyright AAA 2001

The back page, **F**, contains Downtown maps or Areas of Special Interest.

MAP F

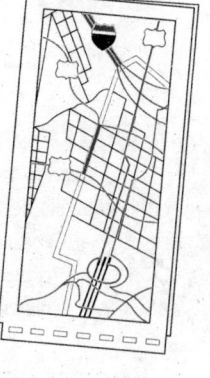

MAP G

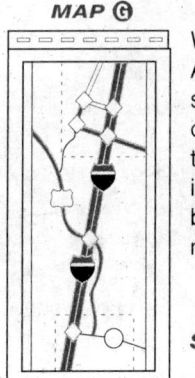

When a City or Special Area map adjoins a Regular strip map, the red dashed outline at terminals on the Regular strip map, **G**, illustrates the relationship between the two strip maps.

SPECIAL APPROACH MAP

MAP H

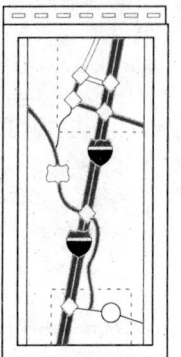

Approach maps, **H**, are used for certain large metropolitan areas to show those major or direct routes that avoid congestion.

COMPUTING DISTANCE

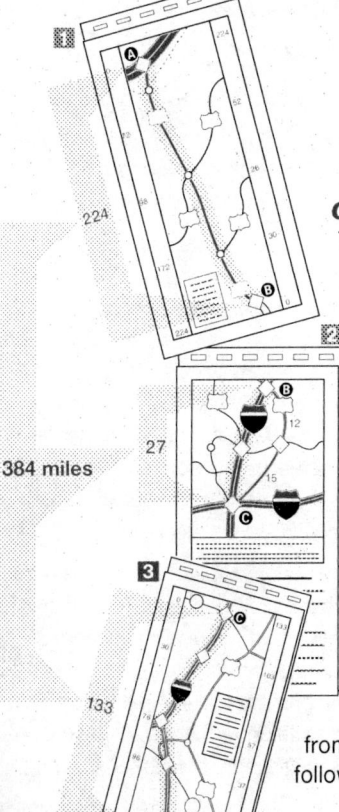

384 miles

To compute overall distance for your specific TripTik® routing, combine the red cumulative mileage or kilometer figures appearing in the margins of Regular strip maps with the distances shown in red on the City maps. For example, the diagram show how the distances between points **A** and **B** of Regular strip map **1** (224 miles), between points **B** and **C** of City strip map **2** (27 miles) and between points **C** and **D** of Regular strip map **3** (133 miles) must be added to give the distance from **A** to **D** (384 miles) via routes followed on each of these three maps.

information about an individual to merit an entry. The exceptions are the men for whom there is little data but who are mentioned so frequently they could not be left out, and in all cases those who were wounded or killed in action. In the fashion of Ernie Pyle, we have listed each man's hometown in parentheses. The individuals who are not identified as replacements are, of course, the originals who came overseas with G Company. We have paid perhaps undue attention to promotions in rank and position because these are indicators of the men's military achievements. [P.R.]

Sgt. Lee E. Allen (St. Louis, MO), 3rd Platoon. Replacement, 19 Nov 44. Rose from pvt to become asst leader, 3rd Squad, 19 Jan 45. WIA at Saarlouis-Roden 17 Feb 45 (fragment of mortar shrapnel in left lower leg). Returned to duty 5 Jun 45. After the war, returned to St. Louis, worked as carpenter 36 yrs until retiring Feb 82. Lives in nearby Ballwin.

Capt. Arma E. Andon (Pelham, NY), CO, H Company. Drafted in 1942; joined H Co Feb 44. WIA on Hoecker Hill (Germany), 14 Mar 45 (multiple shrapnel wounds in left leg and in lower abdomen). Suffers continuing pain and atrophying in leg and knee. After discharge had own business in TV sales and marketing; then worked for Group W Television Sales until retirement 1 May 85. Lives in West Hampton Beach, Long Island, where he has served three terms as mayor.

S/Sgt. Stanley A. Aras (Chicopee, MA), Supply Sgt. Drafted Mar 41. With G Co from activation of 328th Regt in Feb 43. Missed no duty while overseas. After the war, returned to pre-Army job as stock clerk with American Bosch (now United Technologies) until retirement in 1972. Has lived in Chicopee all his life.

S/Sgt. John V. Austin (Mt. Vernon, WA), 2nd Platoon. Volunteered for draft in spring '43. Joined G Co in Mar 44 from ASTP (engineering) at Providence College. Rose from pfc to become leader 1st Squad in Dec 44. WIA at Mon Schumann, Luxembourg, 5 Jan 45 (shrapnel tore tendon in right thumb); returned to duty 14 Mar 45. Rotated home 3 Apr 45. After discharge returned to Washington State College, rec'd degree in architecture. Practiced for 30 yrs in Tacoma. Now retired.

T/Sgt. Benoit A. Bergeron (South Hadley, MA), 2nd Platoon. Volunteered for Army 13 Mar 41. With G Co from activation of 328th Regt in Feb 43. Rose from asst squad leader to platoon sergeant in aftermath of Moncourt. WIA (shrapnel through left instep) by same mortar round that wounded Lt Otts on Hoecker Hill (Germany) 13 Mar 45. Spent eight months in hospital, has 10% disability. Before retiring in 1977, ran garage and tire shop in South Hadley, where he still lives.

Pfc. Joseph A. Bergeron (Chicago), 1st Platoon. WIA at Moncourt, France, 8 Nov 44. Returned to G Company (3rd Platoon) 28 Feb 45. Whereabouts since war unknown.

Pfc. William A. Bergeron (Chicago), 4th Platoon. Brother of Joseph. KIA at Moncourt, France, 8 Nov 44.

Sgt. Henry D. Bilendy (Bayonne, NJ), 4th Platoon. KIA near Woelfling, France, 10 Dec 44.

S/Sgt. Alfred Bruno (Granville, MA), 2nd Platoon. Rose from pvt to platoon guide. A colorful and recklessly brave man, he seems to have developed battle fatigue under the strain. Hospitalized 10 Mar 45, never returned to G Co. Whereabouts since war unknown.

S/Sgt. Willis E. Burhans (Ohio), E Company. ASTP until program terminated; assigned to E Co, 328th Regt, Mar 44. Promoted to squad leader; then guide, 2nd Platoon. Taken POW at Eschdorf, Luxembourg, on 25 Dec 44; liberated by British 28 Apr 45. Together with Bob Pennington from Mar 44 on. Discharged 2 Dec 45 and attended Ohio State, rec'd degree (accounting) 1948. Worked for Price Waterhouse; then Diamond Shamrock Corp until retiring Mar 83. Lives with wife, Pat, in Mentor, OH.

Pfc. Marvin L. Busby (Tulare, CA), Cook. KIA 12 Jan 45 near Mon Schumann, Luxembourg.

S/Sgt. Joseph A. Byrne (Maynard, MA), 1st Platoon. Rose from sgt to squad leader after Moncourt. Hospitalized with trench foot 13 Nov 44; returned to duty 10 Mar 45. Whereabouts since war unknown.

Capt. Paul F. Carrier (Belmont, MA), CO, G Co, until transferred to Hq Co, 328th Regt, 18 Nov 44. Awarded Silver Star. Postwar career unknown. Now lives in Middle Haddam, CT.

1st Sgt. Rocco F. Clemente (Utica, NY), 1st Sgt. Joined G Co in Mar 44 from ASTP at Harvard (civil engineering). Soon became communications sgt. Appt 1st Sgt in Jan 45. After war received degree in civil engineering from Clarkson U. Has spent his career in that field, with state of New York and city of Utica, chiefly in highway design work. Semi-retired (part-time consultant), still lives in Utica. Married, two adult children.

Pfc. Melvin "Billy" Cross (Williamsburg, MA), 1st Platoon. Rec'd Distinguished Service Cross for heroic action at Moncourt. Has been in lumber business in Williamsburg ever since the war.

Pfc. Carl Cullison (Attica, KS), 1st Platoon. Replacement (along with Egger), 27 Oct 44. Wounded at Moncourt, France, 8 Nov 44; returned to duty 14 Mar 45. Returned to Attica after discharge and died of a heart attack in Jan 72.

S/Sgt. Daniel D. Dafoe (Alma, MI), 3rd Platoon. Replacement, 19 Nov 44. Appt leader 2nd Squad, 10 Dec 44, while still pvt. WIA (bullet through upper left arm) at Eschdorf, 24 Dec 44; returned to duty 14 Mar 45. Appt platoon guide 15 Apr 45. After discharge worked as operating engineer at Mich State U power plant 25 yrs. Retired, lives in Lansing.

Pvt. William S. Davidson (hometown unknown), 4th Platoon. Replacement, 27 Oct 44. Taken POW on Dieuze Plateau (France) 14 Nov 44; liberated by French at Strasbourg 24 Nov 44. Transferred to L Co, 328th Regt, 12 May 45. Whereabouts since war unknown.

1st Lt. William P. Dean (West Point, GA), Leader, 1st Platoon. WIA at Moncourt, France, 8 Nov 44. Returned to duty late Feb 44 as CO, E Co. KIA on Hoecker Hill (Germany) on 13 Mar 45.

Pfc. William DeSoto (Miami, FL), 3rd Platoon. Replacement, 19 Dec 44. WIA on Hoecker Hill 13 Mar 45. Returned to duty 1 Jun 45. Whereabouts since war unknown.

Pfc. Robert L. Dixon (hometown unknown), F Company. Replacement, 27 Oct 44. KIA at Moncourt, France, 8 Nov 44.

Pfc. Reginald H. Drew (Providence, RI), 3rd Platoon. Replacement, 27 Jan 45. Died of wounds suffered at Saarlouis-Roden, Germany, on 18 Feb 45.

S/Sgt. Bruce E. Egger (McCall, ID), 3rd Platoon. In ASTP (engineering) at Kansas State, assigned to 97th Div at Ft. Leonard Wood Mar 44. Replacement to G Co, 27 Oct 44. Rose from pfc to become leader of 3rd Squad. Missed no duty. After discharge attended U of Idaho, rec'd degree in forestry in 1951. Served in U.S. Forest Service for 29 yrs before retiring in 1979. Now makes his home in Prineville, Oregon, with his wife, Leora. They have four adult children.

Pfc. Kenneth O. Erickson (hometown unknown), F Company. Replacement, 27 Oct 44. KIA at Moncourt, France, 8 Nov 44.

Pfc. Albert Evans (Bay City, MI), 3rd Platoon. Replacement, 19 Nov 44. WIA (piece of shrapnel in neck) 5 Jan 45 near Mon Schumann, Luxembourg; returned to duty 21 Jan 45. WIA second time (shrapnel in leg) 13 Mar 45 on Hoecker Hill (Germany); returned to duty Jun 45. After the war, returned to Bay City, where in later yrs he worked as custodian at a bank and was active as a coach in youth baseball. Died of a stroke in Jan 80; survived by three adult children and his wife, Virginia.

Pfc. Edward J. Evans (Indianapolis, IN), 3rd Platoon. KIA at Moncourt, France, 8 Nov 44.

Pfc. Jasper E. Fockler (Alma, MI), 3rd Platoon. Replacement, 19 Nov 44. On 8 Jan 45 was hospitalized for frostbite in both feet (now on 10% disability); never returned to G Co. After the war worked for Lobdell-Emery Manufacturing Co in Alma until retirement in 1984. Lives in nearby Elwell.

S/Sgt. Charles N. Foster (Oak Park, IL), 3rd Platoon. WIA at Moncourt, France, 8 Nov 44; returned to duty 11 Nov 44. Rose from pfc to become leader 2nd Squad in mid-Nov. WIA 2nd time near Woelfling, France, 11 Dec 44; never returned to G Co. Whereabouts since war unknown.

Cpl. William P. Frost (Chicago), Forward Clerk. Sophomore at Purdue U when he volunteered for Army May 43. ASTP at Harvard (civil engineering) with Clemente; joined G Co Mar 44. Missed no duty while overseas. Rec'd degree (mechanical engineering) from Purdue Aug 47. Worked for DuPont in various locations for 28 yrs as safety and fire protection supervisor, ending up in 1965 in La Place, LA, where he lives with his wife, Myrtle. Retired 31 Dec 79.

2nd Lt. Edward L. Germain (Belchertown, MA), Leader 4th Platoon. Joined Nat'l Guard 1939. With G Co from activation of 328th Regt in Feb 1943. Longtime 1st Sgt of G Co, accepted field commision 7 Jan 45. After the war suffered serious back injury in France; discharged from Valley Forge Army Hospital Dec 46 with 60% disability. Since 1960 was public school teacher and principal in Monson, MA, where he now lives in retirement.

Pfc. Harry D. Gibbs (Logansport, IN), 3rd Platoon. Drafted Jul 44; replacement to G Co, 18 Mar 45. After discharge in Jul 46 returned to Logansport and worked for Wabash Railroad until retirement in 1986.

S/Sgt. Frederick E. Gilluly (Condersport, PA), 2nd Platoon. Volunteered for Army Feb 43. Served in ETO with 551st Anti-Aircraft Bn; in Dec 44 volunteered for infantry. Replacement to G Co, 19 Dec 44. Rose from pfc to platoon guide. By all accounts a remarkably brave man, was awarded Bronze Star and Silver Star. Has lived in Perry, NY, since 1946 with variety of occupations—factory work, bottle gas business, heavy construction, millwright. Currently part-time maintenance manager at an apartment complex. Married since 19 Jan 46 with three adult children.

S/Sgt. Dominic C. Giovinazzo (Ravenna, OH), F Company. Drafted in Nov 42. ASTP at U of South Dakota until program terminated. To 97th Div, Ft. Leonard Wood, Mar 44. Replacement to F Co 27 Oct 44. Rose from pfc to platoon guide. Captured by Germans at Saarlouis-Roden, Germany, on 19 Feb 45 and held POW until 1 May 45, during which time he suffered frostbitten feet. Rec'd degree (industrial engineering) from Ohio State U in 1950. Worked 27½ years in quality control for General Electric. Retired in Jackson, MS.

Capt. E. Gardner Goldsmith (Chicago, IL). Transferred to G Co as CO, 18 Nov 44. Transferred to HQ, 3rd Bn, 328th Regt 29 Jan 45. Promoted to major. Postwar career unknown. Lives in Milwaukee.

T/Sgt. Francis J. Gormley (St. Louis, MO), 3rd Platoon. Drafted

May 44 at age 29 with a wife and two children. Replacement to G Co, 19 Nov 44. Rose from pvt to become a squad leader (27 Dec 45), platoon guide (19 Jan 45), then platoon sergeant (16 Apr 45). Missed no duty. After the war, returned to St. Louis to pre-Army job as typesetter and in 1953 bought the typesetting firm. Retired in 1985.

Pfc. Russell E. Greasor (Logansport, IN), 3rd Platoon. Drafted Aug 44. Replacement to G Co, 18 Mar 45. After 26th Div shipped home, ended up with 42nd Div, rose to 1st Sgt, Regt HQ. Following discharge went to work for General Telephone Co. Was plant service mgr in Elkhart until 1972, then customer relations mgr in Terre Haute. Served almost 25 yrs with Indiana Nat'l Guard and its reserve. Rose to chief of staff with rank of Colonel. Died 9 Feb 89.

2nd Lt. Ernest Greup (Cortland, NY), Leader, 2nd, later 3rd Platoon. Joined Nat'l Guard (108th Infantry) as enlisted man in 1939; unit nationalized Oct 40. Attended OCS in late 1942. Assigned to A Co, 328th Regt in Jan 1944. Transferred to G Co 11 Oct 44. WIA (machine gun bullets in both hands and left arm) on Dieuze Plateau 14 Nov 44. Spent three years in Army hospitals and still has limited use of left hand and arm. Married in 1947 to Red Cross worker at Valley Forge Gen Hosp. After discharge Oct 47 worked on newspaper and in radio broadcasting in Cortland and Durham, NC. BA 1953, MA (television) 1954, both from Stanford, then returned to Durham to help start WTVD-TV, where he held various on-air and mgmt positions until retirement in 1980. He and wife, Jeanne, still live in Durham.

T/5 John N. Grieco (Montclair, NJ), Medic, 3rd Platoon. Hospitalized with yellow jaundice in Mar 45; returned to duty in Jul 45. After war worked in VA hospital in East Orange, NJ, becoming assistant supervisor of admissions. Died of a heart problem in 1984.

Capt. Chester "Jack" Hargrove (Corvallis, OR). Replacement, Leader 3rd Platoon, 19 Nov 44. Became CO G Co, 29 Jan 45. Awarded Silver Star for action on Hoecker Hill (Germany) on 13 Mar 45. After war was personnel manager Litman's Department Store chain in Portland, OR, for 26 yrs. Died in 1972 at age 52 of brain aneurism.

S/Sgt. Vernon E. Hedgpath (Chester, SC), 2nd Platoon. Replacement, 19 Nov 44. Rose from pvt to leader of 3rd Squad. Whereabouts since war unknown.

Pfc. Henry D. Huckabee (Myrtlewood, AL), 3rd Platoon. Replacement, 10 Nov 44. WIA at Saarlautern, Germany, on 13 Feb 45. Whereabouts since war unknown.

S/Sgt. George Idelson (Brooklyn), 2nd Platoon. Drafted in Jun 43 and sent to ASTP in engineering at Citadel; then in Mar 44 to 100th Div at Fort Bragg. Relacement to G Co 16 Oct 44. Rose from pvt to leader of 1st Squad. Settled in Washington, DC, in 1950, working in advertising and public relations. Currently publisher of "The Consumer Affairs Letter."

S/Sgt. Gaetano A. Iovanni (Boston), Leader 3rd Squad, 3rd Platoon. KIA at Moncourt 8 Nov 44.

T/Sgt Francis J. Kelly (Jamaica Plains, MA), Platoon Sgt, 1st Platoon. Rec'd field commission 14 Nov 44, day he was WIA on Dieuze Plateau (France). Postwar career unknown. Lives in Jamaica Plains.

Pfc. Albert C. Krause (Detroit, MI), 2nd Platoon. Replacement, 29 Jan 45. KIA at Hoecker Hill (Germany) 13 Mar 45.

Pfc. Frank Kuchyt (Hadley, MA), 3rd Platoon. WIA on Dieuze Plateau 14 Nov 44; never returned to G Co. Postwar career unknown. Moved to Colorado sometime after the war and died there, date unknown.

Lt. Law Lamar, Jr. (Selma, AL), C Company. Shipped overseas with Lee Otts; replacement platoon leader C Co, 328th Regt, 18 Nov 44. WIA at Saarlouis-Roden (lost an eye). After discharge rec'd law degree at U of Alabama but became a CPA in Birmingham, where he now lives.

Pfc. Arvil Lamb (LaFollette, TN), Medic, 2nd Platoon. Transferred to Regt Aid Station 32 in Apr 45 where he was accidentally shot in stomach with a souvenir German pistol. He recovered but whereabouts since early 1946 unknown.

Pfc. Fonrose H. LeCrone (Sullivan, IL), 3rd Platoon. Replacement, 10 Nov 44. WIA near Mon Schumann 13 Jan 45 (fragment of mortar shrapnel in shoulder); returned to duty 10 Feb 45. Farmer at nearby Sullivan after the war. Now deceased.

Pfc. Harry D. Lee (Quincy, MA), 3rd Platoon. Died of wounds suffered at Moncourt 8 Nov 44.

Pfc. Walter V. Lee, Jr. (St. Louis, MO), 3rd Platoon. Replacement, 19 Nov 44. KIA near Mon Schumann, Luxembourg, 5 Jan 45. Survived by wife and two children.

Pvt. Robert E. Lees (Portland, OR), 3rd Platoon. Replacement, 19 Dec 44. Hospitalized for frostbite 11 Jan 45. Returned to duty 6 Jun 45. Whereabouts since war unknown.

Pfc. Junior L. Letterman (Conway, MO), 3rd Platoon. Replacement, 10 Nov 44. WIA near Mon Schumann 11 Jan 45; returned to duty 16 May 45. Whereabouts since war unknown.

Pfc. W. C. Lundy (Blueridge, TX), 3rd Platoon. Replacement, 19 Dec 44. KIA on Hoecker Hill (Germany) 13 Mar 45.

Pvt. James R. McCowan (Grand Junction, CO), 3rd Platoon. Joined Army from U of Colorado Mar 43. Assigned to ASTP Colorado A&M Sep 43, then to 97th Div, Ft. Leonard Wood, Mar 44. Shipped in replacement draft to ETO Oct 44. Replacement to G Co 10 Nov 44. Appt asst leader, 3rd Squad (20 Nov 44). WIA at Munster 22 Nov 44 (fragment of mortar shrapnel shatterred tibia of left leg just above ankle). In various hospitals until discharged with 30% disability Feb 46. Rec'd BS (Mar 48) and MS (1949), both in pharmacy, from U of Colorado; Ph.D in pharmacy U of Florida 1954. Taught at several universities, last 22 years at U of Arkansas Medical School. Retired in 1988 as Associate Dean. Lives in Little Rock.

Pvt. John A. Marron (Lansdowne, PA), 3rd Platoon. Replacement, 5 Feb 45. WIA at Deggendorf, Germany, 27 Apr 45; never returned to G Co. Whereabouts since war unknown.

Sgt. Frank Micik (Uniontown, PA), 3rd Platoon. Replacement, 19 Dec 44 (originally to 4th Platoon). Rose from T/5 to become asst leader 1st Squad. Awarded Silver Star for action at Deggendorf, Germany, 27 Apr 45. Whereabouts since war unknown.

S/Sgt. Thomas E. Montgomery (Wilmington, DE), 3rd Platoon. Replacement, 19 Dec 44. Rose from pfc to become leader 2nd Squad (8 Mar 45). Whereabouts since war unknown.

Pfc. Alton W. Moores (Bangor, ME), 3rd Platoon. Nat'l Guardsman, unit nationalized in Oct 40. Replacement to G Co 19 Dec 44. Whereabouts since war unknown.

Pfc. Rufies L. Morgan (Lowell, NC), 3rd Platoon. Replacement, 19 Dec 44. Missed no duty. After the war, returned to Lowell, worked as a truck driver. Died in 1988.

Pfc. Wilbur L. Munns (Raleigh, NC), 3rd Platoon. Drafted 10 Apr 42 at age 32. Replacement to G Co 19 Nov 44. WIA near Woelfling, France, 10 Dec 44 (shrapnel in left shoulder). Returned to G Co 21 May 45. After discharge in Jan 46 returned to Raleigh and pre-army job with printing firm. Retired 25 Feb 77, still lives in Raleigh.

S/Sgt. Stanley A. Nachman (Johnson City, NY), 3rd Platoon. Drafted 30 Mar 44 at age 23. Replacement, 10 Nov 44. Rose from pvt to become leader 1st Squad (7 Jan 45). Missed no duty. Returned to Johnson City, worked as tool and die maker for Ansco Camera. Died of cancer 16 Aug 78.

S/Sgt. Paul A. Nickel (Pelham, NY), 1st Platoon. Transferred to 3rd Platoon 10 Nov 44 to be asst leader 1st Squad; appt leader 13 Nov 44. Hospitalized for trench foot 22 Nov 44; never returned to G Co. Whereabouts since war unknown.

Pfc. Charles W. Nunley (Tracy City, TN), 2nd Platoon. Drafted 4 Apr 44. Replacement, 19 Nov 44. WIA at Saarlouis-Roden, Germany, 17 Feb 45 (fragment of same mortar round that killed his Tracy City buddy, Bobby Phipps, hit Nunley in right shoulder). Returned to duty 16 May 45. After war went back to Tracy City, where he operates a small poultry farm.

Pfc. Thomas W. Oakley (Waverly, TN), 3rd Platoon. Drafted Apr 44 (was married with one child); replacement to G Co, 19 Nov 44. WIA 22 Dec 44; returned to duty 13 Feb 45. After discharge returned to Waverly, where he still lives. Worked in building trades until retired.

S/Sgt. Vernon S. Olson (Montrose, SD), 3rd Platoon. ASTP until program terminated. Replacement to G Co 10 Nov 44. Appt leader 3rd Squad (20 Nov 44). WIA near Mon Schumann 13 Jan 45 (fragment of mortar shrapnel in leg). Returned to duty 22 May 45. Whereabouts since war unknown.

1st Lt. Lee M. Otts (Greensboro, AL), Leader 2nd Platoon. Entered Army Aug 43 after graduating U of Alabama. OCS for antiaircraft officers, commissioned 13 Jan 44; then to infantry course at Fort Benning. Shipped to ETO Oct 44. Replacement platoon leader to E Co, 328th Regt, 18 Nov 44. Transferred to 2nd Platoon, G Co 3 Dec 44. WIA at Hoecker Hill (Germany) 13 Mar 45 (fragment of mortar shrapnel broke left jaw; on way to aid station right shoulder broken by sniper bullet). Various hospitals in England and U.S. until discharged 10 Jul 46. Graduated U of Alabama Law School Dec 48. Has lived in Brewton, AL, ever since, still actively practicing law. Married Mary Frances Byrd 4 Sept 48; they have four married daughters.

Pfc. Allan W. Parlee (Wollaston, MA), 3rd Platoon. WIA at Moncourt, France, 8 Nov 44 (shrapnel wounds in right shoulder, left arm, and back). Never returned to G Co. Now retired from the Milton, MA, public school system; has lived since 1981 in Mystic, CT.

Pfc. Charles N. Patti (Ansonia, CT), 3rd Platoon. Replacement, 18 Mar 45. WIA near Martinreuth, Germany, 18 Apr 45; returned to duty 1 Jun 45. Whereabouts since war unknown.

Pfc. Marshall H. Pearcy (Winnsboro, LA), 3rd Platoon. Replacement, G Co 19 Nov 44. Hospitalized from frostbite 11 Jan 45; never returned to G Co. In 1948 moved to West Coast, where he was heavy equipment mechanic. Killed in 1966 by oncoming car while repairing truck on side of highway.

S/Sgt. Robert E. Pennington, Jr. (Texas), E Company. ASTP until program terminated; assigned to E Co, 328th Regt, Mar 44. Promoted to squad leader then platoon sgt, 2nd Platoon. Taken POW at Eschdorf, Luxembourg, on 25 Dec 45; liberated by British 28 Apr 45. With Willis Burhans from Mar 44 on. After discharge attended U of Texas, rec'd degree (chemical engineering) in 1948. Worked for B. F. Goodrich for 32 years and for Ethyl Corp for ten years until retirement 1 Sep 90. Lives in Houston.

Pfc. Bobbie E. Phipps (Tracy City, TN), 2nd Platoon. Replacement, 19 Dec 44. KIA at Saarlouis-Roden, Germany, 17 Feb 45 (by a fragment of same mortar round that wounded his Tracy City buddy, Charles Nunley).

Pfc. Rene J. Poirier (Leominster, MA), 3rd Platoon. Replacement, 19 Dec 44. WIA near Nothum, Luxembourg, 7 Jan 45; returned to duty 14 Feb 45. WIA (2nd time) on Hoecker Hill (Germany) 13 Mar 45. Never returned to G Co. Whereabouts since war unknown.

S/Sgt. Victor M. Popa (Gary, IN), 3rd Platoon. Entered Army 1 Feb 43. ASTP at U of Iowa and Grinnell College (meteorology) until program terminated. Joined G Co 11 Nov 44. Rose from pvt to platoon guide (15 Dec 44). WIA near Mon Schumann, Luxembourg, 13 Jan 45 (shrapnel in stomach hit all vital organs before exiting); recovered completely and returned to duty 16 May 45. After war earned BA and MA (Business Administration) Indiana U. Became asst VP of mortgage co in Merrillville, IN. Drowned with eight-year-old daughter 17 Feb 68 when snowmobile plunged into lake. Widely respected for work with Catholic Charities and CYO. Survived by wife Peggy and four children.

Pfc. William T. Prior (Blackstone, MA), 3rd Platoon. Replacement, 22 Mar 45. WIA near Schmiedfeld, Germany, 8 Apr 45; returned to duty 13 May 45. Postwar career unknown. Now lives in Cumberland, RI.

S/Sgt. Daniel J. Rankin (Jersey City, NJ), 1st Platoon. Moved to 3rd Platoon after Moncourt, promoted from pfc to s/sgt, and made leader of 1st Squad. Hospitalized with trench foot 13 Nov 45; never returned to G Company. Whereabouts since war unknown.

T/5 Frank K. Richardson (Yonkers, NY), 3rd Platoon. Replacement, 19 Nov 44. WIA near Munster, France, 22 Nov 44; never returned to G Co. Whereabouts since war unknown.

Pfc. Thomas L. Roberts (St. Joseph, MO), 3rd Platoon. Replacement, 19 Nov 44. WIA near Woelfling, France, 9 Dec 44; never returned to G Co. Whereabouts since war unknown.

S/Sgt. Stewart B. Rorer, Jr. (Ambler, PA), 3rd Platoon. Drafted Feb 42. With G Co from activation of 328th Regt in Mar 43. WIA at Moncourt, France, 8 Nov 44 (right side of face by shrapnel); returned to duty 18 Dec 44. Rose from pfc to become leader 2nd Squad (19 Jan 45). WIA 2nd time (shrapnel in middle finger, left hand) on Hoecker Hill (Germany) 8 Mar 45; returned to duty 26 May 45. After war worked for U.S. Customs, Port of Philadelphia, until retirement in 1977. Lives in Philadelphia.

Pfc. Solomon Rubin (Brooklyn), 3rd Platoon. Replacement, 19 Dec 45. Rotated to U.S. 16 Apr 45. Whereabouts since war unknown.

Pvt. Frank Santarsiero (Trenton, NJ), 3rd Platoon. Replacement, 19 Dec 44. WIA near Nothum, Luxembourg, 5 Jan 45; returned to duty 1 Jun 45. Whereabouts since war unknown.

S/Sgt. Philip J. Sarro (Brooklyn), 2nd Platoon. Replacement, 19 Dec 44. Rose from T/4 to squad leader (15 Mar 45). Missed no duty. Whereabouts since war unknown.

S/Sgt. John M. Saulenas (Lynn, MA), Leader, 1st Squad, 3rd Platoon. KIA at Moncourt, France, 8 Nov 44.

Pfc. Paul B. Scheufler (Belpre, KS), 3rd Platoon. Drafted Apr 44; replacement to G Co, 19 Nov 44. Served to end of war. After discharge Jun 46 farmed with father and then, after marriage in 1950, on his own farm near Sterling, KS, where he still lives.

Pvt. Harold L. Schroaf (Dayton, OH), 3rd Platoon. Replacement, 19 Dec 44. WIA near Mon Schumann, Luxembourg, 11 Jan 45; never returned to G Co. Whereabouts since war unknown.

1st Lt. William H. Schulze (Evanston, IL), 3rd Platoon. Replacement platoon leader (from 87th Div), 5 Feb 45. KIA at Deggendorf, Germany, 27 Apr 45. Awarded Silver Star. Survived by wife, Bea, and son Randy.

S/Sgt. David F. Seeney (Newton, KS), 2nd Platoon. Replacement, 19 Nov 44. Rose from pvt to squad leader (15 Jan 45). WIA at Fraulautern, Germany, 5 Feb 45; returned to duty 16 May 45. Whereabouts since war unknown.

1st Lt. Stuart C. Shipman (Marion, OH). Principal of elementary school when drafted Jun 42; commissioned 2nd Lt, Feb 43. Went overseas with G Co as Leader 2nd Platoon; assigned as Exec Officer 14 Oct 44; transferred to Regt HQ 18 Nov 44. After discharge 31 Dec 45 rec'd MA (school administration) from Ohio State U, 1947. Supt of Schools, Cambridge, IN, 1949 until retirement in 1971. Lives in Dublin, IN.

Sgt. Dave A. Smith (Kansas City, MO), 2nd Platoon. Replacement, 19 Nov 44. Rose from pvt to leader 2nd Squad. WIA near Hanau, Germany, 28 Mar 45; never returned to G Co. Whereabouts since war unknown.

S/Sgt. Edmond A. Sorel (Winchendon, MA), 3rd Platoon. Leader, 2nd Squad, appt Platoon Guide 10 Nov 44. Hospitalized for trench foot 13 Nov 44; never returned to G Co. Whereabouts after war unknown.

Sgt. Henry C. Sosenko (Binghamton, NY), 3rd Platoon. Drafted Jun 43; assigned to 844th AA BN then to infantry. Replacement to G Co, 27 Jan 45 (originally to 4th Platoon). Appt asst leader, 3rd Squad. Missed no duty. After discharge returned to Binghamton and worked as machinist for Endicott-Johnson Shoe Corp until retirement in mid-1980s.

T/Sgt. Robert J. Starcher (Crooksville, PA), 3rd Platoon. Volunteered for draft in Feb 41. Assigned to 328th Regt I&R Platoon Mar 43, then to G Co, 2nd Platoon. Became platoon sgt 3rd Platoon, 14 Nov 44. Transferred to Hq Co, 2nd Bn, 9 Jan 45. After discharge operated tavern/restaurant in St. Louis area. Moved to Nashport, OH, in 1955 and worked for Kaiser Aluminum until retirement in 1983. Still in

Nashport, where he farms, enjoys his grandchildren, and restores antique aircraft.

Pfc. Alex Stoddard, Jr. (Alliance, NE), 3rd Platoon. Assigned from Co Hq (runner), 20 Nov 44. WIA near Mon Schumann, Luxembourg, 11 Jan 45 (leg broken by shrapnel); never returned to G Co. Whereabouts since war unknown.

T/Sgt. Willard Straw (Florence, MA), 3rd Platoon. Transferred from 2nd Platoon (squad leader) to platoon sgt, 3rd Platoon, 10 Nov 44. KIA on Dieuze Plateau (France) 15 Nov 44.

T/Sgt. Robert W. Streeter (Northampton, MA), 4th Platoon. Promoted from squad leader to platoon sgt 3 Dec 44. Awarded Silver Star for action near Woelfling, France, 12 Dec 44. WIA 3 Feb in Fraulautern, Germany; returned to duty 24 Feb 45. Whereabouts since war unknown.

S/Sgt. Wallace L. Sullivan (Holyoke, MA), Platoon Guide, 3rd Platoon. WIA at Moncourt, France, 8 Nov 44; returned to duty 17 Mar 45. WIA 2nd time at Deggendorf, Germany, 27 Apr 45. Never returned to G Co. After discharge settled in Brunswick, GA, where he owns and operates an office supply business.

Sgt. Donald D. Thompson (St. Joseph, MO), 2nd Platoon. Drafted 4 Mar 44. Replacement, 19 Nov 44. Runner; then promoted to asst squad leader (28 Mar 45). After discharge returned to St. Joseph and worked for 30 yrs in office for railroad. Died 4 Jan 87; survived by wife and three adult sons.

Pfc. Raymond O. Tompkins (St. Johns, KS), 3rd Platoon. Drafted May 44. Replacement, 19 Nov 44. WIA near Berle, Luxembourg, 17 Jan 45 (wounded in arm and leg by mortar shrapnel; right arm was amputated in hospital). After discharge graduated from Kansas State College (agriculture) and worked for soil conservation service. In 1959 moved to California and worked in Orange County for State Dept of Ag. Retired in 1975 and lives in Santa Anna, CA.

T/Sgt. Lawrence Treff (Bronx), 1st Platoon. Drafted Mar 43. ASTP at Providence College (civil engineering) until program terminated. Joined G Co Mar 44. Rose from pfc to leader 1st Squad, 3rd Platoon (20 Nov 44); then to platoon sgt 1st Platoon (7 Jan 45, four days after his 20th birthday). WIA on Hoecker Hill (Germany) 13 Mar 45 (dozen machine gun bullets in right leg and thigh) and taken POW; freed by U.S. troops 13 days later. Approx one year in various hospitals. BA, Duquesne U, 1949, MA Columbia U, 1950 (business). Lifetime career in textile industry; since 1976 in own business as mill agent and merchandise broker. Married, three children. Lives in Oceanside, NY.

Sgt. Joseph S. Treml (Akron, OH), 3rd Platoon. WIA at Moncourt,

France, 8 Nov 44 (shrapnel wound in upper ankle); returned to duty 13 Jan 45. Appt asst leader, 1st Squad. WIA second time on Hoecker Hill (Germany) 13 Mar 45 (shrapnel in thigh); never returned to G Co. After discharge returned to Akron, worked as parts mgr, then salesman, for Buick agency. Died 9 Apr 87.

Pfc. Thomas J. Twardziewski (Greensburg, PA), 3rd Platoon. KIA at Moncourt, France, 8 Nov 44.

Sgt. William D. Van Norman (Lakewood, NY), Runner, 2nd Platoon. Awarded Silver Star for action near Woelfling, France, 12 Dec 44. Became company runner. WIA near Buprich-Huttersdorf, Germany, 22 Mar 45; returned to duty 28 Apr 45. After discharge worked for Army at Ft. Monmouth as painter for 28 yrs until retired in 1987. Lives in Brick Town, NJ; married, with two sons.

T/Sgt. George E. Van Winkle (Paris, MO), 2nd Platoon. Replacement, 19 Nov 44. Rose from pvt to become leader, 3rd Squad (late Nov 44); then platoon sgt 15 Mar 45. WIA near Kaundorf, Luxembourg, 3 Jan 45 (shrapnel in arm); returned to duty 10 Feb 45. Whereabouts since war unknown.

Pfc. Elbridge Walker (Bangor, AL), 3rd Platoon. Replacement 19 Jan 45. WIA on Hoecker Hill (Germany) 13 Mar 45. Returned to duty 18 Apr 45. Whereabouts since war unknown.

Pvt. James R. White (Rome, GA), 4th Platoon. Replacement, 19 Dec 45. KIA at Saarlouis-Roden, Germany, 20 Feb 45.

Pfc. Clay L. Williams (Pontatoc, MS), 3rd Platoon. Replacement 19 Jan 45. WIA on Hoecker Hill (Germany) 13 Mar 45; returned to duty 18 Apr 45. Whereabouts after war unknown.

Pfc. Jesse J. Wiseheart (New Albany, IN), 3rd Platoon. Replacement 19 Jan 45. WIA at Saarlautern 13 Feb 45 (shrapnel broke shoulder in two places and leg in three); never returned to G Co. After discharge returned to New Albany and became general contractor. Died 14 May 72 of heart attack.

Sgt. Wendell W. Wolfenbarger (Neosha, MO), 3rd Platoon. Replacement 19 Nov 44. Appt asst leader, 1st Squad (7 Jan 45). KIA near Berle, Luxembourg, on 17 Jan 45, leaving wife, 15-month-old son and 2½ year-old daughter. Awarded Silver Star for heroism in that action. His widow, Ruby Wolfenbarger, still lives in Neosha.

Sgt. Simon Yonut, Jr. (Warren, OH), 2nd Platoon. Replacement 19 Nov 44. Appt asst leader, 3rd Squad (8 Jan 45). WIA at Saarlouis-Roden, Germany, on 17 Feb 45. Never returned to G Co. After discharge worked in same factory in Warren he had before being drafted. Now retired.

T/Sgt. Edward J. Zabloski (Brockton, MA), Platoon Sgt, 3rd Platoon. Drafted in 1941. With G Co from activation of 328th Regt in Feb

43. WIA at Moncourt, France, 8 Nov 44 (shot in left shoulder and foot); never returned to G Co. Hospitalized three months then assigned to a training battalion outside Paris. After discharge returned to Brockton, where he worked in the shoe industry until retirement. Married with three sons. [P.R.]

Notes

INTRODUCTION

The words of Charles Ardant du Picq in the epigraph are quoted in Richard Holmes, *Acts of War: The Behavior of Men in Battle* (New York: Free Press, 1985), 18.

1. Page Smith, *Trial by Fire*, vol. 5 of *A People's History of the Civil War and Reconstruction* (New York: McGraw-Hill Book Company, 1982), 472–73.

PROLOGUE

1. Related by Wilbur Munns to Bruce Egger at a get-together of old G Company buddies. See also Harold P. Leinbaugh and John D. Campbell, *The Men of Company K: The Autobiography of a World War II Rifle Company* (New York: William Morrow and Co., 1985), 11, where the authors mention the derision infantrymen felt for the former "ASTP boys"—or "Whiz Kids," as they called them—who had been assigned to K Company when their programs were terminated.

2. Russell F. Weigley, *Eisenhower's Lieutenants: The Campaign of France and Germany 1944–1945* (Bloomington: Indiana University Press, 1981), 374.

3. One historian has recently commented on the shortsightedness of the World War II allocation of manpower: "Not only did Army Service Forces drain off the technical specialists they needed, but also the Army Air Forces took a large portion of the men who finished in the two highest categories on the AGCT [the armed forces intelligence test]. As a result, a survey conducted in 1943 indicated, combat soldiers in the Army Ground Forces had lower AGCT scores than men in the Army Service Forces or the Army Air Forces; combat soldiers were also shorter and weighed less. A historian of the Army's Personnel Division went as far as to say, 'Army Ground Forces got the dregs.' But beginning in 1943, priorities began to shift. Army Service Forces lost their skimming privileges and Army Ground Forces were favored. The ASTP men fed into combat units were a valuable transfusion." Lee Kennett, *G.I.: The American Soldier in World War II* (New York: Charles Scribner's Sons, 1987), 38.

4. The 97th Division was never sent to the Pacific, but in March 1945, the last trained division left in the United States; it was sent to the ETO. Weigley, *Eisenhower's Lieutenants*, 571.

5. This short summary of the history of the 26th Division has been culled from *The History of the 26th Yankee Division, 1917–1919, 1941–1945* (Yankee Division Veterans Association, 1955), 1–33; *History of the 26th Infantry Division in World War II* (G-3 Section, 26th Infantry Division, 1945), 1–3; and Sgt. Ralph A. Anderson, Jr., *Handcar White: A History of the Second Battalion, 328th Infantry, European Theatre of Operations* (Hor Vlatavice, Czechoslovakia, 1945), 9.

1. FIRST BLOOD

1. For this brief summary of military developments in France in the summer and early fall of 1944 the editor has relied mainly on Weigley, *Eisenhower's Lieutenants*; Hugh M. Cole, *The Lorraine Campaign* (*United States Army in World War II: The European Theater of Operations*) (Washington, D.C.: Historical Division, United States Army, 1950); and Chester Wilmot, *The Struggle for Europe* (New York: Harper & Row, 1952). For Third Army operations, Aug. 1–Sept. 25, 1944, see "After Action Report Third U.S. Army, 1 August 1944–9 May 1945" (no place or date of publication), vol. 1, 16–84. See also Patton's directive of Sept. 25, 1944, placing the Third Army on the defensive, ibid., 84.

2. Anderson, *Handcar White*, 9–14; S/Sgt. Jerome J. Theise, ed., *History of the 328th Infantry Regiment (26th Infantry Division)* (Verlagsdruckerei Weis, Austria, n.d.), 11; Cole, *The Lorraine Campaign*, 285, 290–91.

3. *History of the 26th Yankee Division*, 40–41.

4. ". . . so capable were German officers in transforming individual soldiers into cohesive units that in the German army the company developed a sufficient sense of comradeship and solidarity to constitute a primary group, whereas in the American army the usual primary group was the squad, or at the largest, the platoon." Weigley, *Eisenhower's Lieutenants*, 29.

5. Cole, *The Lorraine Campaign*, 296–300.

6. Ibid., 301, 303, 318–20; Anderson, *Handcar White*, 18.

7. Weigley, *Eisenhower's Lieutenants*, 24.

8. Ibid., 390–91; Cole, *The Lorraine Campaign*, 321–32.

9. Anderson, *Handcar White*, 21.

10. Theise, ed., *History of the 328th Infantry*, 12.

11. Anderson, *Handcar White*, 23.

12. Weigley, *Eisenhower's Lieutenants*, 24.

2. THE MUD OF LORRAINE

1. Weigley, *Eisenhower's Lieutenants*, 399–400; Cole, *The Lorraine Campaign*, 454; Anderson, *Handcar White*, 27.
2. Cole, *The Lorraine Campaign*, 332, 594. In his classic memoir of World War I, the English poet Robert Graves stated, "'Trench feet' seemed to be almost entirely a matter of morale. . . . [It occurred] only if [a man] did not mind getting trench feet, or anything else—because his battalion had lost the power of sticking things out." He cites the case of a particular battalion that "lost half its strength in two days from trench feet; our Second Battalion [of the elite Royal Welch Fusiliers] had just completed ten days in the same trenches with no cases at all." Robert Graves, *Goodbye to All That* (London: Penguin Books, 1960), 144–45.
3. Cole, *The Lorraine Campaign*, 454–56.
4. Martin Blumenson, *The Patton Papers*, 2 vols. (Boston: Houghton Mifflin, 1972–1974), 2:588–89, quoted in Weigley, *Eisenhower's Lieutenants*, 386.

3. TRANSITION: FROM LORRAINE TO METZ

1. Ladislas Farago, *Patton: Ordeal and Triumph* (New York: Dell, 1970), 634, quoted in Weigley, *Eisenhower's Lieutenants*, 390.
2. "Third Army After Action Report," 154–57.
3. Cole, *The Lorraine Campaign*, 520–33; Anderson, *Handcar White*, 28–30; *The 26th Infantry Division in World War II*, 15–17.
4. Weigley, *Eisenhower's Lieutenants*, 390; Cole, *The Lorraine Campaign*, 310.
5. *The 26th Infantry Division in World War II*, 18.
6. *Ibid.*; Weigley, *Eisenhower's Lieutenants*, 400.
7. *The 26th Infantry Division in World War II*, 20. On Patton's orders to comb out five percent of the men in noncombat units see Cole, *The Lorraine Campaign*, 595.
The "five-percent" idea was actually an improvement over the Army's existing replacement system, which considered that a warm body was the only prerequisite for being a rifleman. One veteran of the 84th Division related, "I trained in the artillery in Mississippi for thirteen months. Then they sent us overseas . . . and they handed me an M1 rifle. . . . I always carried a carbine as an artilleryman. But they give me that M1 gun, give me the nomenclature of it, made me shoot it, disassemble it. And then they said, 'You're a doughboy now.'" Quoted in Leinbaugh and Campbell, *The Men of Company K*, 78.
Weigley states that although 95 percent of the casualties in the ETO were infantrymen, "On D-Day, only 52 percent of the 76,000 replacements in the European Theater were infantry-trained. The May, June, and July shipments of infantry replacements contained, respectively, only 35, 58, and 50 percent riflemen." *Eisenhower's Lieutenants*, 370, 373.

4. INTO THE BULGE

1. For this brief summary of the initial developments in the Battle of the Bulge, the editor has relied mainly upon Wilmot, *The Struggle for Europe*, 573–98; Weigley, *Eisenhower's Lieutenants*, 446–90; and Hugh M. Cole, *The Ardennes: Battle of the Bulge* (*The United States Army in World War II: The European Theater of Operations*) (Washington, D.C.: Office of the Chief of Military History, Department of the Army, 1965).

2. Wilmot, *The Struggle for Europe*, 583.

3. Cole, *The Ardennes*, 305.

4. Wilmot, *The Struggle for Europe*, 589.

5. George S. Patton, Jr., *War As I Knew It* (Boston: Houghton Mifflin, 1947), 191.

6. Weigley, *Eisenhower's Lieutenants*, 498.

7. See "Third Army After Action Report," 168–69 for a discussion of the changes of army and corps zones, the shifts of units, and the transportation, supply, and communications problems this created.

8. Patton, *War As I Knew It*, 236–37.

9. Cole, *The Ardennes*, 509–20.

10. The first contact with the enemy had been made a bit earlier on Dec. 22 by the 1st Platoon of the 26th Cavalry Reconnaissance Troop, which encountered a strong enemy force converging on the town of Rambrouch on the 328th Regiment's left flank. A little later the 104th Infantry encountered other segments of this column, which proved to be a regiment of the 352nd Volksgrenadier Division. It should be noted that the Germans were unaware of III Corps' presence in the area and were caught by surprise by the American attacks on their southern flank. Ibid., 521–22; *The 26th Infantry Divison in World War II*, 22.

11. The official Army history of this campaign, Hugh Cole, *The Ardennes*, is uncertain as to which American unit actually captured Eschdorf. Cole (p. 543) is inclined to believe that elements of E and F Companies managed to maintain themselves within the town over the night of Dec. 25–26. Anderson, *Handcar White* (p. 37), says that the enemy withdrew during the night and that when Company C of the 104th Infantry entered the town during morning of the 26th part of Fox Company was still there.

12. The Combat Infantry Badge, an elongated blue rectangle with a rifle and wreath embossed upon it, was prized by veterans. One ex-GI is quoted as saying, "There's not too many guys could put that Combat Infantry Badge on. You walk with it with a certain pride. I always put that blue badge number one. You could have your Medal of Honor and Legion of Merit, but there's nothing covers that blue badge, nothing tops it." Quoted in Leinbaugh and Campbell, *The Men of Company K*, 291.

13. Charles B. MacDonald, *The Last Offensive* (*The United States Army in World War II: The European Theater of Operations*) (Washington, D.C.: Office of the Chief of Military History, United States Army, 1973), 1, 25; Weigley, *Eisenhower's Lieutenants*, 556–57; Wilmot, *The Struggle for Europe*, 607–8.

5. VICTORY IN THE ARDENNES

1. MacDonald, *The Last Offensive*, 38–41; *The 26th Infantry Division in World War II*, 30.
2. MacDonald, *The Last Offensive*, 42–52; *The 26th Infantry Division in World War II*, 30.
3. Anderson, *Handcar White*, 43.
4. One of the gross inequities of the war was the number of medals lavished upon headquarters personnel and other rear echelon troops. A recent autobiographical account of a World War II rifle company notes: "The fifty-eight officers in our 84th Division Headquarters pulled in about four times as many medals as the men in K Company. Enlisted men in division headquarters received twice as many medals as we did. The MPs and quartermaster troops also outdid us in decorations. We know of several one-hour periods when K Company took more casualties, killed and wounded, than the total casualties sustained during the entire war by all of these rear-echelon outfits lumped together, but that was the way it was." Leinbaugh and Campbell, *The Men of Company K*, 243.
5. In talking about his utter exhaustion Egger raised an issue that apparently never occurred to the generals but which was revealed in postwar studies. The authors of the official report, *Combat Exhaustion*, discovered that "most men were ineffective after 180 or even 140 days. The general consensus was that a man reached his peak of effectiveness in the first 90 days of combat, that after that his efficiency began to fall off, and that he became steadily less valuable thereafter until he was completely useless." This problem was undoubtedly related to the U.S. Army's policy of keeping a unit continuously in the line for long periods. For the combat soldier caught up in this situation, the only release was death or wounds. Quoted in John Keegan, *The Face of Battle* (New York: Viking Press, 1976), 329.
6. MacDonald, *The Last Offensive*, 53–54.
7. Ibid., 42–53; *The 26th Infantry Division in World War II*, 31; Anderson, *Handcar White*, 43.

6. THE SAARLAUTERN INTERLUDE

1. For this brief summary of the situation and activities of the Third Army in February 1945, the editor has relied mainly on MacDonald, *The Last Offensive*, 98, 115, 117; *The 26th Infantry Division in World War II*, 35; and Cole, *The Lorraine Campaign*, 572-88.

7. THE DRIVE TO THE RHINE

1. MacDonald, *The Last Offensive*, 116–34; Weigley, *Eisenhower's Lieutenants*, 589–95; Patton, *War as I Knew It*, 230–56; "Third Army After Action Report," 270–72, 274–75, 277–78, 291.

2. MacDonald, *The Last Offensive*, 135, 183–84; Weigley, *Eisenhower's Lieutenants*, 600.

3. MacDonald, *The Last Offensive*, 135–84; Weigley, *Eisenhower's Lieutenants*, 599–608; Charles B. MacDonald, *The Mighty Endeavor: American Armed Forces in the European Theater in World War II* (New York: Oxford University Press, 1969), 420–25.

4. MacDonald, *The Last Offensive*, 185–235; Weigley, *Eisenhower's Lieutenants*, 617–19, 626–30; MacDonald, *The Mighty Endeavor*, 426–32.

5. MacDonald, *The Last Offensive*, 236–45; Weigley, *Eisenhower's Lieutenants*, 633–35.

6. *The 26th Infantry Infantry Division in World War II*, 36.

7. MacDonald, *The Last Offensive*, 244–61.

8. Anderson, *Handcar White*, 56.

9. MacDonald, *The Last Offensive*, 266–84; MacDonald, *The Mighty Endeavor*, 442–44, 449–50.

10. Patton, *War As I Knew It*, 273. The telegram was from Major General Leonard T. Gerow, commander of the newly activated Fifteenth Army, which was assigned occupation duty in the rear of the advancing American armies.

11. MacDonald, *The Last Offensive*, 264–65.

12. For Patton's prediction see Patton, *War As I Knew It*, 132.

8. THE RACE ACROSS GERMANY

1. MacDonald, *The Mighty Endeavor*, 475–79.

2. Weigley, *Eisenhower's Lieutenants*, 655.

3. MacDonald, *The Last Offensive*, 376–81.

4. Ibid., 384, 421–22; Patton, *War As I Knew It*, 295–99, 302; "Third Army After Action Report," 353–54.

5. Bill Mauldin, *Up Front* (New York: Henry Holt and Company, 1944), 45.

EPILOGUE

1. Kennett, *G.I.: The American Soldier in World War II*, 223–24.

Index

Italicized page numbers refer to entries in Appendix II: Roll Call.

About the Authors

Bruce E. Egger graduated from the University of Idaho with a B.S. in forestry in June 1951. He served in the U.S. Forest Service for 29 years before retiring in 1979. Bruce now makes his home in Prineville, Oregon, with his wife, Leora. They have four adult children.

Lee MacMillan Otts is a graduate of The University of Alabama (AB 1943) and The University of Alabama Law School (LLB 1948). He has practiced law in Brewton, Alabama, since 1949, where he has been an active leader in his church and community. He and his wife, Mary Frances, have four married daughters.

Dr. Paul Roley is Emeritus Professor of Russian and Soviet History at Western Washington University. He and his wife, Joan, who are both from Illinois, have lived in Bellingham, Washington, since 1967. They have three married children.